Programmed learning aid for

BUSINESS and ECONOMIC STATISTICS

Programmed learning aid for

BUSINESS and ECONOMIC STATISTICS

ROBERT D. MASON
The University of Toledo

Coordinating Editor
ROGER H. HERMANSON
Georgia State University

EARNING SYSTEMS COMPANY

A division of
RICHARD D. IRWIN, INC. Homewood, Illinois 60430

Also available through
RWIN-DORSEY LIMITED Georgetown, Ontario L7G 4B3

ISBN 0-256-00119-7

Printed in the United States of America

2 3 4 5 6 7 8 9 0 K 5 4 3 2 1 0 9

Foreword

Students often have found reviewing for examinations a dull and tedious process. This PLAID series was created to provide the user with an effective, efficient, and interesting means of accomplishing this task. It applies the powerful tool of programmed learning to the subject matter areas comprising business and economics.

The method of programming is easy to use and has the following advantages:

1. Correct response to concepts reviewed is *reinforced immediately.*
2. Incorrect interpretations of concepts reviewed are *corrected immediately.*
3. The reader is kept *active* in the review process, and this increases comprehension.
4. The method makes learning seem like a game.

The PLAID for Statistics was used in test edition form by a large number of students who were enthusiastic in their praise of its effectiveness. It can be used as a supplement with almost any textbook designed for use in an introductory course in statistics.

The author is an excellent teacher, has taught statistics for a number of years, and is "student oriented." His continual concern in developing his PLAID was with simplicity of presentation so as to effectively communicate the essential subject matter of statistics to the reader. I'm sure you will agree that he has done so.

ROGER H. HERMANSON
Coordinating Editor

Preface

This Programmed Learning Aid provides a means of self-review of the techniques studied in most introductory courses in statistics. While many of the illustrations are business oriented, the statistical methods are equally applicable in other areas such as the social sciences, education, and engineering. This PLAID also can be used effectively by students entering a graduate studies program, executives participating in management development programs, and persons working or studying in marketing, accounting, and related fields.

The PLAID is designed to be used as a supplement to your textbook. It is organized into chapters. The chapters are in a logical sequence, but the sequence can be altered to that of any statistics textbook. Each chapter is subdivided into a number of short segments called frames. In each frame the reader tests his comprehension of the material by answering questions that are presented. The answer is always given in the margin.

The following example illustrates the technique used. Before reading the material presented in the frame, cover the answers given in the margin. Now read the material and answer the questions.

1

The arithmetic mean is one of the most commonly used averages. It is found by summing all of the items and dividing the sum by the total number of items. For example, the hourly wage rates of four men are $7, $4, $6, and $3 respectively. The arithmetic mean hourly wage is $5, found by $\frac{\$7 + \$4 + \$6 + \$3}{4}$.

The weekly incomes of five employees of the Ace Stamping Company are $400, $350, $600, $750 and $400 respectively. The total weekly payroll is $______, and the arithmetic mean weekly income is $_______.

$2,500

$500, found by $\frac{\$2{,}500}{5}$

A distinctive feature of this programmed learning aid is the Final Self-Review Examination (with answers) found at the end of each chapter. By answering the 10 review questions, an additional evaluation can be made of how well the concepts in the chapter were understood. Other features of the PLAID include a glossary of terms and formulas found in the Appendix and a Topical Outline of Course Content as contained in basic books in this field.

ROBERT D. MASON

Topical outline of course content

Table of contents

Introduction

chapter

1

1

The word *statistics* has several connotations. In one sense, statistics refers to a collection of numerical data. A perusal of several business magazines revealed these statistics. "Bookings for machine tools reached a record $339.6 billion last month, up 9.1% from February and 29% from March 1977." (*The Wall Street Journal*, April 24, 1978, p. 1.) From *Forbes*, "If you look at the market's near-term future through rose-colored glasses, International Business Machines (240) must not be ignored. A multiple of less than 12 times 1978 estimated earnings and a dividend yield approaching 5% would have been unthinkable not long ago." (*Forbes*, May 1, 1978, p. 112.) Some assorted statistics from *Business Week*, "Among 17,000 Harvard University alumni studied over 15 years, those who had practiced strenuous exercise—jogging, swimming, and similar activities—had suffered fewer heart attacks. More than 400 major corporations now have extensive exercise facilities. Smaller companies also are building gyms. A $100 million-a-year homebuilder in Irvine, Calif., just opened a 7,000 sq. ft., $250,000 gym for its employees, clients, suppliers, and bankers." "With the economy entering its third year of recovery, the growth of personal income accelerated nationwide in 1977, according to *Business Week*'s year-end tabulation. The income growth rate for the year was 11.4%, up smartly from the 10.2% recorded in 1976 before adjusting for inflation. But consumer prices also spurted, so the inflation-adjusted income gain was only 4.6." (*Business Week*, April 3, 1978, pp. 91, 100.)

The word *statistics* is also used to identify the science of collecting, organizing, presenting, analyzing, and interpreting data. The Civil Service Commission defines statistics as "a body of techniques for acquiring accurate knowledge from incomplete information, a scientific system for the collection, organization, analysis, interpretation, and presentation of information which can be stated in numerical form."

Note from the foregoing definition that statisticians work with incomplete data. An order for steel wire might specify that the average tensile strength of the wire must be 10,000 pounds per square inch or more. Out of harsh economic necessity, a decision to accept or reject an incoming shipment of the wire must be made on, say, eight pieces selected at random. Since a test for tensile strength destroys the wire, checking all of the incoming wires would not be feasible. The management of another company must make a decision whether or not to market a newly developed molasses-coated cereal based on incomplete information about consumer preference. Sending introductory test packages to nearly 200 million consumers in the United States would be very costly and time-consuming. The usual procedure is to conduct a product test using a panel of about 2,000 families. Inventory control and sales forecasting are but a few other areas where business decisions are based on incomplete information.

Because complete information is not available, there is usually some uncertainty involved in making most decisions. This means that there is a risk of making a wrong decision. Based on the sample of eight pieces of steel wire, the quality control engineer might accept the incoming shipment of wire when it should have been rejected.

If a decision is made to market the molasses-coated cereal based on the test-panel results, there is a chance that the cereal will not be accepted by the public.

Statistical methods are used extensively in areas other than business such as medical research, education, economics, insurance, psychology, the social sciences, and so on. Economists, for example, are interested in measuring the extent of inflation and projecting the demand for labor. Research is being done in education on the effectiveness of newly developed teaching devices and techniques. Medical research is concerned with assessing new vaccines. Demographers use statistical methods in studying and projecting population growth and birth rates.

2

DESCRIPTIVE STATISTICS AND INDUCTIVE STATISTICS

One facet of statistics is called *descriptive statistics*. To illustrate, the following figures were compiled by the International Monetary Fund. They merely describe the percent increase of consumer prices in various countries during 1976 and during a recent 12-month period.

Country	*Price-Rise in 1976*	*Latest Price-Rise*
Switzerland	1.7%	1.1%
West Germany	4.5	3.1
Japan	9.3	4.3
Netherlands	8.8	4.5
Belgium	9.2	5.4
United States	5.8	6.8
France	9.2	9.1
Australia	13.5	9.2
Britain	16.6	9.9
Italy	16.8	14.1

The Wall Street Journal, April 24, 1978, p. 1.

An analysis of the data indicates that Switzerland has the smallest annual rise in consumer prices; in the United States it is about 7%, and in Italy over 14%.

Another facet of statistics, called *inductive statistics* or *statistical inference*, deals with sample data. In most mass-production industries, it is deemed too expensive to check all the parts manufactured. Quality control engineers at Chevrolet, Toledo Division, select a sample of eight short pinion gears at random every half hour. On the basis of certain averages and other computed statistics, a decision is made about all short pinion gears produced during that 30-minute period. The total group is called a ***population***, and the few parts selected from the population are called a *sample*.

sample
population

The eight short pinion gears are called a __________, and all the gears produced during the half hour are called the __________.

3

Suppose that a sample of 84 shoes were strapped to a special rotary machine and "walked" until a hole appeared in the sole. The average mileage was computed to be 87.3 miles. This sample result is called a sample *statistic*. It was decided to give all the shoes produced during the day (24,568 shoes) a life test, and it was found that the

verage mileage of the population was 87.5 miles. This figure (87.5) is called a popula-
ion *parameter.*

The average tensile strength of 10 wires selected at random for an incoming ship-
nent of steel wires was computed to be 14,340 pounds per square inch. The 14,340 psi
s called a ____________________ because ____________________
________.

statistic
It is associated with a sample

4 ____

Statistical data is considered as being either *discrete* or *continuous.* Discrete data can
only be whole numbers and result from counting persons or items. There are 32 chil-
dren in the fifth grade, and the inventory revealed that there are 16,854 different items
n stock.

These are two examples of ____________________ data because the figures
re the result of ____________________.

discrete
counts

Continuous data can have fractional values and result from measuring. That
s, the measurement given could be further subdivided if more precise instruments
were used. Three pieces of steel had lengths of 1.001, 1.000 and 1.003 inches respec-
ively. This is an example of ________________ data because ________________
____.

continuous
the figures are the result of measuring

Final Self-Review Examination

First, answer all of the questions. Then check your answers against those given at the end of this chapter. Scoring: 10 problems × 10 points each = 100 possible points.

5. Sales last month were $1,215,672.42. This facet of statistics which merely describes the situation is called descriptive statistics.

6. Based on the sample survey just conducted, it is estimated that the average income in the proposed shopping area is between $9,800 and $9,900. When sample data is used to make statements about the total, the facet of statistics is called inductive or statistics inference

7. Political pollsters (Harris, Gallup, Roper, and others) usually interview about 1,500 potential voters in a pre-election poll out of the millions eligible to vote. The relatively small number (1,500) is called a sample.

8. The total of all of the voters (the millions eligible to vote) is called the population

9. Out of the 1,500 selected in the pre-election poll, 900, or 60 percent, indicated that they favored the Republican candidate. Because the figure 60 percent is associated with a sample, it is called a statistic.

10. The actual percent when all the voters indicated their preference was 58 percent for the Republican candidate. This figure (58%) is called a population parameter.

11. There are 58,003 persons in the metropolitan area, and 92 different colors are available. These data are considered (discrete/continuous) discrete data

12. The average length of fish caught in the tournament was 12.2 inches, and the length of life of a typical bulb in a traffic signal is 47 months. These data are considered ________ Continuous data

13. One meaning of the word statistics is a collection of numerical data

14. Another meaning of the word statistics is identifying the process of collecting, analyzing, organizing, presenting and interpreting data

Answers to Final Self-Review Examination

5. descriptive
6. statistical inference or inductive statistics
7. sample
8. population
9. statistic
10. parameter
11. discrete
12. continuous
13. The word *statistics* might refer to a collection of numerical data. For example, there were 720,100 persons unemployed, 56,871,900 were employed, etc.
14. Statistics also refers to the science of collecting, organizing, presenting, analyzing, and interpreting numerical data.

The collection and presentation of statistical data

chapter

2

1

COLLECTION OF DATA

The first step toward describing a business phenomenon is to collect the necessary statistical data. The source of the business data may be classified as being *internal* or *external.*

Internal data includes statistics on the company's operations, such as sales statistics and production statistics. The machine records department sent the sales manager these sales figures for the previous three months: $987,651.76, $876,598.89, and $1,023,458.92. The source of the data is considered ________________. internal

Statistical data not associated with the operation of the business firm itself is called *external* data. The sales manager of an automobile manufacturer may need data on the number of automobiles in use in the United States by age, in order to make estimates of sales 5, 10, and 15 years from now. This data is considered ____________ data. external

2

There is a vast amount of external business data in published form which can be found in university and public libraries. For example, population data, by age, is collected every 10 years by the Bureau of the Census and published in the *Census of Population.* The sales manager can find the age distribution of motor vehicles in an annual publication called *Motor Vehicle Facts and Figures* published by the automobile industry.

The federal government is the largest publisher of annual, monthly, weekly, and daily statistics. One annual publication of the Department of Commerce, the *Statistical Abstract of the United States*, contains over 1,000 pages of population, price, education, production, and other data which may be of use to economists, marketing analysts, and others. A few annual statistics selected from various tables are:

260,378,000 projected population of the United States for 2000.
17.8 percent of American families with incomes of $25,000 or over.
604,000 bicycle thefts.

Source: U.S. Department of Commerce, *Statistical Abstract of the United States*, 1977, pp. 6, 176, 441.

A few of the monthly publications of the federal government are the *Monthly Labor Review*, the *Survey of Current Business*, and the *Federal Reserve Bulletin.* As the name implies, the *Monthly Labor Review* contains various monthly labor statistics, such as total civilian employment. The *Survey of Current Business* includes the total monthly department store sales and the Wholesale Price Index. The amount of money in circulation last month and the dollar reserves at the various Federal Reserve banks are but two financial series found in the *Federal Reserve Bulletin.* The total number of business

Survey of Current Business
Monthly Labor Review

Federal Reserve Bulletin

failures can probably be found in the ____________. The total number of persons unemployed last month can be located in the ____________ ____________ ____________ and various monthly financial statistics can be found in the ____________ ____________ ____________. If a search of these sources for specific data is unproductive, one or more of the following reference aids may be consulted. Edwin T. Coman's *Sources of Business Information* has nearly 300 pages of references categorized into foreign trade, marketing, real estate, and so on. Marian Manley's *Business Information—How to Find and Use It*, the *Business Periodicals Index*, and the indexes of *The New York Times* and *The Wall Street Journal* are other reference aids.

3

THE QUESTIONNAIRE AS A SOURCE OF DATA

Statistical data regarding the current opinions of consumers toward specific television programs, newly developed foods, political candidates, and so on cannot be found in published sources. Thus, this type of data must be collected by *personal interview*, by *mail questionnaire*, or by some other means. The Roper, Gallup, and Harris polls use the personal interview technique almost exclusively. The main advantage of this technique is the high percentage of response possible. It is usually more expensive, however, than mailing out questionnaires. Research firms report that the disadvantage of the mail questionnaire as a tool to collect data is the relatively low percent of response to some questionnaires. Telephone interviews, automatic car counters on highways, and audimeters attached to television sets to record the programs watched are a few other techniques used to collect numerical data. A major advantage of a personal interview as a method of collecting data is ____________.
The major advantage of the mail questionnaire as a data-collecting technique is ____________.

high-percent response

relatively low cost

4

PRESENTATION OF DATA

Simple line graphs and simple bar graphs. Either of these two types of graphs can be used effectively to portray the general trend of sales, production, and the like over a period of time.

SALES OF THE COMPANY

Year	Sales (Millions)
1974	$2
1975	4
1976	3
1977	6
1978	8

SIMPLE LINE GRAPH

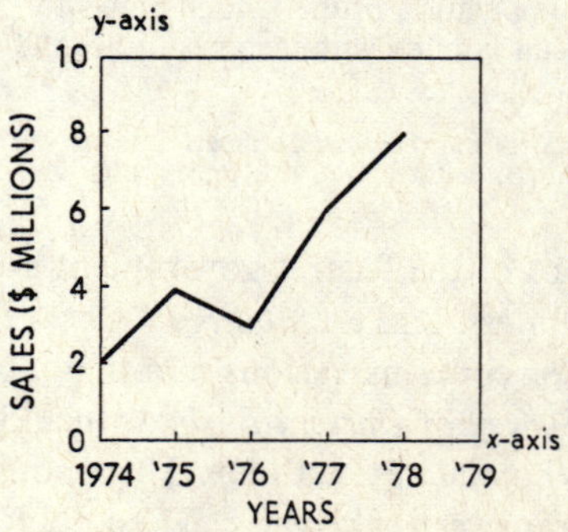

Comments: Note the zero origin on *Y*-axis; years (time) are *always* on *X*-axis.

SIMPLE BAR GRAPH

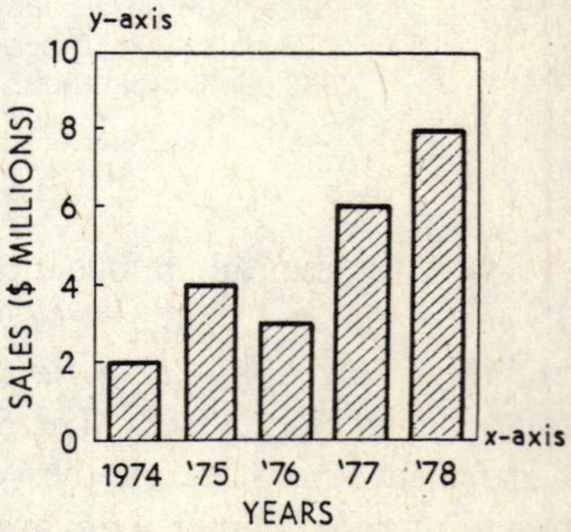

Note: Bars are usually separated (as shown); time usually on *X*-axis.

Masses of statistical data from within the company, from published sources, or ollected using a personal interview or mail questionnaire are usually not in a meanıgful form for analysis. The data should be organized and presented in either *table orm* or *chart form* before any analysis and interpretation are made. If precise figures re needed in a report (such as sales figures in the annual report of a company), the ata should be presented in a table. If not, a graph (chart) may be preferred to attract he attention of the reader.

In the spaces below, portray the following production series in the form of a simple ne graph and a simple bar graph.

PRODUCTION OF A COMPANY

'ear	*Production (000)*
974	4
975	3
976	8
977	12
978	10
979	17

SIMPLE LINE GRAPH

SIMPLE BAR GRAPH

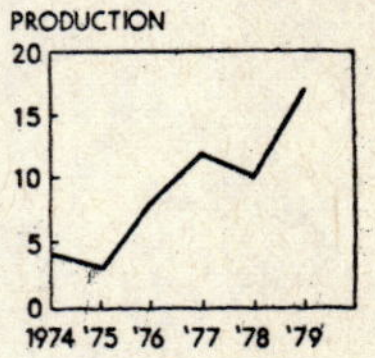

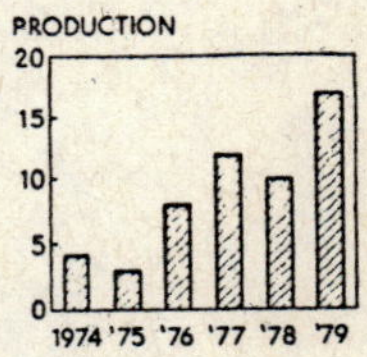

5

Multiple line graph and multiple bar graph. The trend in the exports of two competitors is portrayed graphically. Complete the multiple line graph by plotting the exports of Company B. Use a dashed (- - -) line. Then complete the multiple bar graph by plotting the exports for 1976, 1977, and 1978.

EXPORTS (In Millions)

'ear	*Company A*	*Company B*
1972	$20	$ 2
1973	16	8
1974	12	12
1975	15	13
1976	10	14
1977	7	16
1978	8	19

MULTIPLE LINE GRAPH

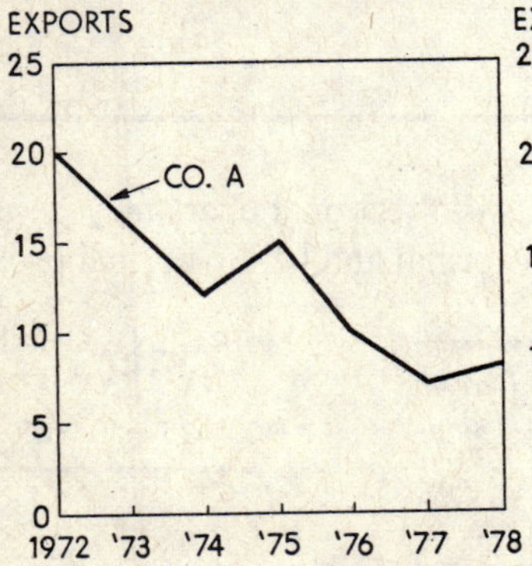

Comments: A dashed line and solid line keep two series separated. If more than 3 or 4 series are plotted it tends to be confusing.

MULTIPLE BAR GRAPH

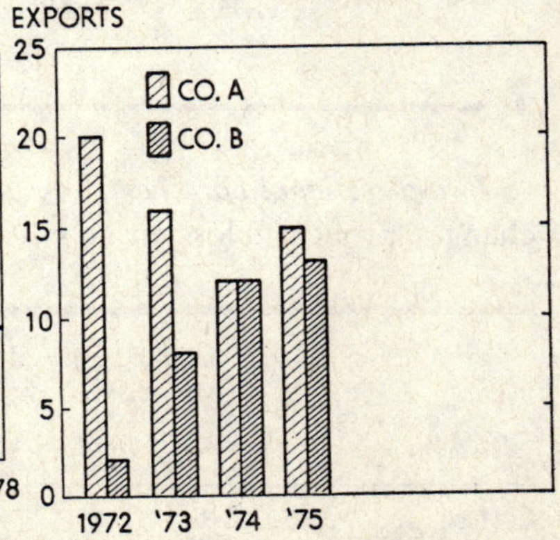

Note: A bar graph is more tedious to construct. Different shadings keep the series separated.

EXPORTS

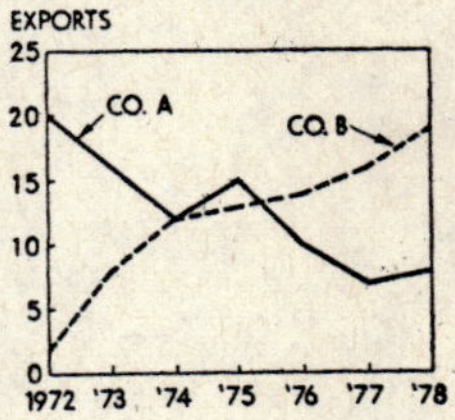

EXPORTS

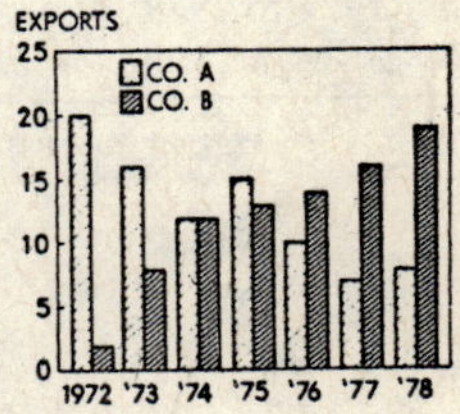

6

Component bar graph. The sales manager of a company manufacturing small radios, replacement parts, and high-fidelity components wishes to graph the total sales for three years and also the change in each component relative to the total. A component line graph (not shown) or a component bar graph could be used. Th steps involved in designing a *component bar graph* are:

Item	*Sales (Millions)* 1977	1978	1979
Small radios	$10	$ 8	$ 3
Replacement parts	4	4	4
High-fidelity parts	2	7	17
Total	$16	$19	$24

To Plot Sales for 1977:		
Step 1	*Step 2*	*Step 3*
Plot sales of $10 million (small radios)	Plot sales of $4 million (replacement parts) on top of radios for $14 million total	Plot sales of $ million (high-fidelity) on top for a $16 million total

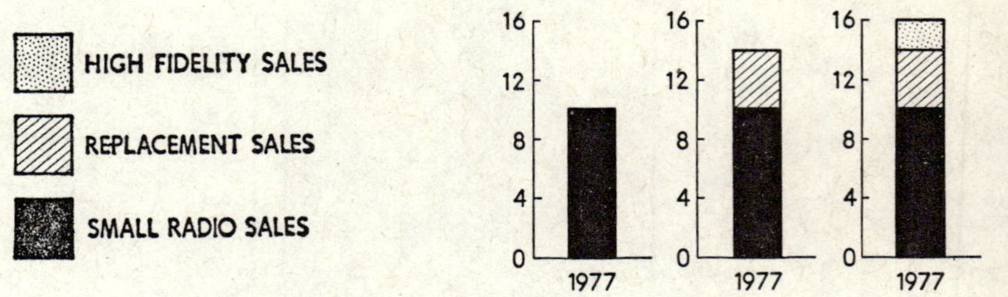

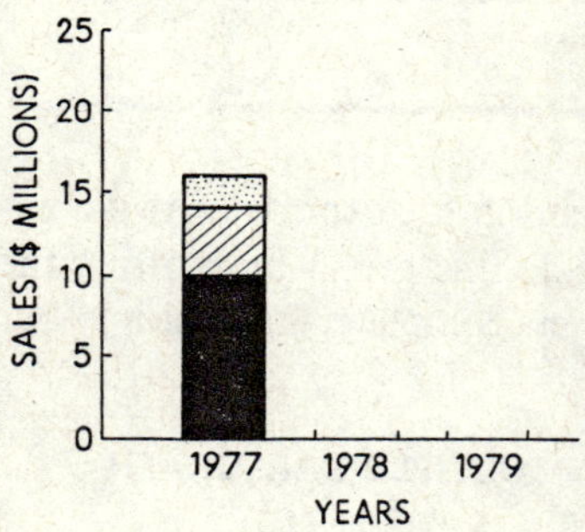

The sales for 1977 (from Step 3) are shown in th adjacent graph. Complete the graph by plottin the sales for 1978 and 1979. The same procedur should be followed, i.e., small radios should b plotted first, then sales of replacement parts plotte on top of radio sales, and finally the sales of high fidelity components.

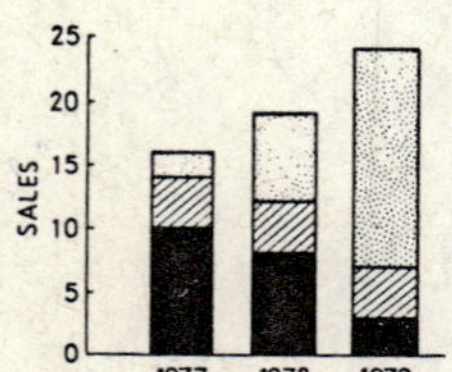

7

Two-directional bar chart. A two-directional chart may be used to show percen changes, profit and loss, or above-normal and below-normal production or sales fron

Division	*Sales (Millions)* 1977	1978	*Percent Change 1977 to 1978*
Eastern	$10	$ 8	−20
Northern	5	7	+40
Southern	2	4	+100
Midwestern	6	3	−50
Far Western	10	11	+10

PERCENT CHANGES IN SALES, BY DIVISION, 1977 to 1978

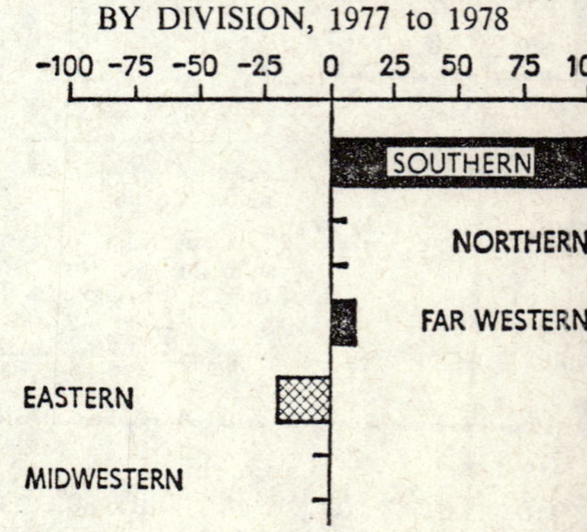

PERCENT CHANGE IN SALES BY DIVISION, 1977 to 1978

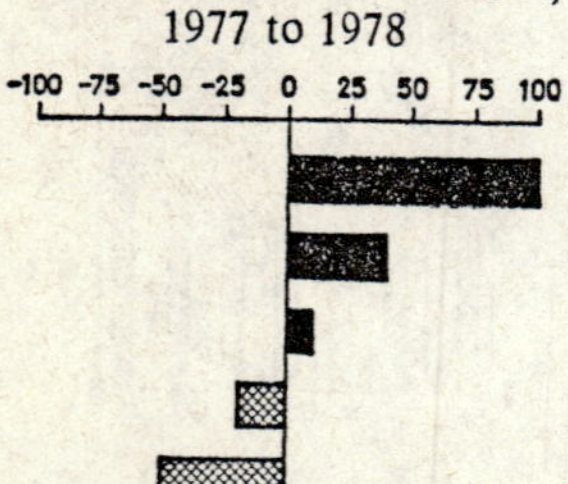

one time period to another time period. For example, the *percent changes* in sales for the five sales divisions from 1977 to 1978 are to be portrayed (not the changes in the dollar amounts). A commonly used technique is to arrange the percent increases shown in the previous table in descending order (+100, +40, and +10 percent), and the percent decreases in ascending order (−20 and −50 percent). These percent changes are then plotted in the same order. Note that the bars go in two directions from zero. Plot the percent changes for the Northern division and the Midwestern division.

The previous graph is called a ______________________. Based on the graph, which division had the largest percent increase in sales from 1977 to 1978? ______________. Which division had the largest percent decrease? __________ __________. This type of graph is especially appropriate to portray ______________ ______________________________________.

two-directional bar chart

Southern

Midwestern

percent changes, profit and loss, or above-normal and below-normal changes.

8

CHART A
COST OF OPERATING A FIRM

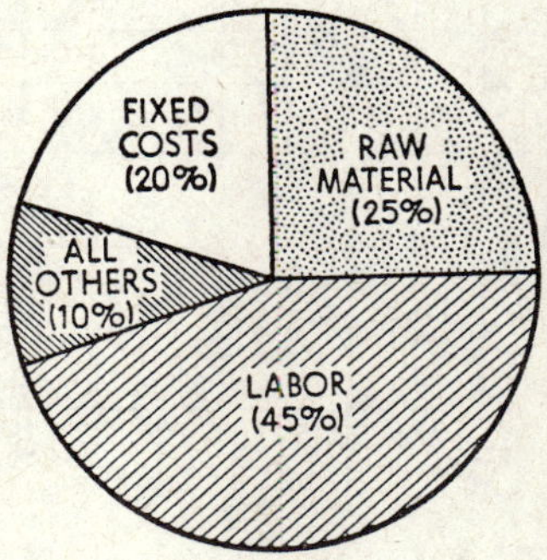

Pie graph. If the relative size of the components of the total are to be emphasized, a pie chart is an appropriate graphic tool. For example, from an analysis of Chart A it is readily apparent that labor costs account for almost half of the total costs. The circumference of the circle represents 100 percent. The usual method of drawing a pie chart is to convert the data into percents of the total. As shown, various shadings can be used to separate the components.

Using the county income data in the following table, design a pie graph. (Plots can only be approximate.)

SOURCES OF COUNTY INCOME, 1979

Source	*Income (Millions)*
Property tax	$12
Income tax	6
All other sources	2
Total	$20

one way is:

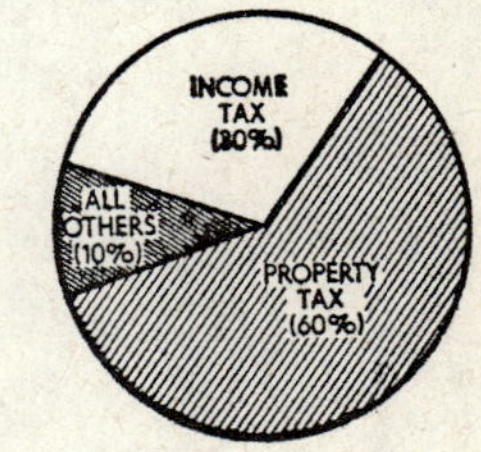

9

The previous graphs were drawn on *arithmetic* paper. Equal distances on arithmetic paper represent equal *amounts*. For example, in the following graph sales increased an equal amount ($1 million) each year.

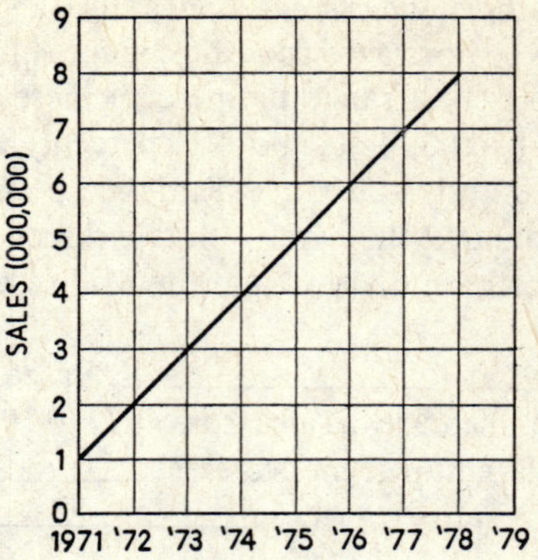

Year	*Sales (Millions)*
1971	$1
1972	2
1973	3
1974	4
1975	5
1976	6
1977	7
1978	8

It appears that sales have been increasing at a steady rate, but a more thorough study of the actual sales shows that between 1971 and 1972 sales increased 100 percent; the second year, 50 percent (from $2 million to $3 million); the next year, 33⅓ percent ($3 million to $4 million); and so on. Although sales have been rising from year to year, the rate of increase has been ________________________. Thus, it may be misleading to plot this type of series (an arithmetic progression) on arithmetic graph paper. Now plot the same sales series on *semilogarithmic* graph paper.

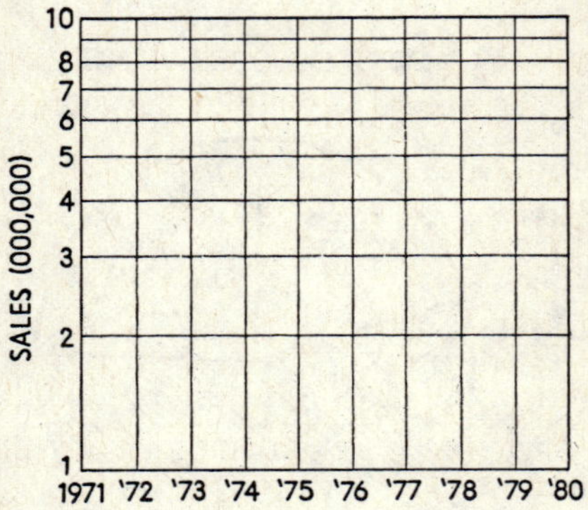

decreasing

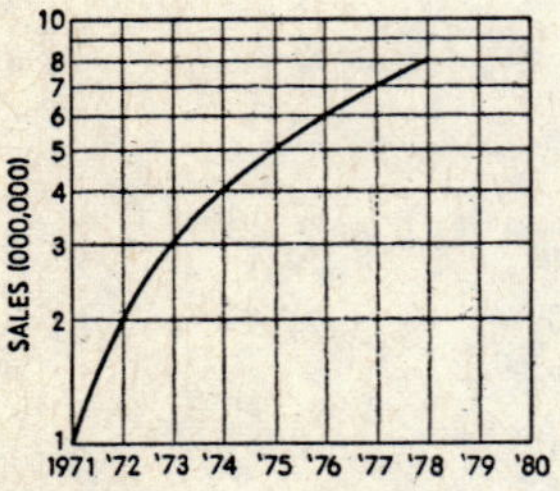

10

The semilogarithmic paper used in the preceding sales illustration is called one-cycle semilogarithmic or ratio paper. Note that the *X*-axis is evenly spaced and has an arithmetic scaling. The *Y*-axis is constructed using logarithms. Equal distances on the *Y*-axis represent equal *percent* changes. The distance between 1 and 2 is the same as between 2 and 4, and also 4 and 8. Each represents a 100 percent increase.

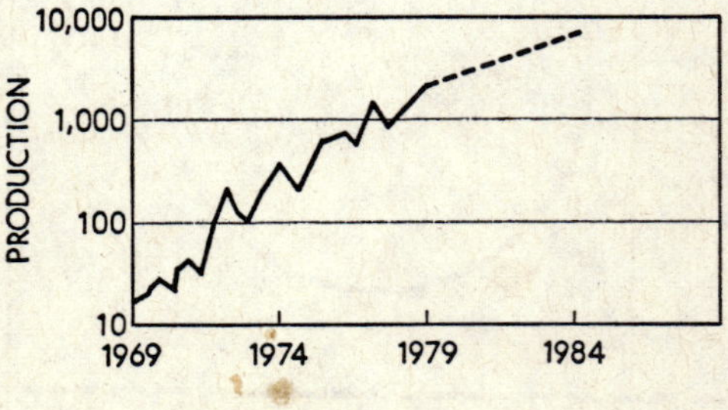

Semilogarithmic paper is very versatile. Suppose production increased drastically from 12 units in 1969 to 6,000 units in 1979 and projected production in 1984 is 9,000 units. The semilogarithmic paper could be designed so that the bottom figure on the *Y*-axis is 10, the top figure of the first cycle would be 100, as shown. Three-cycle semilogarithmic paper would be needed to chart the data.

Note on semilog paper that the distance from the bottom of a cycle to the top of a cycle represents a tenfold increase. The bottom number can be any number except zero. The paper can be purchased in one, two, three, four, five, or six cycles.

Suppose exports have increased from $12 million in 1950 to $642 million at the present time. How many cycles would be needed to plot the data? (Assume the bottom number on the Y-axis is $10 million) ________________. Suppose the debt of a state increased from $122,000 in 1931 to $6 billion at the present time. How many cycles would be needed to plot the data? ________.

2

5

Semilogarithmic paper has other uses, including plotting a *geometric* series. A geometric series increases at a constant rate, such as 12 percent each period. Which paper to use depends on what the statistician wants to emphasize. If the *amount* of change from year to year is more important, ________________ paper should be used. If the *rate* of growth is more important, ________________ paper should be used.

arithmetic

semilogarithmic

Final Self-Review Examination

First, answer all of the questions. Then check your answers against those given at the end of this chapter. Scoring: 10 problems × 10 points each.

11. Data found within a firm is classified as ______ internal ______ data.

12. Total employment in the United States last month, employment in manufacturing, the number of workers in the United States quitting their jobs, and other monthly statistics on the labor force can be found in a monthly publication of the federal government called the ___Monthly Labor Review___.

13. The number of $2 bills in circulation, money turnover, and other monthly financial statistics can be found in a monthly publication entitled ___Federal Reserve Bulletin___.

14. If the search of publications such as the *Statistical Abstract of the United States* does not uncover the data being sought, various reference aids may be consulted. One reference aid is ___Sources of Business Inf___

15. Statistical data may be presented for analysis and interpretation in ___chart table___ form or ___graph___ form.

16. Present the following sales data in a simple line graph. Label.

Year	*Sales (Millions)*
1973	$ 3
1974	7
1975	2
1976	6
1977	8
1978	11

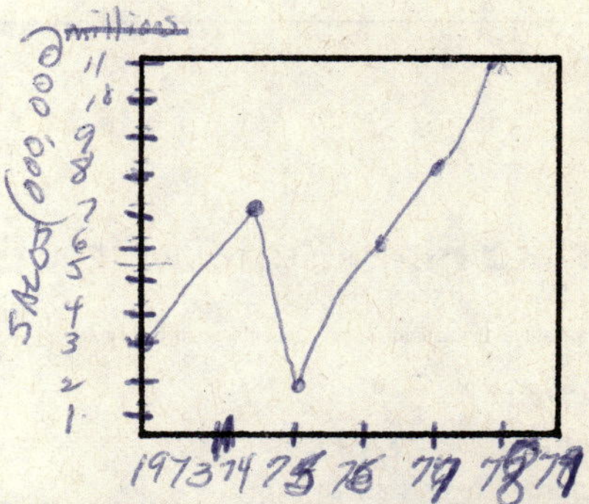

17. Present the following data in a component bar graph. The objective is to show *for each year* the sales of each department as a component of the total. Label. Use the shading given for each department.

Department	*Sales ($000) 1973*	*Sales ($000) 1974*
Suit	$20	$ 9
Shoe	4	4
TV	30	57

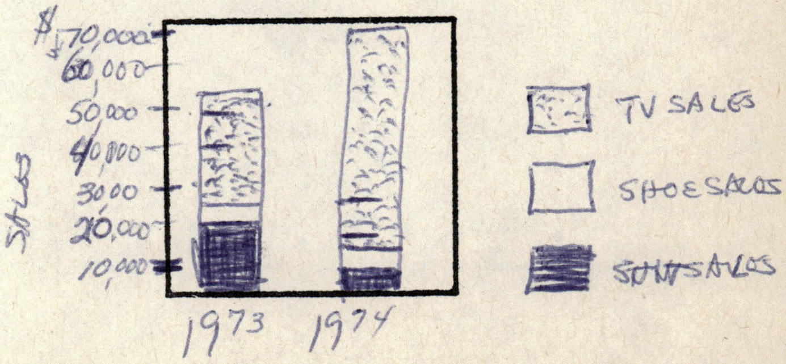

18. The production scheduling department wants to show graphically that the production of some parts increased percentagewise from 1977 to 1978 and others decreased percentagewise. Present the *percent* increases and decreases in a two-directional bar graph. Label.

Part	Production (000) 1977	Production (000) 1978
Beer bottles	500	600
Aspirin bottles	100	70
Medical bottles	1,000	1,600
Perfume bottles	2,000	1,000
Experimental bottles	10	9

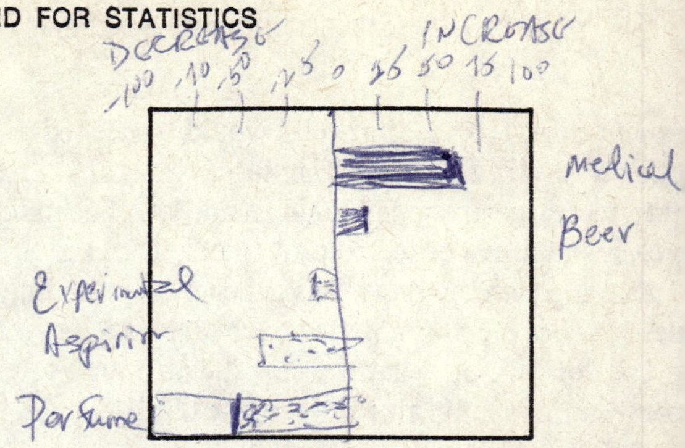

19. Graphs in business and economics are usually drawn on paper having either an ________ scale or a ________ scale.

20. Exports of a company increased from $127,000 in 1951 to $191 million this past year. To portray these export figures, how many cycle semilogarithmic (ratio) paper would be needed? ________.

Answers to Final Self-Review Examination

11. internal
12. *Monthly Labor Review*
13. *Federal Reserve Bulletin*
14. Possible answers are: Index of *The New York Times* or *The Wall Street Journal; Business Periodical Index;* Manley, *Business Information—How to Find and Use It;* Coman, *Sources of Business Information.*
15. table, or graphic form
16.

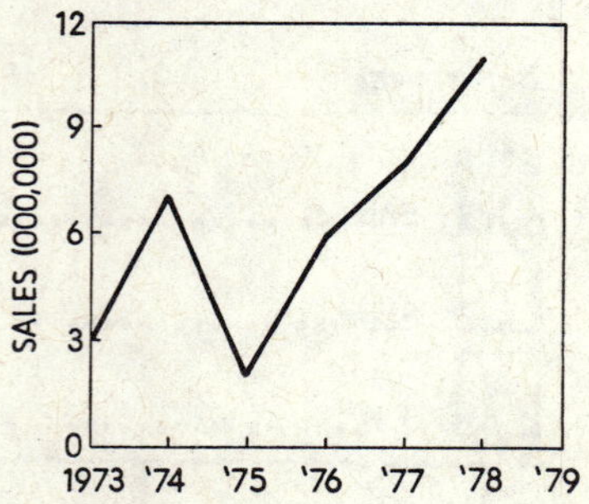

17.

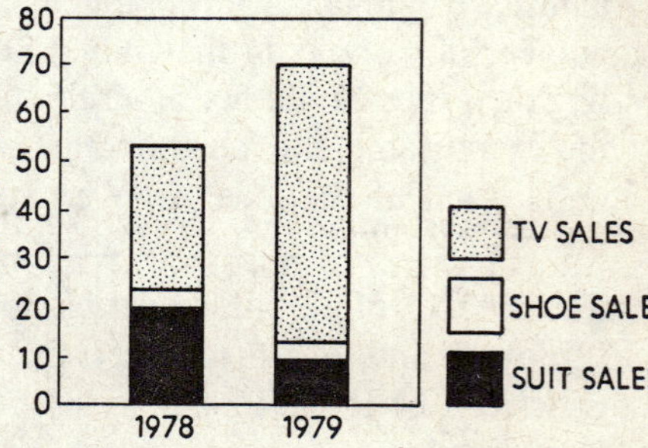

18. PERCENT CHANGE IN THE PRODUCTION OF BOTTLES 1977 to 1978

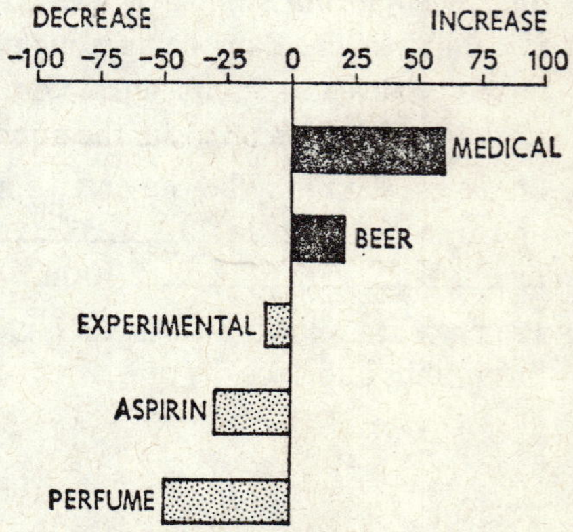

19. arithmetic, semilogarithmic or ratio
20. four

Frequency distributions

chapter

3

1

Business problems involve a large mass of quantitative data which must be organized into some meaningful form before any analysis and interpretation can be made. One commonly used form is the *frequency distribution.* Recall that two types of variables were discussed; namely, discrete and continuous. Frequency distribution analysis is usually concerned with continuous data.

THE ARRAY AND TALLIES

A survey of computer operators in small firms revealed the following monthly incomes (after taxes).

$810	$ 725	$810	$ 875	$850	$ 925	$ 845	$ 880	$750
600	750	790	1,180	850	910	835	1,000	950
875	800	784	800	605	550	1,065	1,175	
770	1,050	987	810	700	890	720	920	
950	545	550	792	825	990	850	900	
850	680	750	600	650	1,075	890	1,050	

The data which are in *ungrouped* form are difficult to analyze, i.e., to determine the low and high incomes, and a central point of concentration, if any. In order to analyze the incomes it is essential, therefore, to organize the data which are in ______________ form into a *grouped* form called a *frequency distribution.* ungrouped

There are two methods of organizing the ungrouped data into a frequency distribution. The first requires setting up an *array* and then *tallying* the incomes into the array. An array is a simple listing of all the monthly incomes arranged in order from the lowest income to the highest income, or vice versa. It was arbitrarily decided to start with the lowest monthly income. The lowest income is ______________. All possible monthly incomes would then be listed in ascending order. Next, the income of each computer operator would be tallied opposite the appropriate amount. See example. $545

Income	*Tally*
$545	/
546	
547	
548	
549	
550	/ /
etc.	

2

THE CLASSES AND THE CLASS INTERVAL

To make a frequency distribution from the array and tallies shown in the previous frame, the incomes could be arbitrarily grouped into *classes* with an interval of, say, $100. The $100 is called the *class interval.* The class interval is merely the range of monthly incomes for each class. A convenient way to determine it is to find the difference between the *lower limits* of two adjoining classes. If the classes were $500 up to $600, $600 up to $700 and so on, the difference between the two lower limits of $500 and $600 is $100 (the class interval). The monthly income grouping of $500 up to $600

class — is called a ________________, ________________. Note that it (does/does not) ________________
does not — ________________ contain the income of $600. The tallies in each of the income classes would then be counted to construct a frequency distribution.

3

A second, or alternative method of organizing the ungrouped data into a frequency distribution is usually less time-consuming. The class interval and the classes are determined first, and the data are tallied directly into the classes. (See the following exhibit.) Fill in the blanks.

Monthly Incomes after Taxes	*Tallies*	*Number of Operators*
$ 500 up to $ 600	///	3
600 up to 700	~~////~~	5
700 up to 800	~~////~~ ~~////~~	10
800 up to 900	~~////~~ ~~////~~ ~~////~~ //	—
900 up to 1,000	~~////~~ ///	—
1,000 up to 1,100	~~////~~	5
1,100 up to 1,200	//	2
Total		—

17
8
50

4

Now an analysis of the incomes of the computer operators can be made. Referring to the frequency distribution, the largest concentration of incomes is in the ________________
$800 up to $900 — ________________ up to ________________ class. Based on the frequency dis-
$500 — tribution, the lowest monthly income is about ________________ and the
$1,200 — highest about ________________.

5

If the classes were 14 up to 18 pounds, 18 up to 22 pounds, and so forth, the distance
class interval — between the classes, called the ________________ is 4 pounds. The limits for the 14 up to 18 pound class are 14 pounds for the *lower limit* and 18 pounds for the *upper limit.* If there were 5 fish weighing between 14 and 18 pounds, the number of fish (5) is called the *frequency.*

Referring to the distribution of monthly incomes of computer operators in frame #3,
$500 lower — the limits of the lowest income class are ________________ for the ________________
$600 upper — ________________ limit and ________________ for the ________________ limit. The fre-
3 — quency for that $500 up to $600 class is ________________. The total of the
50 $100 — frequencies is ________________. The class interval used is ________________.

6

The income classes could have been stated in a number of ways, such as $500–$599.99, $500 through $599.99, and $500 up to but not including $600. The interval between the
$100 — classes (the class interval) in each of these illustrations is ________________.

THER CRITERIA FOR THE CONSTRUCTION OF A FREQUENCY ISTRIBUTION

In practice, the total number of classes usually varies from a minimum of 5 to a aximum of 15. Too few or too many classes might not reveal the essential character- tics of the data. For example, if the incomes of the computer operators were organ- ed into just two classes:

Monthly Incomes	Number of Operators
$500 up to $ 850	26
850 up to 1,200	24

n analysis of the frequency distribution (would/would not) ______ reveal much about the income pattern of the computer operators in the small rms.

would not

henever possible, the intervals between all of the classes in a frequency distribution ould be equal. Unequal class intervals present problems when graphing and com- ting averages and other statistical measures. The class interval in the following dis- bution of tensile strengths is (equal/unequal) ______.

unequal

Tensile Strength of Wires (In Pounds per Square Inch)	*Number of Wires*
Under 12,000	6
12,000 up to 15,000	18
15,000 up to 20,000	7
20,000 up to 50,000	4
50,000 pounds and over	2
	37

e distribution of tensile strengths in frame #8 is also an illustration of a frequency stribution with *open-end* classes. One open-end class is "under 12,000 pounds" and e other is ______. The distribution of tensile strengths ould be difficult to graph, and measures such as the arithmetic mean and standard viation studied in subsequent chapters could not be computed.

50,000 pounds and over

Finally, the class interval selected should result in but one point of concentration in ntrast to two or more peaks.

As noted in Chapter 2, it is often desirable to graph quantitative data in order to in the attention of the reader. Also, a graph may reveal certain relationships which ght not be clearly discernible from an analysis of a frequency distribution table. ree graphs associated with frequency distributions are the *histogram*, the *frequency lygon*, and the *cumulative frequency polygon* or *ogive*.

10

THE HISTOGRAM

The income distribution of the computer operators is used again to illustrate th construction of a histogram. Note that three operators earned between $500 and $6C after taxes. Vertical lines are drawn from $500 and from $600 on the *X*-axis to 3 on th *Y*-axis. This area is enclosed to form a bar. (See exhibit.) Next, a bar is drawn to repr sent the five men who earned between $600 and $700. Complete the histogram.

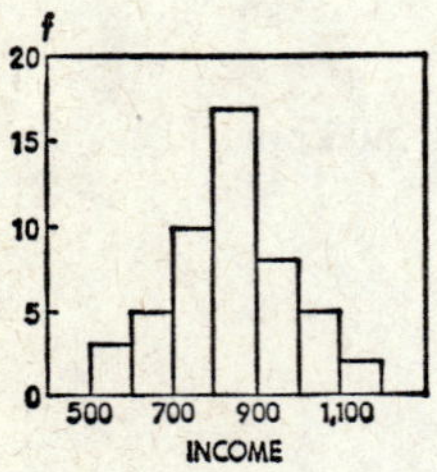

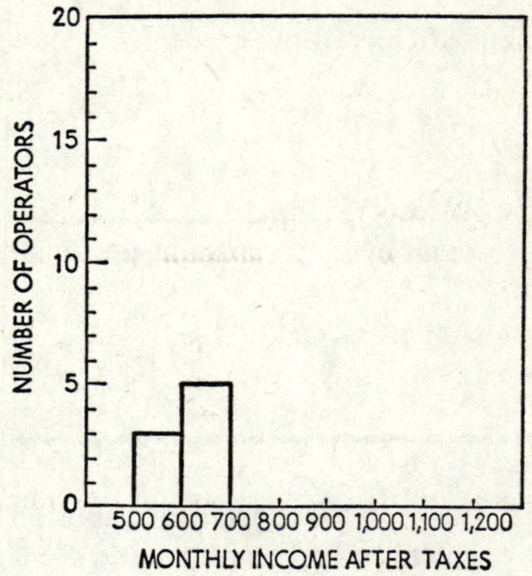

Monthly Income (After Taxes)	*Frequencies*
$ 500 up to $ 600	3
600 up to 700	5
700 up to 800	10
800 up to 900	17
900 up to 1,000	8
1,000 up to 1,100	5
1,100 up to 1,200	2

11

Y-axis
X-axis
histogram
$800 up to $900

As shown, the frequencies are always plotted on the (*X*-axis/*Y*-axis) ____________ ____ and the variable such as income on the (*X*-axis/*Y*-axis) ____________ The graph, called a ________________, reveals that more operators are in th ____________________ up to ____________ income class than in any other class

12

$550
3

$550 and 3

THE FREQUENCY POLYGON

The frequency distribution may also be portrayed graphically in the form of *frequency polygon*. The *midpoints* of each class are used to represent the typical incom of the computer operators in that class. For example, the midpoint of the $500 up t $600 class (frame #10) is ________________. This mid-value is assumed to be th typical income of the (number) ________________ operators in the $500-up-to $600 income bracket. Thus, the coordinates of the point on the frequency polygon ar ____________________ and ____________ operators.

13

The coordinates of the first plot of $550 and 3 frequencies (*f*) is shown. Fill in th blanks and draw the frequency polygon by plotting the remaining points. Then connec the points by straight lines. The usual practice is to extend the lines to the midpoints c the classes above and below the extremes ($450 and $1,250).

Monthly Income after Taxes	*Midpoints*	*f*
$ 500 up to $ 600	$550	3
600 up to 700	—	5
700 up to 800	—	10
800 up to 900	—	17
900 up to 1,000	—	8
1,000 up to 1,100	—	5
1,100 up to 1,200	—	2

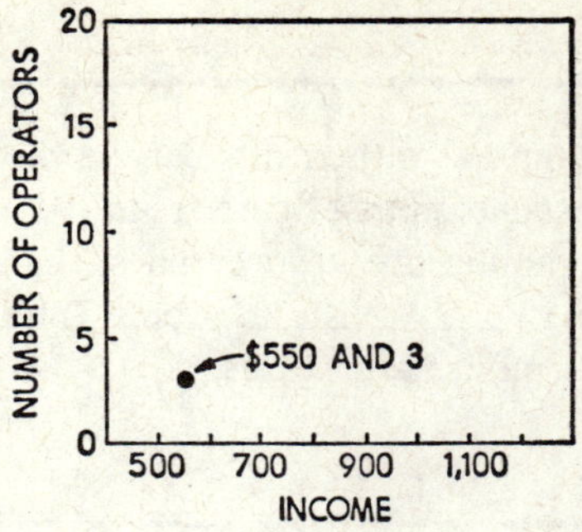

Midpoints are:

$650	$ 950
750	1,050
850	1,150

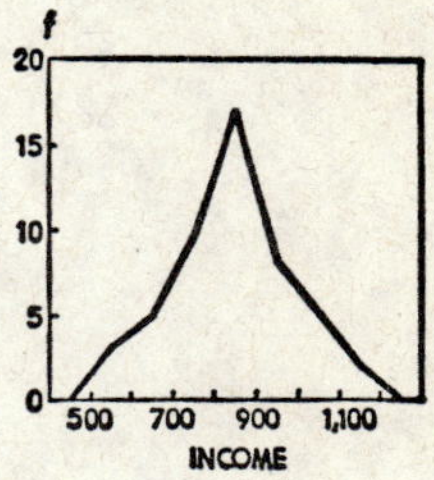

14

THE CUMULATIVE FREQUENCY

There are two cumulative frequency polygons (often called ogives). One is a *less-than-cumulative frequency polygon* and the other a *more-than-cumulative frequency polygon.*

The less-than-ogive is constructed from a less-than-cumulative frequency distribution. To design the cumulative frequency distribution, the frequencies are cumulated starting with the lowest income class and continuing through the highest income class. Now fill in the cumulative frequencies in the following table (extreme right column).

The upper limits of the income classes are also needed to construct the less-than-cumulative frequency polygon. (Insert the upper limits in the spaces provided.)

Monthly Income	*Upper Limit of Class*	*Frequency in Class f*	*Number Receiving Less than Upper Limit of Class CF*
$ 500 up to $ 600	$600	3	3
600 up to 700	700	5	8
700 up to 800	—	10	—
800 up to 900	—	17	—
900 up to 1,000	—	8	—
1,000 up to 1,100	—	5	—
1,100 up to 1,200	—	2	—
		50	

Upper Limits	Cumulative
$ 800	18
900	35
1,000	43
1,100	48
1,200	50

15

The upper limits of the income classes and the corresponding cumulative frequencies are plotted to construct the less-than-cumulative frequency polygon. The first plot in the adjacent exhibit indicates that 3 computer operators earn less than $600, the second plot that 8 earn less than $700, and so on. Complete the less-than-cumulative frequency polygon. Connect the points by straight lines. (Note: the usual practice is to extend the line to the *X*-axis as shown.)

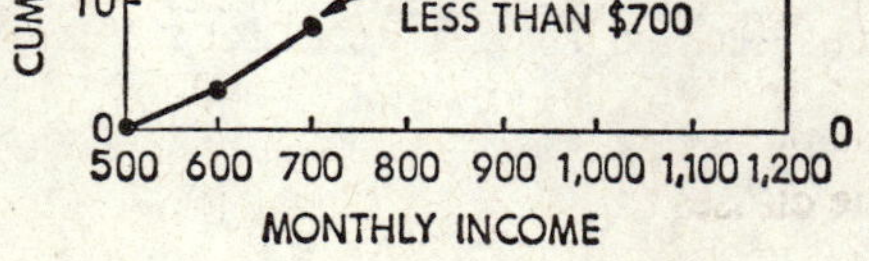

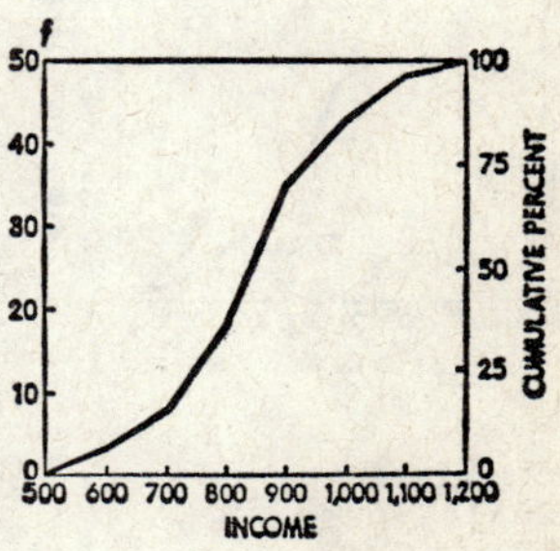

$930
$840
18

16

The cumulative percents can be plotted (as shown) on the right side of the graph. A few *approximate* figures read from the less-than-ogive are: Seventy-five percent of the computer operators earn less than ______________. Half of the operators earn less than ____________. About (number) ______________ operators earn less than $800 a month after taxes.

17

The *more-than-cumulative frequency polygon* is constructed from a more-than-cumulative frequency distribution. Starting with the *highest* income class the frequencies are cumulated up to the lowest income class. The *lower limits* of each class are also needed to construct the more-than-ogive. Accumulate the frequencies and indicate the lower limits in the following distribution of operator incomes. Start with the highest income class.

Monthly Income	*Lower Limit of Class*	*Frequencies f*	*Number of Operators Receiving More than Lower Limit of Class CF*
$ 500 up to $ 600	$ ___	3	___
600 up to 700	___	5	___
700 up to 800	___	10	___
800 up to 900	___	17	___
900 up to 1,000	___	8	___
1,000 up to 1,100	___	5	7
1,100 up to 1,200	1,100	2	2
		50	

Lower Limits	*CF*
$ 500	50
600	47
700	42
800	32
900	15
1,000	7
1,100	2

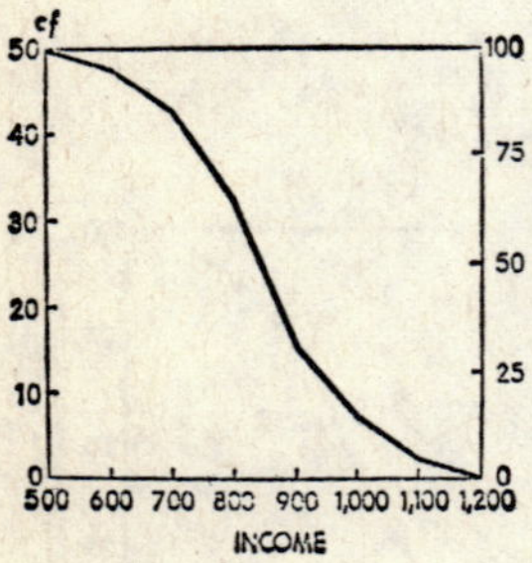

18

A MORE-THAN-CUMULATIVE FREQUENCY POLYGON

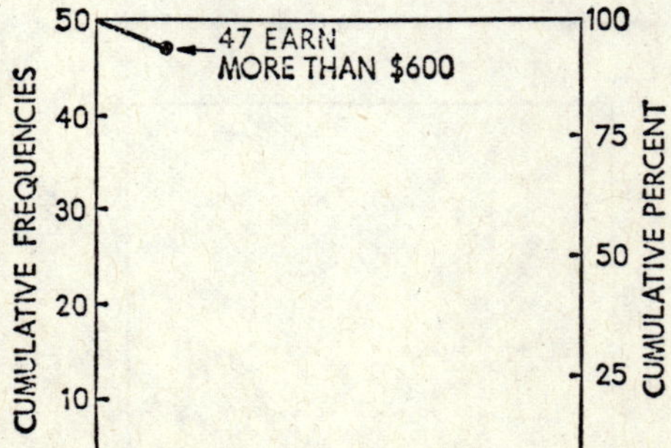

The lower limits of the income classes and the corresponding cumulative frequencies are plotted to construct the more-than-cumulative frequency polygon. The first plot in the adjacent exhibit indicates that all 50 operators earn more than $500, the second plot that 47 earn more than $600, and so forth. Complete the more-than-cumulative polygon. Connect the points by straight lines. Extend the line to the *X*-axis indicating that none of the operators earned $1,200 or more.

9

A few *approximate* figures read from the more-than-ogive are: None of the operators earn more than __________. 50 percent of them earn more than __________. About (number) __________ operators earn $750 or more. All of the operators earn __________ or more after taxes.

$1,200 $840
39
$500

Final Self-Review Examination

First, answer all of the questions. Then check your answers against those given at the end of this chapter. Scoring: 10 problems × 10 points each = 100 possible points.

20. The outside diameter of a shaft is measured by a special gauge. In order to organize the measurements, the following was designed.

Measurement	
62	/
63	////
64	//
65	~~////~~ //
etc.	

The data are considered (discrete/continuous) (*a*) continuous. The ordered numbers 62, 63, 64, etc., are called an (*b*) array, and the ~~////~~ / are (*c*) tallying

21. The measurements were then organized as follows:

Outside Diameter	*Number of Measurements*
62 up to 65	7
65 up to 68	17
68 up to 71	26
71 up to 74	14
74 up to 77	6

The previous table of outside diameters is known as a (*a*) frequency distribution. The data in the table is considered (grouped/ungrouped) (*b*) grouped.

22. In the table of outside diameters (frame #21), the size of the class interval is (*a*)__________, and the numbers on the right (7, 17, etc.) are called (*b*)__________.

23. Present the data on outside diameters (frame #21) in the form of a *histogram* in the following left grid. Label axes and insert essential numbers.

24. Present the data on outside diameters (frame #21) in the form of a *frequency polygon* in the right grid. Label axes and insert essential numbers.

25. Using the same distribution of outside diameters (frame #21), portray the data in a *less-than-cumulative frequency polygon* (left).

26. Now on the right draw a *more-than-cumulative frequency polygon* using the same distribution (frame #21). Include essential numbers.

27. Based on any of the graphs, answer the following questions. The largest concentration of outside diameters are in the (*a*)________________ up to ________________ class. One-fourth of the outside diameters measured less than (approximately) (*b*)________________

28. (Refer again to the graphs.) Approximately half of the outside diameters measured more than (*a*)________________. About (*b*)________________ percent of the shafts measured more than 71 on the special gauge.

29. Briefly, indicate the purpose(s) of organizing data into a frequency distribution and drawing various graphs.____
____
____.

ıswers to Final Self-Review Examination

!0. (*a*) continuous
(*b*) array
(*c*) tallies

!1. (*a*) frequency distribution
(*b*) grouped

!2. (*a*) 3
(*b*) frequencies

!3. Histogram

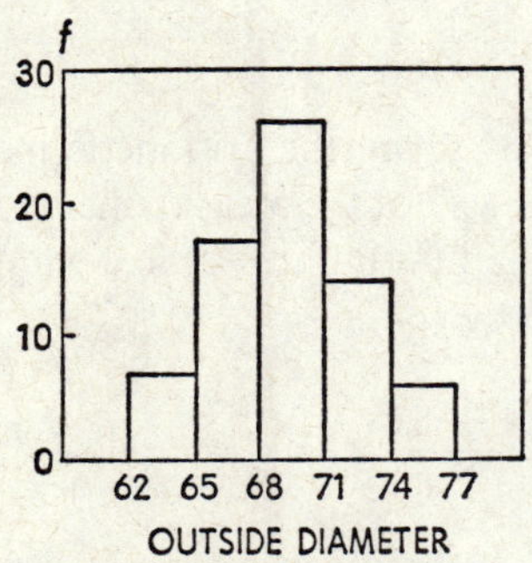

!4. Frequency Polygon

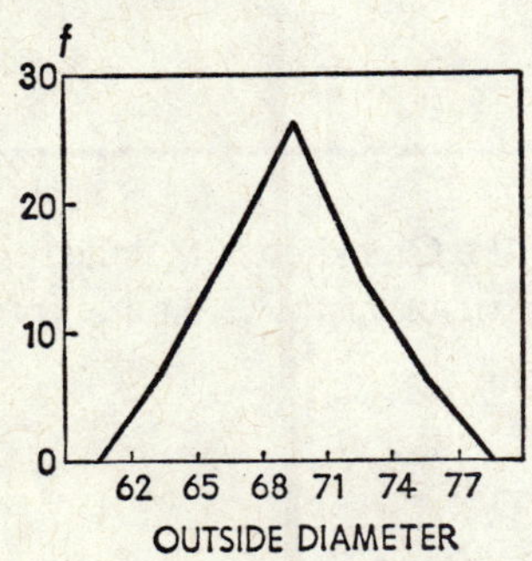

25. Less-than-cumulative frequency polygon

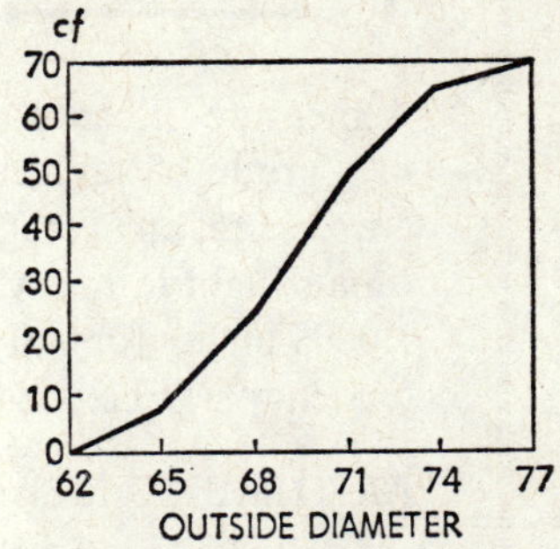

26. More-than-cumulative frequency polygon

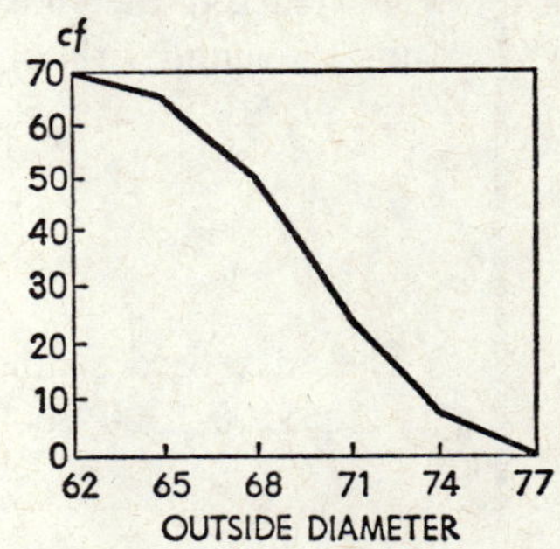

27. (*a*) 68 to 71 class
(*b*) 67 or 66

28. (*a*) about 69 or 70
(*b*) 30 percent

29. Purpose is to organize the ungrouped data into some meaningful form. If the data are continuous (or even discrete), the frequency distribution, the histogram, and other graphic forms reveal points of concentration and other important characteristics and relationships not easily discernible from a perusal of the ungrouped data.

chapter

4

Measures of central tendency

1

A measure of central tendency is a single number which represents the central value of a group of variables. These measures are commonly called "averages." A few examples are: an average family income of $8,200 a year, a 60.2-pound average weight of tuna caught in the Atlantic Fishing Tournament, and an average outside diameter of 1.0003 inches for valve stems machined during the last hour. Four measures of central tendency will be considered: the *arithmetic mean, median, mode,* and *geometric mean.*

ARITHMETIC MEAN

Ungrouped data. If the data are in ungrouped form, the arithmetic mean (often shortened to the "mean") is calculated by summing all of the measurements and dividing the sum by the number of measurements. The hourly rates of five employees are $3, $2, $6, $4, and $2. The mean is $3.40, found by:

$$\frac{\$3 + \$2 + \$6 + \$4 + \$2}{5}$$

$400 The advertised selling prices of an older-model automobile at several used car lots were: $500, $300, $600, and $200. The arithmetic mean price is ________.

2

For simplicity, the plus signs can be replaced by the Greek letter Σ, called sigma. The variable is designated as x, n stands for the number of variables, and $\bar{X}$ (pronounced X bar or bar X) is the symbol for the mean. Thus:

$$\bar{X} = \frac{\Sigma x}{n}$$

Several firms submitted bids for a new building: the Jones Company, $6 million; Ace Construction $10 million; and Arno, Ltd., $5 million. The symbol for the arithmetic mean is ________. In this problem, Σx represents the ________ ________, and n stands for ________. The formula for the arithmetic mean, the essential numbers, and the arithmetic mean bid is:

$\bar{X}$ sum of the bids number of firms

$\bar{X}$ = ________ = ________ = ________ million

$\frac{\Sigma x}{n} = \frac{\$21}{3} = \$7$

3

If n and $\bar{X}$ are known, Σx can be found. For example, the mean wage for the 30 employees of the Betz Stamping Plant for the week of July 1 was $120. The total employee payroll for the week was ________.

$3,600

Grouped data. The tensile strengths of several wires (in pounds per square inch) re 6, 6, 7, 7, 7, 8, 8, and 9.4 pounds. The tensile strengths were grouped into a freuency distribution.

The midpoint of each class is used to represent the class. The midpoint of the class lesignated as x) is then multiplied by the number of frequencies in that class. The um of these products is divided by the total number of frequencies to give the arithetic mean. In terms of a formula:

$$\bar{X} = \frac{\Sigma fx}{n} \quad \text{or} \quad \frac{\Sigma fx}{\Sigma f}$$

nsert the missing numbers:

Tensile Strengths (Pounds per Square Inch)	*Number of Wires* f	*Midpoint of Class* x	fx
5.50 up to 6.50	2	6	12
6.50 up to 7.50	3	7	—
7.50 up to 8.50	2	—	—
8.50 up to 9.50	1	—	—
	8	Total	—

x	fx
	21
8	16
9	9
	58

---

he formula for the mean of grouped data, the essential numbers and the mean tensile rength are:

$\bar{X}$ = ________ = ________ = ________ pounds per square inch.

$$\frac{\Sigma fx}{\Sigma f} = \frac{58}{8} = 7.25$$

---

he mean of the original ungrouped data (6, 6, 7, 7, 7, 8, 8, and 9.4) is ________ ounds. Note that the mean of the grouped data (7.25) and the mean of the ungrouped ata (7.3) are not identical. The difference is due to the loss of accuracy when the data ere grouped. The mean would probably be another value if a different class interval ad been selected.

7.3

---

he annual sales of selected firms were organized as follows.

Annual Sales (In Millions)	*Number of Firms*
\$ 5 up to \$15	3
15 up to 25	5
25 up to 35	6
35 up to 45	4
45 up to 55	2

The arithmetic mean annual sales is \$________. ________ million.

$$\bar{X} = \frac{\Sigma fx}{\Sigma f} = \frac{\$570}{20} = \$28.5$$

8

MEDIAN

Ungrouped data. The median is the value of a point on a scale above which half the values are found and below which the other half of the values lie. To determine th median of ungrouped data, the values are first arranged from low to high. Arrange th incomes of five individuals in ascending order. The incomes are: $12,000, $10,00 $22,000, $17,000, and $100,000.

$10,000
$ 12,000 — $__________
$ 17,000 — $__________
$ 22,000 — $__________
$100,000 — $__________

$17,000 median

The middle income is __________. This income is called the ________

9

The median income of $17,000 seems to be a typical income since all but one inc vidual are in the $10,000-up-to-$22,000 income range. The median is a mo representative measure of central tendency than is the arithmetic mean which

$32,200

________.

Thus, the median is usually a more appropriate measure if one or more extreme

high

__________ (or low) observations are included. What would the media income be if the highest income were $1 million instead of $100,000? ________

same $17,000

_____. Had the lowest income been $2,000 instead of $10,000, the median incon would be __________.

same $17,000

10

If there is an even number of ungrouped observations, the median is halfway betwe the two center observations. A sample of prices of Grade D pine lumber at four lumb yards revealed prices of $0.28, $0.32, $0.22, and $0.21. To determine the median pric the prices must first be ________________. The median price __________. (Note that no lumber yard had a price of exactly $0.2

arranged from low to high
$0.25

11

Grouped data. There is a minimal amount of work involved in arranging a few u grouped observations from low to high and selecting the middle value. A large numb of observations, however, presents a problem of ordering the data and finding t middle item. Instead, the quantitative data may be tallied directly into classes and t median approximated from the resulting frequency distribution. Also, in many cas the original data from which the frequency distribution was designed are not availab and the median must be estimated from the grouped data.

The 60 junior executives in a firm were rated by top management on a scale from up to 100. The composite ratings were then organized into a frequency distribution f further study.

Ratings of Junior Executives	*Number* f	*Cumulative Number* CF_i
50 up to 60	9	9
60 up to 70	15	24
70 up to 80	20	44
80 up to 90	11	55
90 up to 100	5	60
Total	60	

The problem involves estimating the composite rating of the junior executive in the middle of the distribution. He is the ____________th junior executive counting down from the lowest rated. 30

12

The position of the 30th junior executive is shown schematically as follows.

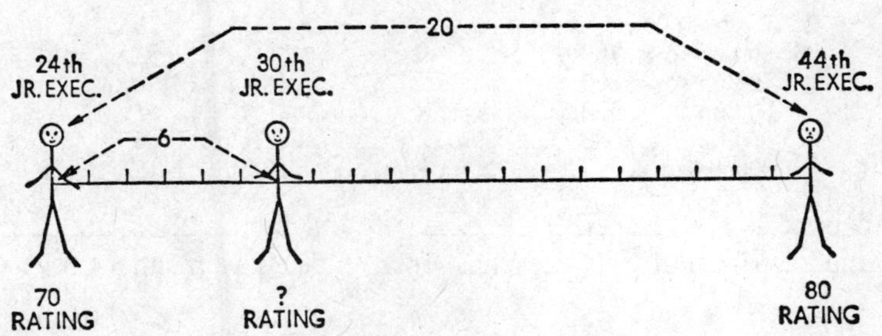

Interpolating, the rating earned by the 30th junior executive is ________/20 of the distance between a rating of 70 and ____________. This amount (6/20 of 10, or ________) is added to 70. Thus, the median rating of the junior executives is ________. 6 80 3 73

13

One assumption when interpolating the median is that the ratings are evenly distributed between 70 and 80. If the ungrouped data were available, the median rating might not be exactly 73. Thus, it probably should be said that *about* half of the junior executives had a rating less than ____________ and *about* half more than ________. 73 73

14

The median may also be computed using the formula:

$$\text{Median} = L + \frac{\frac{n}{2} - CF}{f}(i)$$

where: L is the lower limit of the class in which the median falls. The 30th junior executive accumulated from the lowest rating is found in the ________ up to ______ 70 up to 80

70 ______ class and ______ is the lower limit of that class. n is the total num-
60 ber of junior executives, or ______ (number). CF is the cumulative fre-
24 quency for the class immediately below the median class. There are ______ (number) junior executives accumulated below the median class. The frequency (f) in
20 the median class is ______ (number). The letter i stands for the width
10 of the class interval of the median class. The width in this problem is ______.
Thus, the formula for the median, essential numbers, and the answer:

$$L + \frac{\frac{n}{2} - CF}{f}(i)$$

$$= 70 + \frac{\frac{60}{2} - 24}{20}(10) = 73$$

Median = ______ = ______ = ______ (answer)

Note that the answer is the same as found previously (frame #12).

15

The prices paid for a three-piece livingroom suite were tabulated by the assistant buyer into the following frequency distribution.

Price Paid for Suite	*Number of Sales*
Up to \$600	20
\$ 600 up to \$ 700	83
700 up to 800	122
800 up to 900	91
900 up to 1,000	66
1,000 and over	18

\$779.51, \$700 + 97/122 of \$100

The median price is ______, found by: ______.
Note that the distribution of prices has open ends. The mean cannot be found.

16

MODE

Ungrouped data. The *mode* is defined as the value of the observation which appears most frequently. If there is only one mode, the distribution is called *unimodal.* If there are two values which appear most frequently, the distribution is called *bimodal.* The ages of a group of draftees are: 19, 21, 20, 21, 20, 21, 21, and 24 years. The data are
ungrouped (grouped/ungrouped) ______ and the distribution is (unimodal/
unimodal 21 years bimodal) ______. The mode is ______. Hourly production of individuals making identical assemblies are 5, 8, 8, 7, 9, 10, 10, 8, 10, and 11
bimodal units. The distribution is (unimodal/bimodal) ______. The modes are
8 units, 10 units ______ and ______.

17

Grouped data. The *crude* or *observed* mode for data grouped into a frequency distribution is the midpoint of the class in which the greatest number of frequencies are
\$750 found. The observed mode for the distribution in frame 15 is ______.

18

GEOMETRIC MEAN

The geometric mean is defined as the nth root of the product of n numbers. The formula is:

$$\text{Geometric mean} = \sqrt[n]{(x_1)(x_2)(x_3)\ldots(x_n)}$$

ne important business application is determining the average percent increase in sales, roduction, or other variable over a period of time. A modification of the formula is:

$$\text{Geometric mean} = \sqrt[n-1]{\frac{\text{Value for the last period of time}}{\text{Value for the first period of time}}} - 1$$

'or example, sales for 1979 were \$180 million, and for 1973 they were \$100 million. Vhat is the average annual percent increase in sales from 1973 through 1979? Note iere are seven years.

$$\text{Geometric mean} = \sqrt[7-1]{\frac{\$180}{\$100}} - 1 = \sqrt[6]{1.80} - 1$$

'sing logarithms to find the 6th root of 1.80:

$$\frac{\text{log of } 1.80}{6} = \frac{0.2553}{6} = 0.0426$$

The antilog of 0.0426 is approximately 1.103. Then 1.103 − 1 = 0.103. Sales in-reased 10.3 percent per year on the average from 1973 to 1979.

Similarly, the approximate average (geometric mean) annual percent increase of a tock which rose from \$20 in 1970 to \$117 in 1978 is____________ percent (near-st whole percent).

about 25 percent

9

ELATIONSHIP OF THE MEAN, MEDIAN AND MODE

If a frequency distribution is bell-shaped (symmetrical), the mean, median, and ode are equal. (See the following exhibit.) However, if the frequency distribution is ot symmetrical (called asymmetrical, or skewed) the relationship among the averages anges. The graph on the right portrays a *positively skewed* distribution. Suppose at it represents the distribution of family incomes contiguous to a proposed shopping nter. The arithmetic mean is the highest of the three averages, the median is the next rgest, and the mode the smallest. The mean income is the highest because it is being fluenced by a few extremely high incomes.

A SYMMETRICAL DISTRIBUTION

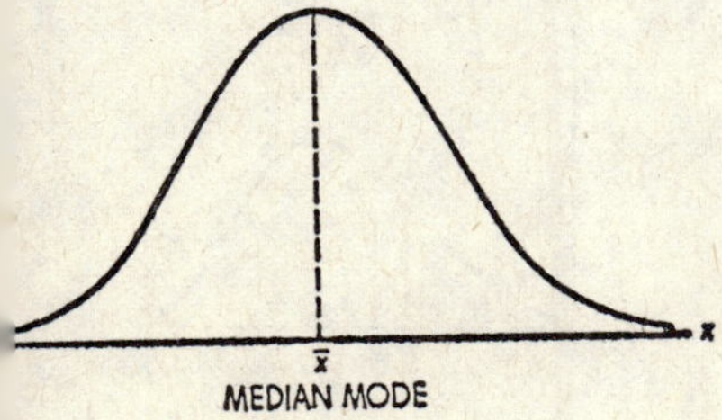

A POSITIVELY SKEWED DISTRIBUTION

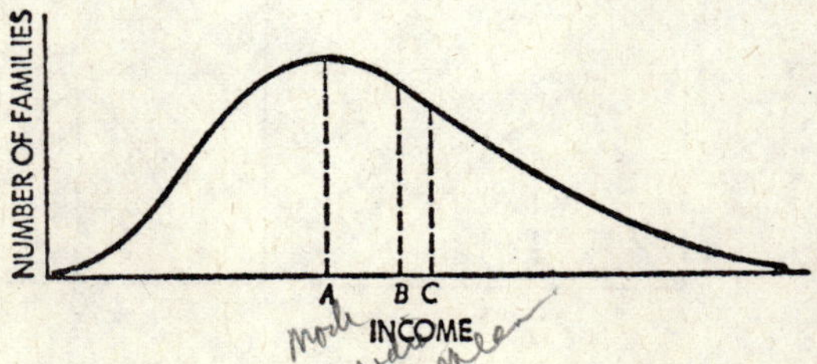

verage A is the ________________, B is the ________________ and the __________.

Mode Median Mean

20

If the distribution is only moderately skewed, one average can be approximated if th other two are known by either:

$$\text{Mode} = \text{mean} - 3(\text{mean} - \text{median})$$

$$\text{Median} = \frac{2(\text{mean}) + \text{mode}}{3}$$

$$\text{Mean} = \frac{3(\text{median}) - \text{mode}}{2}$$

$12,000

If the modal family income were $9,000 and the median $11,000, the approximat mean income is ________________. (Note that the median is about two thirds o the distance between the mode and the mean.)

50 years

If the ages of a group were organized into a frequency distribution and the mea age computed to be 60 years and the mode 30 years, the median age is approximatel ____________ years.

21

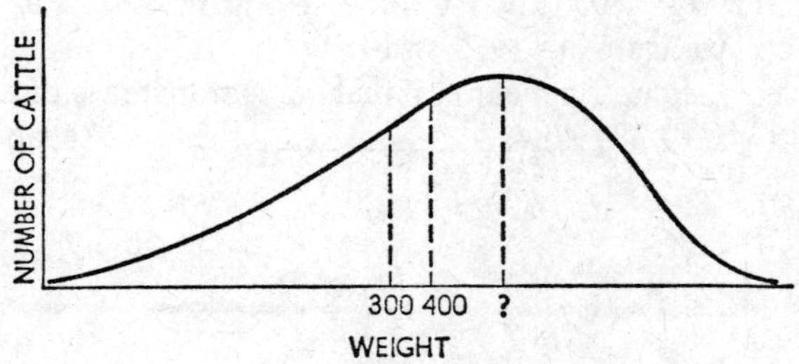

600
400 600
negatively

The arithmetic mean in a *nega tively skewed* distribution is th smallest of the three averages.I is affected more than the me dian or mode by extremely lov values. The next largest averag is the median and the mode i the largest. In the following dis tribution of the weights of cattl sold at the stockyards, the mode is about ____________ pounds. Half of the cattl weighed less than ______________ pounds. More cattle weighed ____________ ______ pounds than any other weight. The distribution is ________________ skewed.

22

positively skewed
bell-shaped or symmetrical
negatively skewed

In review, describe the shape of the distribution in Figure A ______________ ______________, in Figure B ________________________________, and Fig ure C ________________________________.

FIGURE A

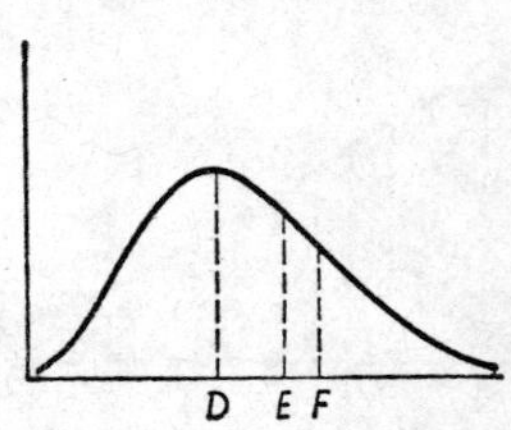

FIGURE B

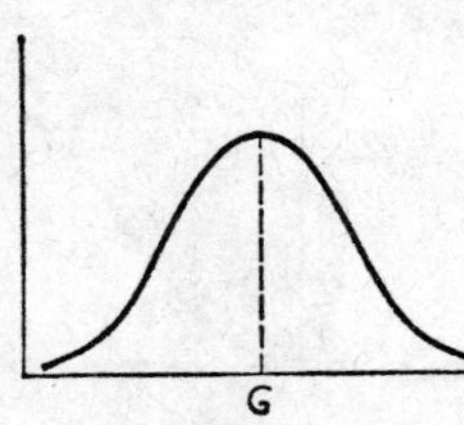

FIGURE C

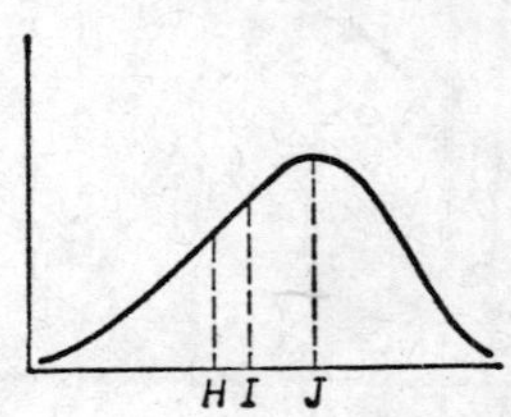

mode
mean
also $200

The letter D represents which average? ________________. The letter F ________________. The mode in Figure B is $200. The median is ____________ ______. In Figure C, the mean is 80 inches and I is 100 inches. What is the value of J

__________ inches. In Figure C, half of the values are over __________ inches. 140 100

23

SUMMARY OF THE CHARACTERISTICS OF MEASURES OF CENTRAL TENDENCY

The arithmetic mean is the most commonly used average. All the values are needed for its computation. If all of the values are clustered near the mean, and if the distribution is somewhat symmetrical, the mean can be considered a representative average. Extremely high (or low) values unduly affect it, and an unrepresentative average may result. Generally speaking, if the distribution of values is skewed, the (average) __________ is considered a poor average to use to represent the group. arithmetic mean

The median, however, is not affected by extreme values and better represents the group of values when the distribution is skewed. Also, the median can be computed if the distribution has open ends. The arithmetic mean cannot be determined for an open-end frequency distribution because __________. midpoints (X) are not available

The mode is not used as often as the mean or median but is a very appropriate average to use if one value near the center of the distribution appears quite frequently. If the distribution is symmetrical or slightly skewed the mode (can/cannot) __________ be determined. Also, the mode (can/cannot) __________ be computed if the distribution has open ends. can can

The geometric mean is infrequently used partly because logarithms are needed for its computation. It is the only average, however, that gives the correct answer in problems involving __________. average annual percent increase

Final Self-Review Examination

First, answer all of the questions. Then check your answers against those given at the end of this chapter. Scoring: 10 problems × 10 points each = 100 possible points.

24. The ages of several typists are 22, 26, 29, 23, and 18 years. The median age is (*a*)__________ years. The arithmetic mean age is (*b*)__________ years.

Questions 25 through 28 are based on the following frequency distribution.

Hourly Wages of Workers	*Number of Workers*
\$ 2 up to \$ 4	1
4 up to 6	3
6 up to 8	20
8 up to 10	4
10 up to 12	2

25. The arithmetic mean hourly wage is __________ (nearest cent).

26. The median hourly wage is __________ (nearest cent).

27. The observed mode is __________.

28. Based on the three measures of central tendency, the distribution of wages can be considered (positively skewed/negatively skewed/symmetrical) __________.

29. If a frequency distribution is only slightly skewed, *but has open ends*, which of the following measure, or measures, of central tendency *cannot* be computed? (arithmetic mean/median/mode) __________.

30. The production of a small plant increased from 40 units in 1977 to 74 units in 1978. The average annual percent increase in production is ________________ percent. (Note: nearest whole percent. It is not necessary to interpolate.)

31. Most of the prices paid for 120 antique silver pieces at an auction varied between $5 and $12 except for one rare piece which brought $71,000. Which of the three most commonly used averages (arithmetic mean/median/mode) would not be a representative average to use? ________________.

32. The following frequency polygon portrays a distribution of tensile strengths of copper wire. The letter A represents an average called the (*a*)________________ and the letter B represents the (*b*)________________ tensile strength. Is the distribution (symmetrical / positively skewed/ negatively skewed)?(*c*) ________________.

DISTRIBUTION OF TENSILE STRENGTHS

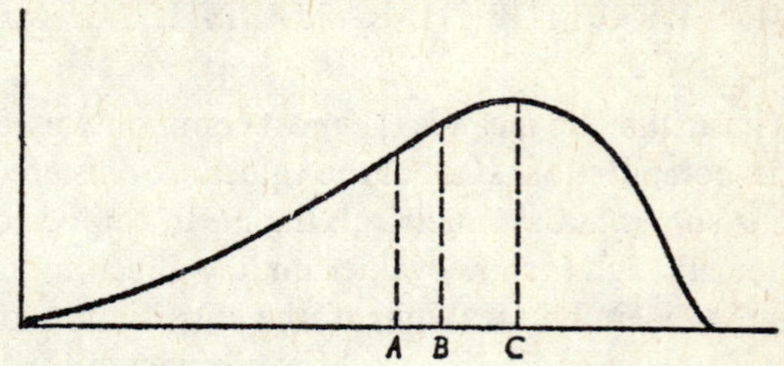

33. It was found that a distribution of incomes in a suburb was moderately skewed. The mean income was computed to be $15,000 and the median income $14,000. The approximate modal (mode) income is ________________.

Answers to Final Self-Review Examination

24. (*a*) 23, (*b*) 23.6 years
25. $7.20, found by $216/30
26. $7.10, found by $6 + 11/20 of $2
27. $7.00
28. positively skewed
29. arithmetic mean
30. about 13 percent
31. arithmetic mean
32. (*a*) arithmetic mean
    (*b*) median
    (*c*) negatively skewed
33. $12,000

Measures of dispersion and skewness

chapter

5

he basic concept of *dispersion*, alternatively called *variation* or *spread*, can be illus- ated by analyzing the weekly incomes of two groups of employees; namely, the roduction employees and the office employees.

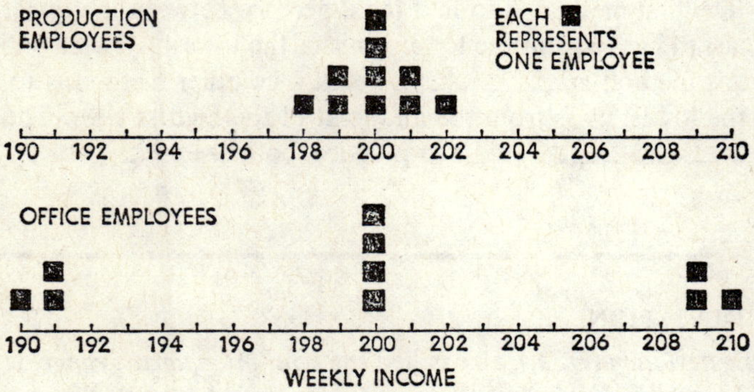

he arithmetic mean weekly income of both groups is ______. Any comparison of the come structure of the two groups based only on the average, however, would be mis- ading. This is so because the incomes of the ______________ employees are oread out more than the incomes of the ______________ employees. Thus, dditional statistical measures to describe the dispersion, also called ______________ ___ or ______________, are needed. Five measures of absolute dispersion are udied. They are the *range*, the *quartile deviation*, the *average deviation*, the *variance*, nd the *standard deviation*.

$200

office
production
variation or
spread

2

IEASURES OF ABSOLUTE DISPERSION: RANGE

Ungrouped data. The lowest paid employee in the office (frame #1) earned $190 a eek and the highest, $210. The difference of $20 is called the *range*. The range of the eekly incomes for the production group is ______________________.

$4, found by $202 − $198

---

here is more spread in the incomes of the office employees than in the incomes of the roduction employees because the range of ______________ is greater than ______. he range of $4 for the production employees compared with the range of $20 for e office employees indicates that the incomes of the production employees tend to uster more about the mean. It also indicates that the mean income of ______________ r the production employees is a (more/less) ______________ representative average an the $200 mean income of the office employees.

$20 $4

$200
more

4

Grouped data. The same concept is used if the data are grouped into a frequenc distribution. Suppose the ages of the office employees were grouped as follows.

Ages	*Number of Office Workers*
15 up to 25 years	12
25 up to 35 years	51
35 up to 45 years	16

There are two methods of determining the range from data grouped into a frequenc distribution. The first method is to find the difference between the upper limit of th highest age class (45 years) and the lower limit of the lowest age class (15 years). Th
30 range using this method is ________ years. The other method is to subtract th midpoint of the lowest class from the midpoint of the highest class. The range usin
20 this method is ________ years. In practice, both are used.

5

QUARTILE DEVIATION

The *quartile deviation* (Q.D.), also called the *semi-interquartile range*, is a positiona measure similar to the range. The value of the range is based solely on the differenc
lowest and highest between the ________ and ________ observations. The quartile deviation i based on the difference between the first quartile (Q_1) and the third quartile (Q_3). Th first quartile is the value corresponding to the point below which 25 percent of the ob servations lie. The third quartile is the value corresponding to the point above whic 25 percent of the observations lie. Thus, between Q_1 and Q_3 can be found the middl
50 ________ percent of the observations.

6

The concept of the first quartile (Q_1) is illustrated by considering the tensile strength of 60 wires. Its computation is very similar to the median (Q_2) studied in the previou chapter.

Tensile Strengths (Pounds per Square Inch)	*Number of Wires f*	*Cumulative Frequencies CF*
600 up to 700	3	3
700 up to 800	6	9
800 up to 900	13	22
900 up to 1,000	20	42
1,000 up to 1,100	10	52
1,100 up to 1,200	8	60
	60	

There are 60 wires. Counting up from the lowest class to include the first quarter of th observations (15)—found by dividing 60 by 4—the point located is called the firs quartile. The tensile strength on the scale below which are located the tensile strength of 15 wires can be interpolated as follows: Counting into the distribution there are 9 wires accumulated up to 800 pounds and 22 wires accumulated up to 900 pounds. Logically, the first quartile is between 800 and 900 pounds. The tensile strength below which are one fourth of the wires is 6/13 the way up from 800 pounds.

$$Q_1 = 800 + \frac{6}{13} \text{ of } 100 = 846.15 \text{ pounds (846 rounded)}$$

Shown schematically:

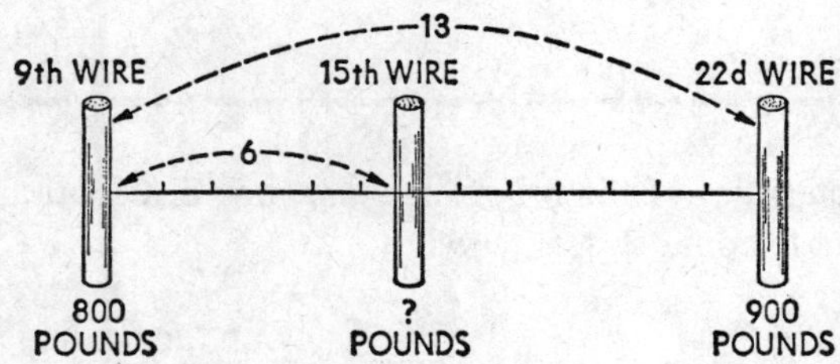

Using this method of interpolation, determine the third quartile, Q_3 = ________________.

1,030 pounds, found by 1,000 + 3/10 of 100

7

Half the distance between the third quartile and the first quartile is *semi-interquartile range*, or the *quartile deviation* (Q.D.). Design a formula, insert the appropriate data, and determine the quartile deviation.

Q.D. = ________ = ________ = ________.

$$\text{Q.D.} = \frac{Q_3 - Q_1}{2} = \frac{1{,}030 - 846}{2} = 92 \text{ pounds}$$

8

If the distribution is symmetrical, the distance between Q_1 and Q_2 (the median) is equal to the distance between ________ and ________. This concept is portrayed in the following distribution representing the annual incomes of middle management.

Q_2 and Q_3

The median is ________. The quartile deviation is ________. If the quartile deviation is subtracted from, and added to, the median, the resulting answers are ________ and ________ respectively. These two amounts are the ________ and ________ quartiles. This relationship between the median and the (measure of dispersion) ________ is only true if the distribution is ________.

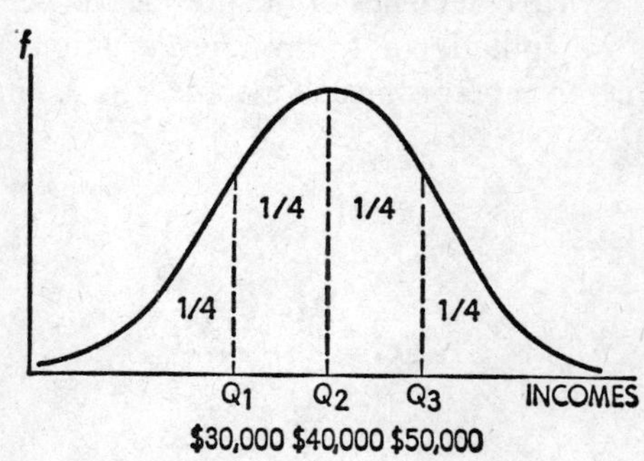

$40,000
$10,000

$30,000 and $50,000

first and third

quartile deviation
symmetrical or bell-shaped

9

If the frequency distribution is skewed *positively*, the distance between Q_1 and Q_2 will be less than the distance between Q_2 and Q_3. For the following ________

positively

any guess over 230 pounds

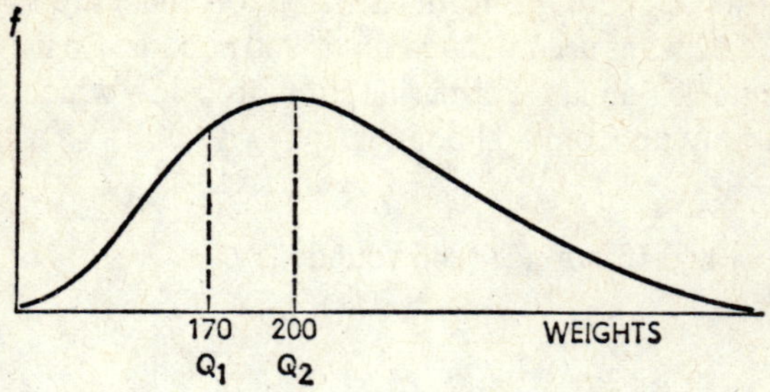

skewed distribution of the weights of football players, guess the third quartile. ________.

Conversely, the distance between Q_1 and Q_2 is larger than the distance between Q_2 and Q_3 in a *negatively* skewed distribution.

10

yes
yes yes
yes
no (because of the open end)

Two unusual characteristics of the following frequency distribution are an open-end (under 20 years), and unequal class intervals.

Ages of Visitors	*Number of Visitors*
Under 20 years	16
20 up to 30 years	32
30 up to 40 years	83
40 up to 60 years	29
60 up to 90 years	10

Can the median age be computed? (yes/no) ________, Q_1 ? ________, Q_3? ________ Q.D. ? ________. The range? ________.

11

AVERAGE DEVIATION

Ungrouped data. The *average deviation* is also called the *mean deviation.* As the name implies, it is computed by averaging the deviations from the mean, or median, disregarding the algebraic signs. The sign || signifies that plus and minus signs are to be ignored. The formula is:

$$\text{A.D.} = \frac{\Sigma|X - \bar{X}|}{n} \quad \text{or} \quad \frac{\Sigma|X - \text{median}|}{n}$$

The weekly incomes of the production employees from frame #1 are used to illustrate the computation of the average deviation. The mean income is \$200. First, the absolute difference between each income and the mean income was found.

Then:

Weekly Income of Production Employees

X	$X - \bar{X}$
\$198	−\$2
199	− 1
199	− 1
200	0
200	0
200	0
200	0
201	+ 1
201	+ 1
202	+ 2
	\$8

$$\text{A.D.} = \frac{\Sigma|X - \bar{X}|}{n} = \frac{\$8}{10} = \$0.80$$

\$5.60, found by \$56/10

Now compute the average deviation for the incomes of the office employees from frame #1; namely, \$190, \$200, \$200, \$209, \$191, \$200, \$210, \$200, \$191, and \$209. The average deviation is ________.

2

comparison of the two average deviations indicates that there is less dispersion in the comes of the ______ workers because ______ is less than ______. Also, the average income of the production employees is more repre- ntative than the average income of the office employees because ______ ______.

production $0.80
$5.60
$0.80 is less than $5.60

The average deviation of grouped data is seldom encountered.

3

ARIANCE AND THE STANDARD DEVIATION

Ungrouped data. The *variance* is also based on the deviations from the mean. To nd the variance (s^2) of the income figures for the production employees, the deviations om the mean ($X - \bar{X}$) are squared $(X - \bar{X})^2$, then summed $\Sigma(X - \bar{X})^2$ and averaged by ividing by the number of men or n. The formula, essential work, and the answer for e variance follows.

Income X	*Income − Mean* $X - \bar{X}$	$(X - \bar{X})^2$
$198	−$2	$ 4
199	− 1	1
199	− 1	1
200	0	0
200	0	0
200	0	0
200	0	0
201	+ 1	1
201	+ 1	1
202	+ 2	4
		12

$$s^2 = \frac{\Sigma(X - \bar{X})^2}{n} = \frac{\$12}{10} = \$1.20$$

Now compute the variance for the incomes of office workers; namely, $190, $200, 200, $209, $191, $200, $210, $200, $191, and $209. The variance is ______ ______.

$52.40, found by $524/10

4

gain, a comparison of the two measures of dispersion (a variance of $52.40 for the ffice employees and $1.20 for the production employees), indicates that there is less ispersion in the incomes of the ______ employees because $1.20 is ss than $52.40. Also, the average income for the production employees is more repre- entative for the same reason, i.e., ______ is less than ______.

production

$1.20 $52.40

5

he variance is difficult to interpret. In this problem, the unit of variance is (dollars)^2. o convert this vague concept to dollars, the square root of the variance is computed. he square root of the variance (s^2) is the *standard deviation*, or (s).

The variance of the incomes of the production employees was found to be $1.20. he square root of the variance, called the ______ ______ is ap- roximately $1.10. (See Appendix Table III for square roots.)

standard deviation

$7.24
production

The variance of the incomes of the office employees was computed to be $52.40. Th standard deviation is $________. Again a comparison of the two standard devi ations indicates that there is less dispersion in the incomes of the ________ employees.

16

Grouped data. To illustrate the computation of the standard deviation for groupe data consider the following wages of welders. First, the midpoint (X) of each wage clas is found. Then each X is squared (X^2) and multiplied by the appropriate number of fre quencies in the class to give fX^2. In terms of a formula, the standard deviation fo grouped data is:

$$s = \sqrt{\frac{\Sigma fX^2}{n} - \bar{X}^2} \quad \text{or} \quad \sqrt{\frac{\Sigma fX^2}{n} - \left(\frac{\Sigma fX}{n}\right)^2}$$

Complete the following table.

Hourly Wages of Welders	*Number of Men* f	*Midpoint* X	X^2	fX^2	fX
$3 up to $5	2	$4	$16	$32	$8
5 up to 7	5	__	__	__	__
7 up to 9	3	__	__	__	__
Total	__			__	__

	$6	$36	$180	$30
	8	64	192	24
10			$404	$62

$$s = \sqrt{\frac{\Sigma fX^2}{n} - \left(\frac{\Sigma fX}{n}\right)^2}$$
$$= \sqrt{\frac{404}{10} - \left(\frac{62}{10}\right)^2}$$
$$= \$1.40$$

Give the formula for the standard deviation, insert figures from the table, and find th standard deviation.

$s =$ $\qquad$ $=$ $\qquad$ $=$ ________ (answer)

17

diemakers
diemakers

Now that the standard deviation has been computed to be $1.40, how is it interpreted Unfortunately, it cannot be as easily defined as the range or median. However, th standard deviation can be considered a unit of measurement similar to the ton, foot, o pounds per square inch tensile strength. The standard deviations from two distribu tions can be used as a common denominator to compare the dispersion of two distri butions and the representativeness of the two means. Assuming that the two means ar approximately equal, standard deviations of $1.40 for the welders and $1 for a distri bution of the wages of diemakers indicates that the mean of the (welders/diemakers ________ is more representative and that there is less dispersion in th wages of the (welders/diemakers) ________.

18

Another use of the standard deviation as a tool of analysis is in its relationship to th mean of a *normal distribution*. (It is sufficient at this point to indicate that the norma curve is often referred to as the Gaussian distribution after Karl Gauss. It is symmetri cal and smoothed. Theoretically, the tails of the curve move off to infinity.) One relationship is in terms of the percent of the observations within one standard deviation below the mean and one standard deviation above the mean. In a normal distribution, exactly 68.3 percent of the values lie within plus and minus one standard deviation of the mean. (See the graph.)

THE AREAS UNDER THE NORMAL CURVE

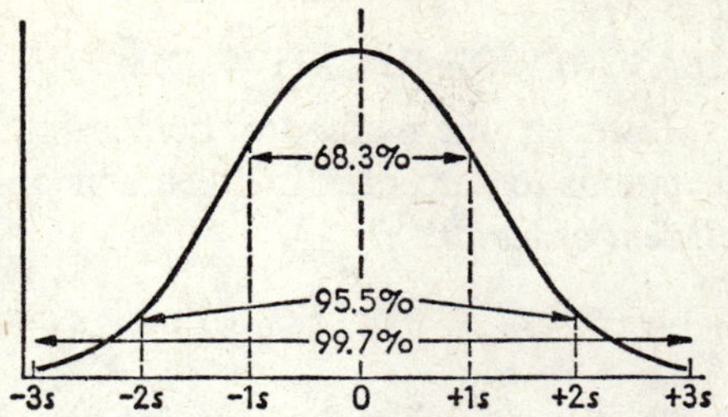

Further, the mean ($\bar{X}$) plus and minus (written $\pm$) two times the standard deviation includes approximately 95 percent of the observations. The $\bar{X} \pm 3(s)$ includes about 99.7 percent of the observations.

The quality control department of a tire manufacturer tested the durability of a proposed new tire by taking a large sample of the tires and running them on a test machine until each disintegrated. The mileage of each at the time of the blow-out was organized into a frequency distribution. The mean mileage of the tires was 40,000 miles, the standard deviation 2,000 miles.

Reading from the following graph:

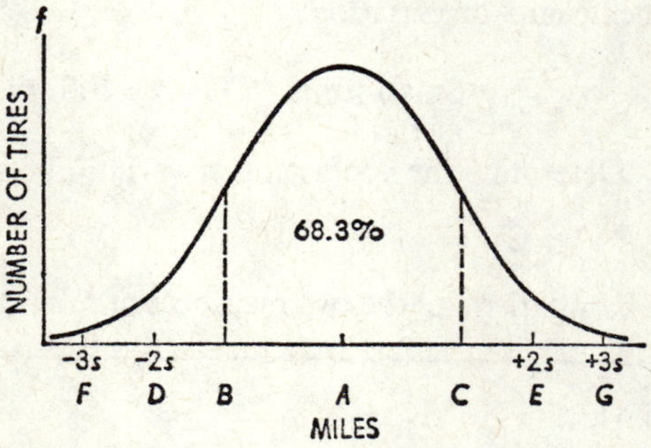

1. For this analysis, *A* is the measure of central tendency called the mean and is ________ miles.
2. The distance between *B* and *C* represents the $\bar{X} \pm$ ______ *s*.
3. The value of *B* is ________ miles and *C* is ________ miles.
4. The values of *D* and *E* are ________ miles and ________ miles respectively.
5. The value of *F* is ________ miles and *G* is ________ miles.
6. The percent of the observations between *D* and *E* is approximately ________ percent.
7. The percent of the observations between *F* and *G* is ________ percent.
8. The smoothed curve is called a ________ curve.

1. 40,000
2. 1
3. 38,000 42,000
4. 36,000 44,000
5. 34,000 46,000
6. 95
7. 99.7
8. normal, bell-shaped, or symmetrical

19

In the previous discussion, a *direct* and meaningful comparison of two standard deviations (or other measures of dispersion) could be made because the means were approximately equal. Frequently, however, the means are quite far apart or two dissimilar groups must be compared. A direct comparison of the standard deviations would be meaningless. For example, a meaningful comparison of the incomes of the presidents of the top 100 firms in the United States and the incomes of migrant workers (could/could not) ________ be made using means and standard deviations. Similarly, the distribution of the incomes of the presidents and a distribution of their ages are (similar/dissimilar) ________ and (should/should not) ________ be compared *directly*.

could not

dissimilar

should not

20

MEASURES OF RELATIVE DISPERSION

However, one method of comparing two distributions is to convert the standard deviations to percents. Karl Pearson (1857–1936) originated a measure called the *coefficient of variation.*

$$CV = \frac{s}{\bar{X}}(100)$$

To illustrate, the distribution of the profits of a selected group of small firms and the profit of a selected group of large firms are to be compared. Both distributions are somewhat normally distributed.

Small Firms	*Large Firms*
$\bar{X}$ = \$100,000	$\bar{X}$ = \$2,000,000
s = \$ 10,000	s = \$ 200,000

There is a tendency to conclude that there is more dispersion in the distribution of the large firms because the standard deviation of \$200,000 is greater than the standard deviation for the distribution of small firms (\$10,000). However, converting the data to coefficients of variation:

$$\text{Small firms: } CV = \frac{s}{\bar{X}}(100) = \frac{\$10{,}000}{\$100{,}000}(100) = 10 \text{ percent}$$

Determine the coefficient of variation for the distribution of large firms.

CV = ______ = ______ = ______.

A comparison of the two measures of relative dispersion indicates that ______
______.

10 percent, found by [\$200,000/\$2,000,000] (100)
The relative dispersions of the two distributions are equal

21

MEASURES OF SKEWNESS

Karl Pearson also developed a *coefficient of skewness* (*Sk*) to measure the amount and direction of skewness. For example, in a negatively skewed distribution of the ages of executives, the mean was computed to be 50 years, the median 60 years and the standard deviation 5 years.

$$Sk = \frac{3(\bar{X} - \text{median})}{s} = \frac{3(50 - 60)}{5} = -6$$

The coefficient of skewness for a comparative group of teachers was found to be −9.3. The skewness for the group of teachers is also negative and a comparison of the two groups indicates that the distribution of the ages of teachers is more highly skewed.

Computations for distributions of the outside diameters of a shaft were: mean outside diameter 1.00025, median 1.00020, standard deviation 0.00010. The coefficient of skewness is ______.

If $Sk = 0.00$, what would it indicate? ______
______.

+1.5, found by [3(1.00025 − 1.00020)]/0.00010
no skewness, or a symmetrical (normal) distribution

Final Self-Review Examination

First, answer all of the questions. Then check your answers against those given at the end of this chapter. Scoring: 10 problems × 10 points each = 100 possible points.

Questions 22 through 25 are based on the following sample of hourly wages: \$3, \$7, \$2, and \$8.

22. The range is \$__________.
23. The average deviation is \$__________.
24. The variance is \$__________.
25. The standard deviation is \$__________.

Questions 26 through 28 are based on the following distribution of amounts allocated by firms for capital improvements.

Amounts Allocated for Capital Improvements (In Millions)	*Number of Firms*
\$1 up to \$ 3	4
3 up to 5	7
5 up to 7	10
7 up to 9	6
9 up to 11	3
Total	30

26. The range is \$__________ millions.
27. The quartile deviation is \$__________ millions.
28. The variance is \$__________ millions and the standard deviation is \$__________ millions.

Questions 29 through 31 are based on the following production figures for three groups of workers. The three groups are identified by the name of the supervisor. The production figures were recorded over a long period of time and represent weekly production.

	Supervisor		
Measure	*Jarnow*	*Arn*	*Smith*
Arithmetic mean	800	780	820
Median	800	790	810
Mode	800	810	790
Standard deviation	20	40	60
Average deviation	16	32	48
Quartile deviation	14	28	40

29. The production of which group is the most erratic? (*a*)__________. The distribution of which group is negatively skewed? (*b*)__________.
30. The middle one half of the weeks, Supervisor Jarnow's group produced between (*a*)__________ and __________ units. The middle 95 percent of the weeks, Supervisor Jarnow's group produced between (*b*)__________ and __________ units.
31. The coefficient of variation for the production distribution of Supervisor Jarnow's group is (*a*)__________. The coefficient of skewness for the production distribution of Supervisor Smith's group is (*b*)__________.

Answers to Final Self-Review Examination

22. \$6
23. \$10/4 = \$2.50
24. \$26/4 = \$6.50
25. square root of \$6.50 = \$2.55
26. either \$10 or \$8
27. $Q_1 = \$3 + 3.5/7$ of $\$2 = \$4$

    $Q_3 = \$7 + 1.5/6$ of $\$2 = \$7.50$

    Then $\text{Q.D.} = \dfrac{\$7.50 - \$4}{2} = \$1.75$
28. $\text{Variance} = \dfrac{\$1{,}172}{30} - \left(\dfrac{\$174}{30}\right)^2 = \$5.43$

    $\text{Standard deviation} = \sqrt{\$5.43} = \$2.33$
29. (*a*) Smith's group because distribution has largest measures of dispersion.

    (*b*) Arn's group
30. (*a*) 786 and 814 units

    (*b*) 760 and 840 units
31. (*a*) 20/800 (100) = 2.5 percent

    (*b*) 3(820 − 810)/60 = 0.5

chapter

6

A survey of probability concepts

1

Methods of descriptive statistics were examined in the first five chapters. These methods dealt mainly with data collection (questionnaires and library sources), organization and presentation of data (frequency distributions, tables, and graphs), and data analysis (measures of central tendency and dispersion). Descriptive measures merely describe the business phenomena, such as the trend of sales the past 20 years, and an average annual increase of 3.4 percent. The businessman using these basic techniques of description does not take any risk of making an error, such as maintaining a too high level of inventory, or building a new plant and then finding it was not needed. (The only "error" he might make is entering a wrong number in the calculator or plotting data incorrectly on a graph.)

A second facet of statistics is called inductive statistics or statistical inference. It deals with inferences about the population based on incomplete (sample) data. To put it another way, inductive statistics are concerned with reasoning from the partial to the general. And, because only partial information is available, there is a risk of making an error. For example, the Roper, Gallup, and Harris opinion-gathering polls use sample data almost exclusively to predict the outcome of an election. Based on a relatively small group of potential voters, there is always the risk of an incorrect prediction (such as in 1948 when Thomas Dewey was favored to win). The level of inventory to maintain, and the strategy to be followed in marketing a new product, are but two business decision problems with the built-in danger of making an error. Seldom, if ever, does the decision maker have complete information on which to make a decision. If he is trying to determine how many television sets to make during the forthcoming year, the potential consumer demand for each model, possible changes in the price of raw materials, and the possible effect of a recently announced increase in a competitors warranty to seven years are but a few factors which must be assessed. Obviously, it would be impossible to study all relevant factors which might affect the decision on the number of each model to be produced during the year. Therefore, most business decisions are made under conditions of (certainty/uncertainty) ____________________ and there is (no risk/risk) ____________________ involved.

uncertainty
risk

2

Thus, under conditions of uncertainty it is assumed that there is a risk involved regardless of the level of inventory, or production, decided upon. Probability theory has often been referred to as the science of uncertainty. The use of probability theory allows the decision maker with only limited information available to him to analyze the risks and minimize the gamble inherent in establishing the inventory at level A, level B, or level C. Thus, a knowledge of the concepts of probability is essential before discussing sampling (Chapters 8 and 9), tests of hypotheses (Chapter 10), decision making (Chapter 11), and Bayesian statistics (Chapter 12).

INTERPRETATIONS OF PROBABILITY

The *objective* interpretation of probability has been the dominant one in statistics until recent years. There is concern with events which can be repeated over and over under the same conditions. To illustrate, a balanced coin can be tossed into the air many times and the number of heads and tails recorded. A head will appear face up in about half of the tosses, i.e., the probability of a head is ½, or 0.50. The probability of a tail is $P =$ ________________. If the first production run of 10,000 parts resulted in 100 defective parts, the quality control engineer would no doubt estimate the probability of a defective to be ____________.

½, or 0.50

100/10,000 or $P = 0.01$

3

In the past two decades, a new interpretation of probability called *subjective* or *personal* probability has been growing rapidly in the area of business decision making. Subjective probability measures the *strength of personal belief.* For example, a weather forecaster might state that (in his opinion) the chance of rain tomorrow is 10 percent, or $P = 0.10$. Another forecaster using the same set of weather data and maps might put the probability at 0.20. An economist after reviewing inventory level, unemployment, and so on might indicate that there is a 40 percent chance of a recession during the forthcoming summer. Another economist using the same data might believe the probability of a recession is 0.20. These degrees of belief are called ____________ probabilities. The use of the subjective approach to probability will be examined in more detail in the chapter on decision making under uncertainty (Chapter 11), and in Chapter 12.

subjective or personal

4

It will become apparent in the following discussion that there is no necessary conflict between the two interpretations. In fact, in many problems, both the objective and subjective notions will be of value. Many of the rules for manipulating and combining probabilities apply both to objective and subjective probabilities.

The science of probability has been of concern to mathematicians since the early 1600's. Much of the early study was devoted to mathematical problems involving games of cards, dice, roulette, and other games of chance. Many mathematicians earned their livelihood working out and instructing wealthy patrons in "knowing the odds." Marquis de Laplace (1749–1827) interpreted probability "simply as a fraction whose numerator is the number of favorable cases and whose denominator is the number of all the cases possible." To illustrate, suppose there are four cards lying face down on a table. There is a spade, a diamond, a heart, and a club. What is the probability of selecting one of the cards at random and finding it to be a diamond? ____________.

¼, or 0.25

5

These probabilities are designated as *a priori.* A priori probabilities then can be determined *before* an experiment, trial, or any sampling is done. For example, it is common knowledge that a coin has a head on one side and a tail on the other side. It can be reasoned beforehand, therefore, that should a large number of coins be tossed in the air about half of them will have a head showing face up. That is, $P(\text{head}) = \frac{1}{2}$. It should be noted that *a priori probabilities are confined to events that can be repeated and have equally likely outcomes.*

A single die has six sides numbered 1, 2, 3, 4, 5, or 6. How many *equally likely* outcomes are there? ______________. What is the probability that a 4 will appear on a throw of the die? ______________. Can this probability be considered a priori? (yes/no) ______________. Explain ______________________________

6
$\frac{1}{6}$ yes
Probability can be determined before an experiment is conducted.

6

However, in many business problems, it is inconceivable that the probability of an event can be determined beforehand. And furthermore, the equally likely assumption may not be realistic. For example, it is not realistic to assume that before a new model color television set is introduced on the market, an equal number of persons will buy one, two, and three sets for their homes next year. Thus, two characteristics of this early approach to probability which may not be applicable to many real business problems are ______________________________ and ______________________________.

(in any order) probability of an outcome cannot be determined beforehand and probability of various outcomes are not equally likely

7

A Russian mathematician, A. N. Kolmogorov, suggested a *relative frequency* interpretation of probability in the 1930's which has since become synonymous with the objective interpretation. A probability is interpreted as the *relative frequency resulting from a long series of trials or observations.* This interpretation of probability differs in one important respect from the earlier classical approach. The classical notion is that the probability of an outcome happening can be determined (before/after) ______________ an experiment. The relative frequency approach is that the probability is computed (before/after) ______________ a series of trials or observations. Probabilities computed after a sample (trials) (experiment) (observations) are called *posteriori*, or *empirical* probabilities. Thus, the relative frequency interpretation of probabilities relies on past experience.

before
after

A probability computed prior to throwing a die can be considered an exact probability. A probability computed from sampling data cannot be exact, but rather it is only an estimate. If, out of a sample of 2,000 employees, 1,600 were in favor of a guaranteed annual wage, the probability of 0.80 is only an estimate because a larger sample would give a more precise (and, no doubt, different) probability, such as 0.79 or 0.82. Thus, empirical probabilities can be considered as being (exact/estimates) ______________ and a priori probabilities as being (exact/estimates) ______________.

estimates
exact

8

A canning company keeps a constant check on the weight of the content of the cans. Although the machine is set to give the weight specified on the label, the content of some cans is under what is specified and others are overweight. The results of frequent checks at the beginning of the

Content	*Number of Cans*	*Probability of Occurrence*
Underweight	100	0.
Correct weight	1,700	.
Overweight	200	.
Total		.

0.05
.85
.10
1.00

ew canning season were organized into the previous table. Compute the probabilities nd record the answers in the spaces provided. What is the probability that a can icked at random will be overweight? ________________. Is it an a priori or emirical probability? ____________________. Are the outcomes equally likely? ʼes/no) ______________.

200/2,000 or 1/10 or 0.10
empirical
no

---

s noted in the previous example, the sum of the probabilities for all possible outcomes annot exceed ____________ One six-sided die is tossed. The probability of an 8 appearng is ____________. Thus, the lowest value a probability assumes is ________ ____________ and the highest ____________. Is the probability of −1.0 possible? ʼes/no) ____________.

1.0
0.0 0
1
no

0 ---

the problem cited previously, a can was either underweight, overweight, or had the orrect weight. Thus, the outcomes of an event are considered to be *mutually exclusive*, eaning that a can selected at random cannot *at the same time* be underweight, overeight, and have the correct weight. To put it another way, *mutually exclusive outomes means that simultaneous occurrence is not possible.* Referring to the random lection of one of the four cards lying face down on the table (a diamond, a spade, a ub, and a heart), are the outcomes mutually exclusive? (yes/no) ____________. xplain ____

yes
A card chosen at random can only be one suit.

1 ---

he English logician, J. Venn, (1834–88) developed a diagram to portray graphically e mutually exclusive concept and various other rules for combining probabilities. o construct a Venn diagram, a space is first enclosed which represents the total of all ossible outcomes. This space may be any shape and is called the *sample space*. Some utcome (such as a tail appearing on the toss of a coin) is called a *sample point*. Thus, e total of all sample points equals the ________________________.

The following Venn diagram represents the mutually exclusive concept. If a head (event A) occurs, a tail (event B) does ot. There is no overlapping of events, i.e., the events are ______ ________________________.

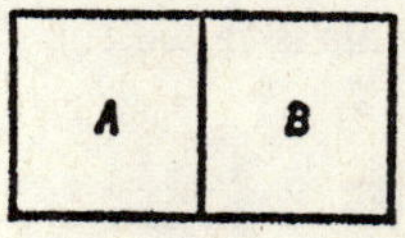

sample space
mutually exclusive

2 ---

he next Venn diagram shows the possible outcomes on the roll of a die. oes the diagram, called a ________________ ______ diagram, account for all possible outcomes? ʼes/no) ________________. The total area ncompassed by the heavy black line is called the ________________________.

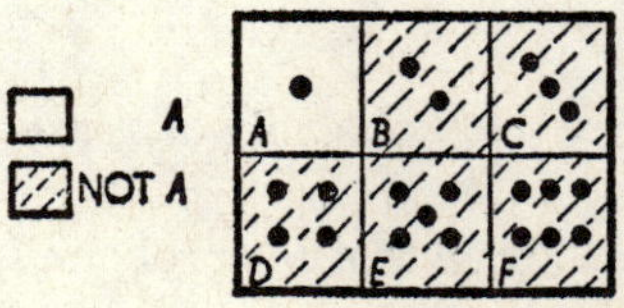

Venn
yes
sample space

sample points

The individual areas marked A, B, C, D, E, and F are called ____________________________.

1/6
5/6

The probability that event A would occur is ____________________. The proba bility that event A would not occur (written ∼A) is ____________________.

13

any shape such as:

Referring again to the previous problem of four cards (a diamond a club, a spade, and a heart) lying face down on a table, draw a Venn diagram in the space provided to show the mutually exclu sive nature of the outcomes.

14

Rules for manipulating and combining probabilities

Several computations involving probabilities have already been examined. In frame #8 the probability of a can selected at random being underweight (event A) was com puted to be 0.05. Other probabilities were: correct weight (event B) 0.85, and over weight (event C) 0.10. It was noted that:

$$P(A) + P(B) + P(C) = 1$$

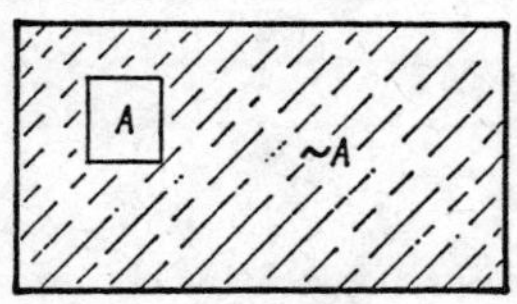

Also, the probability that a can selected at random was underweight $P(A)$, plus the probability it was not under weight, written $P(\sim A)$, must equal 1. Shown symbolically:

$$P(A) + P(\sim A) = 1$$

The Venn diagram might appear as shown.

$P(A) + P(\sim A) = 1$ can be revised to read:

$$P(A) = 1 - P(\sim A)$$

The rule is often referred to as the *complement rule.* The probability that an ace will be chosen at random from a standard deck of 52 cards is 4/52. What is the probability that it will not be chosen? ____________________, found by ____________________. This is called the ____________________ rule.

48/52 found by 1 − 4/52
complement

15

In the foregoing discussion, another rule in dealing with probabilities was used but it was not identified as the *addition* rule. Returning to a simple example to illustrate it, a head (event A) or a tail (event B) may occur on the toss of a coin. The outcomes are mutually exclusive. Then:

$$P(A \text{ or } B) = P(A) + P(B)$$

So, the probability of a head (A) or a tail (B) (written $P(A \text{ or } B)$), occurring is 1, found by ½ + ½.

Recall that the probability a can would be underweight is 0.05, the correct weigh

0.85, and overweight 0.10. What is the probability that a can selected at random will contain the correct weight or be overweight? ______________. (Note the addition rule applies even though the letters are different and there are more than two possible outcomes.)

0.95, found by $P(B \text{ or } C) = P(B) + P(C)$
$= 0.85 + 0.10$

Ages of the respondents to a questionnaire were grouped as follows:

Number of Respondents	*Ages*
40	Under 18 years
100	18 up to 30 years
30	30 up to 50 years
20	50 up to 70 years
10	70 years and over

What is the probability that if a questionnaire were chosen at random the respondent would be either under 18 years, or 30 up to 50 years, or 70 years and over? ______________. This is an application of the ______________ rule. What is the probability that the respondent is not in one of these three age groups? ______________. This is an illustration of the ______________ rule. The outcomes are ______________ exclusive.

0.40
addition
0.60, found by 1 − 0.40
complement
mutually

16

The adjacent ______________ diagram illustrates two outcomes which are not mutually exclusive, i.e., there is an overlapping of outcomes. This means that there is some chance that both A and B can occur at the same time. It is usually written $P(A,B)$ or $P(A \text{ and } B)$, and is called the *compound* event, or the *joint* probability of A and B. It seems logical that to compute the probability of A or B that the joint probability of A and B should be subtracted or it will be added twice. Thus, to compute the probability of A or B:

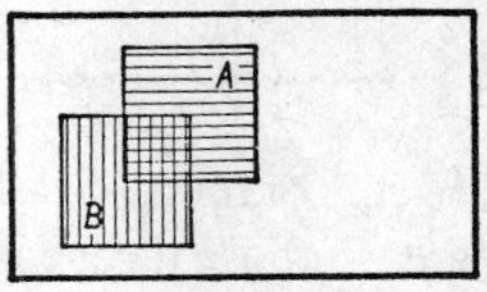

$$P(A \text{ or } B) = P(A) + P(B) - P(A,B)$$

Venn

17

Again, a simple illustration involving a standard deck of cards containing 52 cards. The probability that a card chosen at random from the deck is either a king or a diamond is 16/52 or 0.3077, found by: (event A is a king, event B is a diamond).

$$P(A \text{ or } B) = P(A) + P(B) - P(A,B)$$
$$= 4/52 + 13/52 - 1/52$$

Are the possible outcomes mutually exclusive or nonmutually exclusive? ______________ exclusive. Explain ______________

What is the probability that a card selected at random is either a jack or a diamond or a club? ______________.

nonmutually
The king of diamonds is both a king and a diamond. Because of this overlapping, the joint probability of A and B is subtracted to prevent it from being added twice.
28/52, found by 4/52 + 13/52 + 13/52 − 1/52 − 1/52.

18

Two coins are to be tossed in the air—either simultaneously or one and then the other. The action, or outcome, of one coin will in no way affect the other. This concept is known as *statistical independence.* If the two outcomes are independent, then the probability of a head occurring on one coin, written $P(A)$, and the probability of a head occurring on the other coin, written $P(B)$, is:

$$P(A \text{ and } B) = P(A) \cdot P(B) = 1/2 \times 1/2 = 1/4$$

This can be shown by listing all of the possible outcomes. Two heads is only one of the four possible outcomes.

	H	H
or	H	T
or	T	H
or	T	T

The foregoing illustrates the *multiplication rule* when the outcomes are independent. Using the multiplication rule, design an equation and then solve for the probability that three heads will appear on the toss of three coins.

The equation is ______

The probabilities are: ______

The answer is ______

$P(A \text{ and } B \text{ and } C) = P(A) \cdot P(B) \cdot P(C)$
$\frac{1}{2} \times \frac{1}{2} \times \frac{1}{2}$
$\frac{1}{8}$ or 0.125

19

The rule of multiplication is also used when the probabilities are *conditional.* To illustrate, suppose a scheme has been devised to raise money for charity. A total of 100 sealed boxes are to be placed on a table, and the donors may buy one or more of them. There are prizes in 10 of the boxes and the remaining 90 are empty. A prominent donor has the privilege of selecting the first two boxes. One might wonder what his chance is of winning two prizes. The probability that he will win a prize on the first draw, designated as $P(A)$ is 10/100. Then the probability that he will win two prizes depends on whether he won a prize on the first draw. Thus, the probability of a prize on the second draw is conditional on the results of the first draw. This conditional probability is designated as $P(B|A)$ and is interpreted as the probability of B happening given that A has happened. The probability of winning two prizes on the first two draws is found by:

$$P(A \text{ and } B) = P(A) \cdot P(B|A) = \frac{10}{100} \times \frac{9}{99} = \frac{1}{110}, \text{ or slightly less than 1 percent}$$

Note that the probability $P(B|A)$ of 9/99 assumes that a prize was chosen the first draw and only 9 prizes were left in the remaining 99 boxes. The concept of conditional probability is, therefore, based on the assumption that the two (or more) events are (dependent/independent) ______.

dependent

A survey is to be conducted by interviewing 10 executives. One executive is in the mining industry, three in the service industry, and the remaining in manufacturing. The names of the executives to be interviewed will be picked at random. What is the probability that the first two executives chosen will be in the manufacturing industry?

The equation is ______. $P(A \text{ and } B) = P(A) \cdot P(B|A)$

The probabilities (fractions) are ______. $\frac{6}{10} \times \frac{5}{9}$

The answer is ______. ⅓ or 0.33

What is the probability that three executives in the manufacturing industry will be [ch]osen on the first three selections? ______. ⅙ or 0.17, found by $\frac{6}{10} \times \frac{5}{9} \times \frac{4}{8}$

[1]0

[P]ermutations and combinations

Determining the total number of possible outcomes in a problem involving prob[a]bilities may be difficult. Rules of *permutations* and *combinations* merely facilitate [c]ounting. Both permutations and combinations use a notation called "*n* factorial." [T]his is written $n!$ It means the product of $n(n-1)(n-2)(n-3)\ldots[n-(n-1)]$. [F]or example, 6! would be computed by $6(6-1)(6-2)(6-3)(6-4)[6-(6-1)]$. [T]hat is, $6 \cdot 5 \cdot 4 \cdot 3 \cdot 2 \cdot 1 = 720$. What does 4! equal? ______. 24

The numbers $4 \cdot 3 \cdot 2 \cdot 1$ are products. Therefore, they can be canceled when in the [n]umerator and denominator. To illustrate:

$$\frac{5!3!}{4!} = \frac{5 \cdot \not{4} \cdot 3 \cdot 2 \cdot 1(\not{3} \cdot \not{2} \cdot \not{1})}{\not{4} \cdot \not{3} \cdot \not{2} \cdot \not{1}} = 30$$

$$\frac{6!2}{3!} = \underline{\hspace{6cm}}$$ 240

[1]1

Permutations. Three machines (a grinder, a drill press, and a shaper), are to be [p]laced on the floor of the plant. The problem is to determine how many different ways [th]e three machines can be placed on the floor. The number of permutations is deter[m]ined by:

$$P = \frac{n!}{(n-r)!}$$

[I]n this equation, P is the number of permutations or ways the machines can be placed; [n] is the number of machines; and r represents the number of machines to be placed [o]n the floor at a time. There are three machines ($n = 3$), and all three are going to be [p]laced on the floor ($r = 3$). Note that there are three different machines making [r]epetition impossible. For example, it is not possible to place three grinders on the [fl]oor. It should be noted before solving the problem that, by definition, $0! = 1! = 1$. [T]hen:

$$P = \frac{n!}{(n-r)!} = \frac{3!}{(3-3)!} = \frac{3!}{0!} = \frac{3!}{1!} = 6$$

[T]he six ways are ABC, ACB, BCA, BAC, CBA, and CAB.

The formula for permutations is applicable when it is desired to count the number [o]f ways (permutations) of n things taken r at a time. The ordering of the different [it]ems is important, i.e., ABC is one order of the items, BCA is another order, and [s]o on.

It has been decided that only five colors are to be used in decorating an office build[in]g. The colors are always to be used in groups of three, such as red, yellow, and blue.

60, found by $\frac{5!}{(5-3)!}$

How many ways can the five colors be arranged in groups of three? ________________________.

22

If repetitions are permitted, then $P = n^r$. To illustrate, two letters, A and B, are to be taken two at a time. With repetitions, such as AA, there are four ways (permutations) possible, found by 2^2. The four ways would be AB, BA, AA, and BB. If repetitions were not allowed, how many ways can the two letters be arranged? ________________.

2

In the previous frame, it was found that there were 60 different ways five colors could be used three colors at a time. If repetitions were allowed (such as red, yellow, yellow), how many permutations could there be? ________________

125, found by 5^3

23

Combinations. In computing the number of permutations of n things taken r at a time, the order of things was important. In the office decoration problem, the decorator could use red on the floor, yellow on the walls, and blue on the ceiling in one room, and in another room the order could be changed to yellow on the floor, blue on the walls, and red on the ceiling, and so on. It was calculated that there were 60 such permutations of five colors taken three at a time.

Suppose the decorator has just decided that a combination of any three colors will be used only once in the building. This means that if red, blue, and yellow are used in Room No. 6, no other room can be decorated with these three colors. In effect, the many different ways of ordering the three colors is being disregarded. That is, the combination of red, blue, and yellow is considered the same as blue, yellow, and red. One might now ask, how many different *combinations* of the five colors taken three at a time are possible. The answer is 10, found by:

$$C = \frac{n!}{r!(n-r)!} = \frac{5!}{3!(5-3)!}$$

210, found by $\frac{10!}{4!\,(10-4)!}$

There are 10 union stewards in the plant and 4 are to be picked at random to attend a convention. How many different combinations of stewards are possible? ________. (Note that a combination recognizes a group of four stewards comprised of Smith, Jones, Miller, and Stevens is the same as Jones, Stevens, Miller, and Smith.)

Final Self-Review Examination

First, answer all of the questions. Then check your answers against those given at the end of this chapter. Scoring: 10 problems × 10 points each = 100 possible points.

24. Discuss the difference between the objective and subjective interpretation of probability. ______________________________.

25. The following is called a (*a*)______________________. The probabilities are (mutually exclusive/non-mutually exclusive. (*b*)______________. The block A is called a (sample space/ sample point) (*c*)______________________.

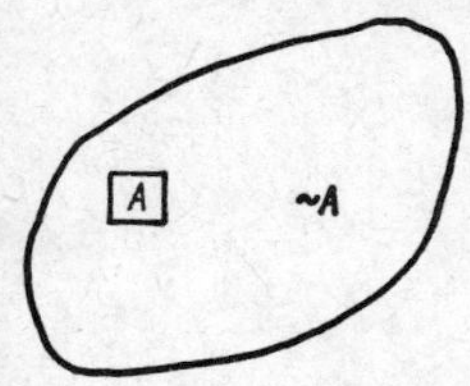

26. A random sample revealed that 100 parts were poorly machined, 700 parts were satisfactorily machined, and 200 parts were exceptionally well machined. It would, no doubt, be estimated that the probability of an exceptionally well machined part is (*a*)______________. The probabilities are considered as being (a priori/empirical) (*b*)______________.

27. Four disks were polished on one side but left dull on the other side. If the disks were tossed in the air, what is the probability that all four would land with polished sides facing up? (*a*)______________. Are the outcomes dependent or independent? (*b*)______________.

28. It is known that 3 parts in a batch of 10 parts are defective. What is the probability that the first three parts selected at random will be defective? (*a*)______________. Are the outcomes conditional or nonconditional? (*b*)______________.

29. A round-robin tennis match involving 10 people must be scheduled. (A round robin means that each person plays every other person. Usually, the person winning the most number of matches wins the grand prize.) How many matches must be scheduled? (Hint: If Sam plays Joe, it is the same as Joe playing Sam.) ______________.

30. Four firms are considering merging to form one company. A ten-man delegation, including the president and nine other men, from each of the four firms met to discuss the proposed merger. The four firms are Armcoe Ltd., Smith Steel, NoFarm Products, and Casper Aluminum. It was decided to divide into small committees of three members each to study various aspects of the merger. Each committee is to be picked at random. The rules committee is to be chosen first. What is the probability that the first member of the rules committee chosen will be either a president, or a man from Smith Steel, or a man from Casper Aluminum? (*a*)______________.

31. The Intelligence Bureau is designing a secret code based on six letters—A, B, C, D, E, and F. Only two letters are to be transmitted, such as AA, or AB, or BA. Note that repetitions are permitted. How many code signals are possible? ______________.

32. The production planning department has the problem of determining the most efficient way of assembling four pieces into a sub-assembly. The four pieces can be assembled in any order, such as 1, 2, 3, 4, or 2, 1, 4, 3, and so on. How many different ways can the four pieces be assembled? ______________.

33. The same production planning department has another problem concerning soldering. There are six parts. The first operation will involve connecting two parts with a wire, such as (A)(B). In this operation, it does not matter which two are connected (AB or AC or CD or DF, etc.). Note, however, that connecting AB is the same as connecting BA. How many ways can the six parts be connected, taking them two at a time? ______________.

Answers to Final Self-Review Examination

24. The objective interpretation of probability is that a probability can be determined beforehand (a priori), such as the probability of a four spot appearing on the toss of a die. A probability can also be determined on the basis of experience. An illustration of this is the probability of a defective after observing that 100 out of a sample of 1,000 parts selected at random were defective.
The subjective interpretation of probability is one of personal belief. For example, if an executive strongly believes that the level of demand for a multicolored automobile tire will be high, he might assign a probability of 0.90 to this high level, 0.07 to an average level of demand, and 0.03 to a low level of demand.

25. (*a*) Venn diagram
(*b*) mutually exclusive
(*c*) sample point

26. (*a*) 0.20
(*b*) empirical

27. (*a*) 1/16, found by $1/2 \times 1/2 \times 1/2 \times 1/2$
(*b*) independent

28. (*a*) $6/720 = 1/120$ ($\cong 0.008$) found by

$$P(A \text{ and } B \text{ and } C) = P(A) \times P(B|A) \times P(C|B)$$
$$= \frac{3}{10} \times \frac{2}{9} \times \frac{1}{8}$$

(*b*) conditional

29. 45, found by $C = \dfrac{n!}{r!(n-r)!}$
$$= \frac{10!}{2!8!}$$

30. 22/40, found by
$$P(A \text{ or } B \text{ or } C) = P(A) + P(B) + P(C) - P(A,B) - P(A,C)$$
$$= \frac{4}{40} + \frac{10}{40} + \frac{10}{40} - \frac{1}{40} - \frac{1}{40}$$

31. 36, found by 6^2

32. 24, found by $P = \dfrac{n!}{(n-r)!}$
$$= \frac{4!}{(4-4)!}$$
$$= \frac{4!}{1} \text{ (by definition)}$$

33. 15, found by $C = \dfrac{n!}{r!(n-r)!}$
$$= \frac{6!}{2!(6-2)!}$$

robability distributions

chapter

7

'he *Bernoulli, or binomial probability distribution*, the *Poisson probability distribution*, nd the *normal probability distribution* are but three probability distributions. The pplication of these theoretical distributions to probability-type problems can assist ie quality control engineer in making a decision to accept or reject an incoming lot of ansistors based on the discovery of, say, two defective transistors in a sample of 100 lected at random from the lot. The public opinion pollsters and the marketing re-earch analysts use various theoretical probability distributions (as will be shown in ie following chapters) in preelection polling and in analyzing consumer surveys and st market data.

HE BERNOULLI OR BINOMIAL PROBABILITY DISTRIBUTION

The Bernoulli probability distribution (named after Jacques Bernoulli, who in the 500's also developed the concept of permutations) is applicable when only two out-omes are possible. For example, in a true-false test, an answer to a question is either ght or wrong. Other illustrations:

Valve stem is defective	Will not vote for the incumbent
Valve stem is not defective	Will vote for the incumbent
Does not like the toothpaste	Cannot identify the brand name
Does like the toothpaste	Can identify the brand name

ince there is no measurement involved, the Bernoulli probability distribution, also alled the ________________ probability distribution is a discrete istribution. Could a distribution of the tensile strengths of wires be described by a inomial distribution? (yes/no) ____________. Explain ____________ ______________________________.

binomial

no Tensile strengths are measurable; thus, the data are continuous.

'he binomial probability distribution can be expressed several different ways.

$$(q + p)^n \quad \text{or}$$

$$\Sigma_n C_r (p)^r (q)^{n-r} \quad \text{or} \quad \sum \frac{n!}{r!(n-r)!} (p)^r (q)^{n-r}$$

o illustrate, suppose that it is desired to compute the probability of guessing 0, 1, 2, 3, id 4 questions correct out of four questions on a true-false test and to construct a inomial probability distribution. First, to compute the probability of guessing four ut of four correctly using the formula:

$$P(r) = \frac{n!}{r!(n-r)!} (p)^r (q)^{n-r}$$

here n is the total number of items, or 4 questions in this problem.

r is the number of correct answers (4) out of the total.
$n - r$ is the number of incorrect answers (0) out of the total, found by 4–4.
p is the probability of guessing an answer correctly (0.50).
q is the probability of not guessing an answer correctly (0.50).

Thus, to compute the probability of guessing 4 out of 4 correctly:

$$P(r) = \frac{n!}{r!(n-r)!}(p)^r(q)^{n-r}$$

$$P(r) = \frac{4!}{4!(4-4)!}(0.50)^4(0.50)^{4-4}$$

$$= \frac{4!}{4!0!} \qquad (0.50)^4(0.50)^0$$

recall from the previous chapter that $0! = 1$. Also, $(p)^0$ or $(q)^0 = 1$. Thus, $(0.50)^0 = 1$. Then:

$$= (1)\,(0.50)^4(1)$$
$$= 0.0625$$

.2500, found by (4) $(0.50)^3(0.50)^1$
.0625, found by (1) $(0.50)^0(0.50)^4$

Compute the probability of guessing three out of four correctly 0. __________, and the probability of guessing 0 out of four correctly. 0. __________.

3

The complete distribution of probabilities for guessing 0, 1, 2, 3, and 4 correct out of four follows. A histogram has been constructed to show the symmetrical nature of the distribution.

HISTOGRAM REPRESENTING THE BINOMIAL PROBABILITY DISTRIBUTION, $n = 4, p = 0.50$.

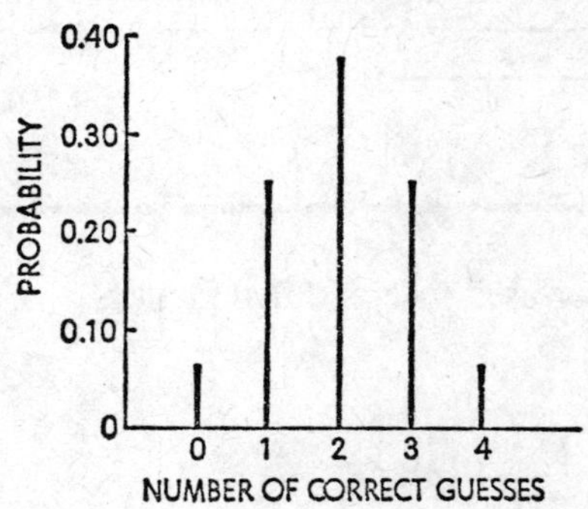

BINOMIAL PROBABILITY DISTRIBUTION FOR $n = 4, p = 0.50$

Number of Correct Guesses	*Probability*
0	0.0625
1	.2500
2	.3750
3	.2500
4	.0625
	1.0000

The binomial expansion $(q + p)^n$ could have been used to find the probabilities. [The expansion is also written $(p + q)^n$.] Recall from algebra:

$$(q + p)^1 = q + p$$
$$(q + p)^2 = q^2 + 2qp + p^2$$
$$(q + p)^3 = q^3 + 3q^2p + 3qp^2 + p^3$$
$$(q + p)^4 = q^4 + 4q^3p + 6q^2p^2 + 4qp^3 + p^4$$

and so on.

In this problem, q is the probability of guessing the answer correctly and p is the probability of guessing it incorrectly. The probabilities shown in the previous table for $n = 4$ could have been computed using the binomial expansion $(q + p)^4$. The first term q^4 is $(0.50)^4$, or 0.0625, and is the probability of guessing none correct out of four. The second term of $4q^3p$ represents the probability of guessing one correct out of four, and so on. Without referring to the answer given in the previous table, compute the probability of guessing three correct out of four using the binomial expansion. 0.________________, found by ____________________.

.2500
$4qp^3$ or $4(0.5)(0.5)^3$

4

The numbers in front of each of the terms are called *binomial coefficients*. The binomial coefficients in the previous problem where $n = 4$, are 1, 4, 6, 4, and 1. When q and p are 0.50, the terms yield a symmetrical binomial probability distribution. These binomial coefficients can be obtained from *Pascal's triangle* (developed by Blaise Pascal in the 17th century).

Number in Sample n	*Binomial Coefficients*	*Sum*
1	1 1	2
2	1 2 1	4
3	1 3 3 1	8
4	1 4 6 4 1	16
5	1 5 10 10 5 1	32
6	1 6 15 20 15 6 1	64
7	1 7 21 35 35 21 7 1	128
8	1 8 28 56 70 56 28 8 1	256
9	1 9 36 84 126 126 84 36 9 1	512
10	1 10 45 120 210 252 210 120 45 10 1	1,024

The terms for the binomial expansion for 10 true-false questions would be $(q + p)^{10}$. To find the probability of getting 0 correct out of 10, using Pascal's triangle, the first term would be $1q^{10}$. And, $q^{10} = (0.5)^{10} = 0.0009766$. The second term would be $10q^9p^1$ and represents the probability of guessing 1 out of 10 correct. Thus, $10(0.0009766) = 0.0098$. Note that the sum of the powers applied to q and $p = n$. That is, $9 + 1 = 10$.

Using the binomial expansion (and Pascal's triangle), the next number (45) would be the binomial coefficient for ____________ correct out of 10. The term would be ____________________. The probability of guessing two out of ten correct is 0.________________.

2
$45q^8p^2$
.0439, found by
45(0.0009766)

5

The main purpose of the foregoing discussion was to show that a binomial probability distribution is a theoretical distribution which can be generated mathematically using the binomial expansion method. In practice, however, these calculations need not be done, as a table for the binomial distribution is available (Appendix Table VII). To find the probability of guessing 2 out of 10 in a true-false test ($n = 10, r = 2$), it is first necessary to locate the n of 10. Then move down to the r of 2. Finally, move horizontally in that row until the number under the p of 0.50 is located. It is 0.0439, the same as calculated in frame #4. What is the probability of guessing 6 out of 10 correctly in a true-false test? 0.________________. This means if there were 10,000 students

.2051

2,051

in a class, and a 10-question true-false test were given, approximately ______ students would guess 6 out of 10 correctly. (This assumes that the students had no knowledge of the subject and were just guessing.)

6

The probabilities for the 10-question true-false test are presented in the following table. Complete the table. Then draw a histogram representing the binomial distribution.

.1172
.0439
.0098
.0010
1.0000

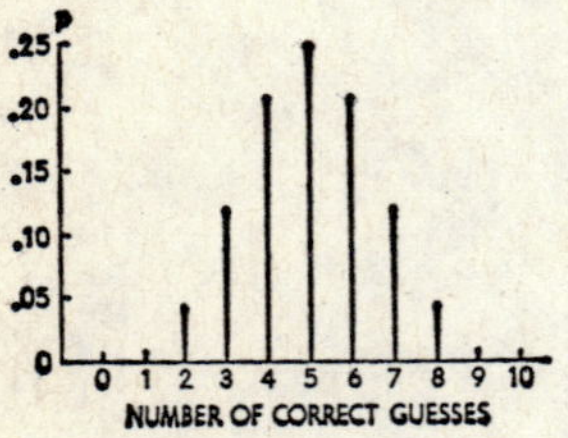

HISTOGRAM REPRESENTING THE BINOMIAL PROBABILITY DISTRIBUTION FOR $n = 10, p = 0.50$

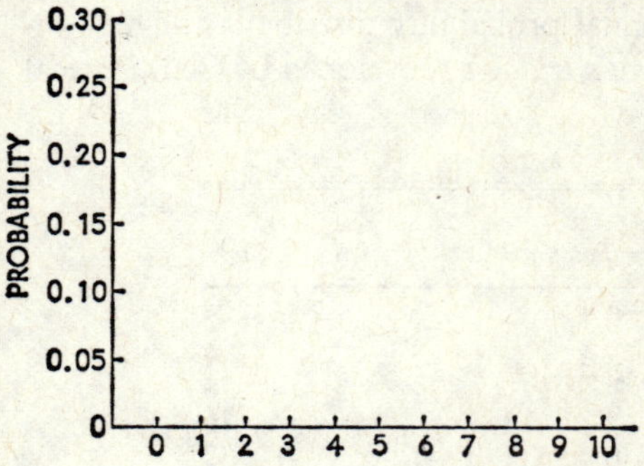

BINOMIAL PROBABILITY DISTRIBUTION FOR, $n = 10, p = 0.50$

Number of Correct Guesses	*Probability*
0	0.0010
1	.0098
2	.0439
3	.1172
4	.2051
5	.2461
6	.2051
7	____
8	____
9	____
10	____
Approximate Total	____

7

38 percent

The instructor indicated that 60 percent or more (6 or more out of 10) will be a passing grade in the test. Approximately what percent of the students will pass? ______.

8

The probability of an event occurring (p) and the probability of an event not occurring (q) may not be equal (0.50). If the probabilities are not equal, the binomial distribution is not symmetrical but instead is skewed. If the probability of a defective part (p) is 0.05, q (the probability of a nondefective part) is 0.95. The binomial expansion method may be used to determine the probability of 0, 1, and 2 defectives chosen at random out of two ($n = 2$). (Refer to frame #3 for the binomial expansion.)

The probabilities of:	0	1	2 defectives
are computed by:	q^2	$+ 2qp$	$+ p^2$
inserting q and p:	$(0.95)^2$	$+ 2(0.95 \times 0.05)$	$+ (0.05)^2$
the probabilities are:	0.9025	+ 0.0950	+ 0.0025 = 1.0

Of course, the total of all possible outcomes must equal 1.0. As noted previously, it is not necessary to calculate the probabilities. They have already been determined and are in Appendix Table VII for $n = 2$, $p = 0.05$. Again, note that the distribution of probabilities is skewed.

INOMIAL PROBABILITY DISTRIBUTION FOR $n = 2, p = 0.05$

Number of efective Parts	*Probability*
0	0.9025
1	.0950
2	.0025
Total	1.0000

HISTOGRAM REPRESENTING THE BINOMIAL PROBABILITY DISTRIBUTION FOR $n = 2, p = 0.05$

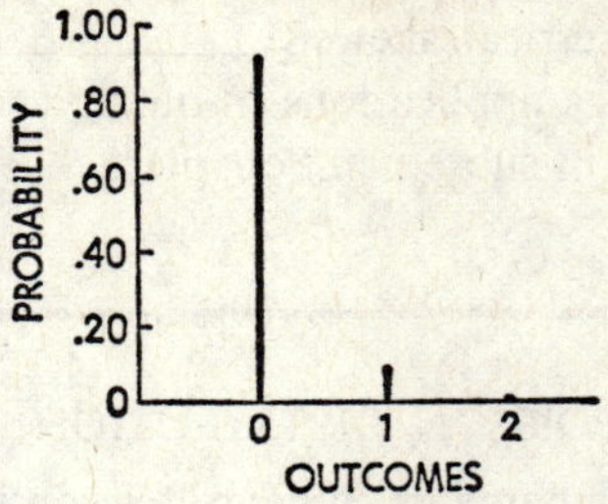

A multiple-choice examination consisting of 10 questions has been designed. There re four possible answers to each question. Thus, $p = 0.$ ________. Assume at none of the students taking the multiple-choice test attended class or studied for e examination (a common occurrence). Design a binomial probability distribution or guessing 0, 1, 2, ... 10 correct out of 10 on the examination. Then draw a stogram representing the distribution.

.25, found by ¼

INOMIAL PROBABILITY DISTRIBUTION FOR $n = 10, p = 0.25$

. . . .	0.______
. . . .	______
. . . .	______
. . . .	______
. . . .	______
. . . .	______
. . . .	______
. . . .	______
. . . .	______
. . . .	______
. . . .	______
Approximate Total	______

HISTOGRAM REPRESENTING THE BINOMIAL PROBABILITY DISTRIBUTION FOR $n = 10, p = 0.25$

.0563
.1877
.2816
.2503
.1460
.0584
.0162
.0031
.0004
.0000
.0000
1.0000

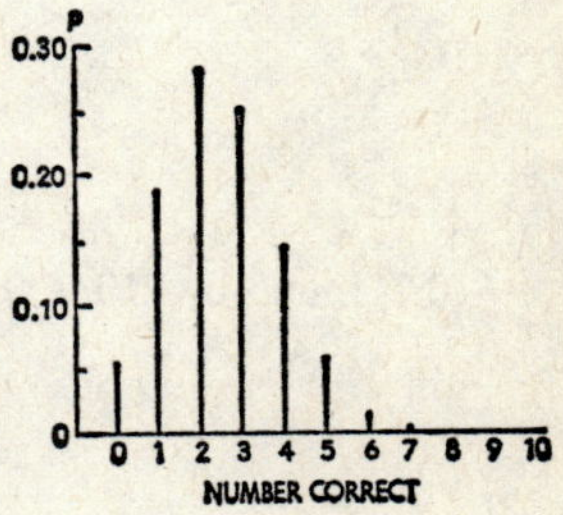

---

e instructor giving the multiple choice test has set 60 percent and above as the passg grades, i.e., 6, 7, 8, 9, or 10 out of ten correct. If there were 100 students in the class, eoretically about how many students would pass the examination? Approximately ________. (This compares with about 38 out of 100 (from Frame #7) who would ass a true-false test with 60 percent or above.)

2 students, found by adding 0.0162, 0.0031, 0.0004, 0.0000, and 0.0000.

0 ---

summary, a binomial probability distribution is also called a ________ probability distribution. It is applicable when (one/two/three or more) ________ outcomes are possible. The Bernoulli (binomial) probability distribution is (discrete/continuous) ________ distribution. When $p =$ 50, the binomial distribution is (symmetrical/skewed) ________.

Bernoulli
two
discrete
symmetrical

reading the probabilities from a table

skewed

The probabilities for the binomial distribution can be determined using the binomia expansion method, or by ______________________ ______________________. If the probability of a "success" (guessing correctly, no defective, and so on) is not exactly 0.50, the Bernoulli probability distribution i (symmetrical/skewed) ______________________. This theoretical probability distribu tion has applications in quality control statistics sampling, and tests of hypothese found in subsequent chapters.

11

THE POISSON DISTRIBUTION

Originated by Simeon Poisson in 1837, the Poisson probability distribution is an other discrete distribution. It is used to describe such phenomena as the distributio of the number of errors in IBM punched cards or the number of scratches and othe imperfections in newly painted panels. To apply the Poisson distribution, n must b large, i.e., a large number of IBM punched cards or a large number of painted panels And, p (the probability of a defect, error, etc.) must be small.

Another characteristic is that there can be 0, 1, 2, 3, 4, ... errors on the card o imperfections in the panel. To illustrate, assume that 300 IBM cards were checked using a verifier, with the following results:

Errors X	*Number of Cards* f
0	162
1	88
2	35
3	10
4	3
5	2
6	0
Total	300

0.7, found by 210/300

The mean number of errors, designated as μ is ______________________.

12

The mean (μ) is needed to construct a theoretical Poisson probability distribution. Th probability of say two errors can be computed by:

$$P(X) = \frac{\mu^X e^{-\mu}}{X!}$$

where

- μ is the mean number of occurrences.
- X is the number of occurrences being considered (2 in this case).
- e is the base of the natural (Naperian) logarithms (2.71828).
- $X!$ is X factorial (and in this case is 2 factorial).

$$P(2) = \frac{(0.7)^2(2.71828)^{-0.7}}{2 \cdot 1}$$

The calculations for the probability of two errors and the probabilities of 0, 1, . . errors have been made and placed in a table. Refer to Appendix Table VI. Readin horizontally, locate $\mu = 0.7$. The probability of no errors is 0.496585. The probability of one error is 0. ____________________. Instead of determining the probability of two errors using the previous equation, the value read from the table is 0.____________________.

.347610

.121663

13

Suppose that records were kept on the number of imperfections per panel which had to be repaired before the panel was shipped to the buyer. The distribution of the number of imperfections (such as burrs, paint globs, and unpainted surfaces) approximated a Poisson distribution. That is, a large number of the panels had no imperfections, some had one imperfection, very few panels had two imperfections, and so on.

The mean number of imperfections per panel was computed to be 0.5. The Poisson probability distribution is (to simplify calculations, copy probabilities to the first *three* figures only):

Number of Imperfections X	*Probability of* X
0	0.____________
1	____________
2	____________
3	____________
4	____________
5	____________

.606
.303
.075
.012
.001
.000

14

An order for 1,000 panels has been received. The cost department must estimate the total cost of repairing the panels *before* the work begins. Past experience revealed that each imperfection costs 10¢ to repair. What is the estimated total cost? (Hint: One imperfection costs 10¢, three imperfections 30¢ to repair, and so on.) ________________.

$49.30, found by:

X		
0	606 × 0 =	$0
1	303 × 10¢ =	30.30
2	75 × 20¢ =	15.00
3	12 × 30¢ =	3.60
4	1 × 40¢ =	0.40

15

The Poisson probability distribution for a μ of 5.0 follows. Plot the probability distributions for a μ of 0.5 and a μ of 2.0 on the same graph.

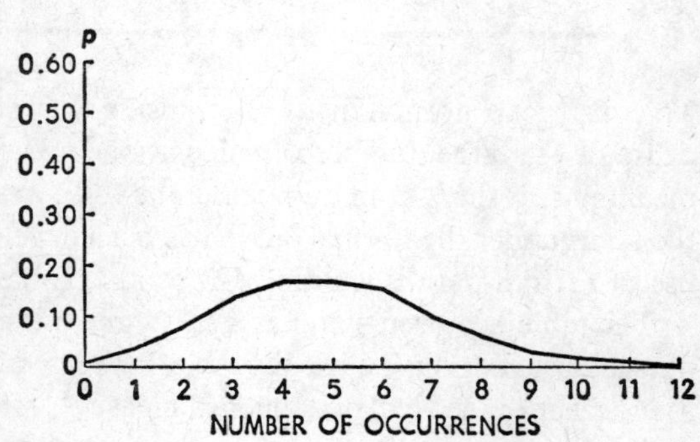

It should be stressed again that the Poisson probability distribution involves counts (discrete data). *Thus, only the points on the graph are important. The fact that lines connect the points does not indicate that there are probabilities between the points.*

An analysis of the adjacent graph containing probability distributions, called ________________ probability distributions, reveals that all three are (symmetrical/skewed) ________________.

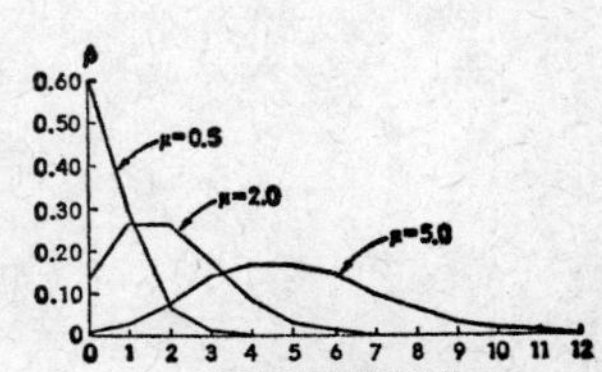

Poisson

skewed

However, note as the mean (μ) becomes larger, the Poisson distribution tends to approach a symmetrical distribution. Reference to the various Poisson distributions in Appendix Table VI reemphasizes this.

Before any Poisson probability distribution is constructed, it is necessary to know one value—namely, the ________________.

mean, denoted as μ

16

THE NORMAL PROBABILITY DISTRIBUTION

The preceding discussion dealt with two discrete probability distributions namely, the ________________ and the ________________ distributions. Conversely, *the normal probability distribution is applicable to measurable data.* Examples of data which tend to follow a normal pattern are the tensile strengths of wire, weight of male children 10 years old, and the length of fingerling trout. Thus, since this type of data can assume fractional values, such as 1,003.583 pounds tensile strength, the normal distribution is a (discrete/continuous) ________________ distribution.

binomial and Poisson

continuous

17

However, a more important use of the normal distribution is in the area of sampling. It has been discovered that regardless of the shape of the parent population, the distribution of the means of samples selected from that population will be normally distributed. The importance of this discovery will become evident in the following chapters in sampling and quality control.

The equation for the normal probability distribution is:

$$Y = \frac{1}{\sigma\sqrt{2\pi}} e^{-\frac{1}{2}(X-\mu)^2/\sigma^2}$$

where μ = mean, σ = standard deviation, $\pi = 3.14159 \cdots$, $e = 2.71828 \cdots$

Note that the μ and the standard deviation σ are needed to construct a normal distribution. In contrast, what was needed to develop a Poisson distribution? ________________. A binomial distribution? ________________ and ________________.

The mean number of errors (imperfections) designated as μ.
The probability of success, designated as p and the number of frequencies (n).

18

To construct a normal distribution using the formula would be a formidable task because of the large number of calculations necessary. (The distribution is continuous, meaning that there is an infinite number of possible values X could assume.) A table of the areas under the normal curve has been developed to facilitate the construction and use of the normal distribution (Appendix Table IV).

The table has been standardized to make it applicable to any problem involving a normal distribution. To use the table, various values must be transformed into a standard measure called z. This standard measure, often called the *z value,* the *standard normal deviate,* the *standard deviate* or the *z transformation,* is found by:

$$z = \frac{X - \mu}{\sigma}$$

To illustrate, suppose a distribution of the weights of ball bearings follows a normal attern with a mean of 100 ounces and a standard deviation of 10 ounces. One might sk, what proportion of the weights were between 100 ounces and, say, 110 ounces $= 100$, $\sigma = 10$, and $X = 110$).

Show the formula, insert the values, and find the z value.

$z =$ ______________ = ______________ = ______________

$$\frac{X-\mu}{\sigma} = \frac{110-100}{10} = 1.00$$

9

ow, referring to Appendix Table IV, the z values are found in the left margin. Locate ne z value of 1.0 and then read horizontally to the proportion given under .00. The roportion is 0. ______________.

.3413

0

ince the normal curve is symmetrical, hat percent of the weights are between 90 unces and 100 ounces? 0. ______________. /hat is the probability that if one of the all bearings is selected at random it would eigh between 90 ounces and 110 ounces, e., between $\mu \pm 1\sigma$? 0. ______________. What is the probability that it ill weigh between $\mu \pm 2\sigma$? 0. ______________. Between $\mu \pm 3\sigma$? About 0. ______________.

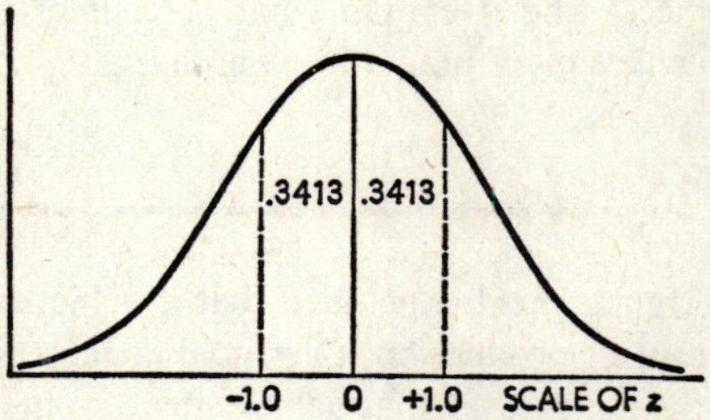

.3413

.6826, found by 0.3413 + 0.3413

.9544

.9973

1

he mean μ divides the normal probability distribution into two equal parts with the roportion above the mean being 0. ______________ and the area below the mean so being 0. ______________. Note that the mean of the standardized normal disibution is zero and the standard deviation is 1. To find the proportion of ball bearings eighing more than 110 ounces, the proportion between 100 and 110 (0.3413) is subacted from 0.5000. The proportion weighing more than 110 ounces is 0. ______________.

.5000

.5000

.1587

Shown schematically:

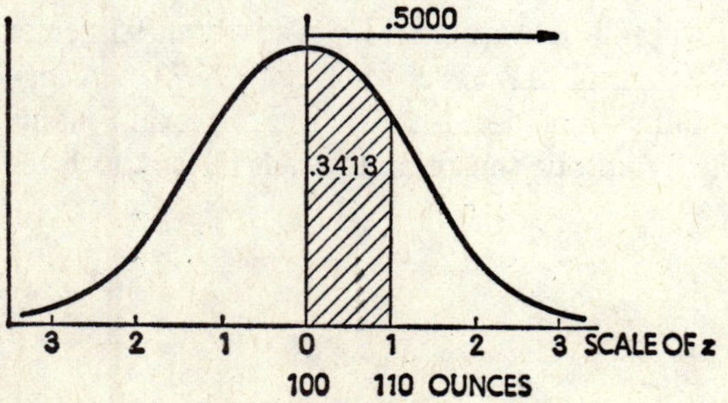

22

Using the same data (mean = 100 ounces, standard deviation = 10 ounces), what is the probability of selecting a ball bearing at random and finding that it weighed between 95 ounces and 122.5 ounces? 0. ____________.

.6793, found by 0.1915 + 0.4878

23

Management is considering awarding achievement points for production over a specified number of pieces in order to increase production. Past records on the production of a small electronic component revealed that the distribution of production was somewhat normally distributed with a mean daily production per employee of 800 pieces and a standard deviation of 50 pieces. The electronic components are counted, and thus the data are considered discrete. However, the normal frequency curve, which was based on a large number of parts produced, allows a reasonable assumption to be made that the distribution is continuous.

It has been suggested that achievement points be awarded on production of 946 pieces and over. On what percent of total production (based on past records) will achievement points be awarded? ____________.

0.0018 (less than 1 percent), found by:

$$z = \frac{946 - 800}{50} = 2.92$$

Then, 0.5000 − 0.4982 = 0.0018

24

Management concluded that if achievement points were awarded on less than 1 percent of production, their goal of increasing production would not be realized. It was then suggested that achievement points be awarded on the highest 5 percent of production (based on past records). If this plan went into effect, achievement points would be awarded on production over ____________ pieces. (Hint: the upper 5 percent represents how many z values?)

882.25 pieces, found by:

$$z = \frac{X - \mu}{\sigma};$$

$$1.645 = \frac{X - 800}{50}$$

25

In summary, the normal probability distribution is a (discrete/continuous) ____________ distribution. It is described by a mean designated as ____________, and a standard deviation designated as ____________. The normal distribution is (skewed/symmetrical) ____________ and appears as a smoothed curve. A *standardized* normal distribution has a mean of ____________ and a standard deviation of ____________. Using z, called the ____________ probabilities can be determined for any normal distribution. It was noted, for example, the probability is 0. ____________ that a value selected at random will fall between $\mu \pm 1\sigma$. And about 95 percent of the values fall between $\mu \pm$ ____________. Practically all (99.73 percent) of the values in a normal distribution fall within $\mu \pm$ ____________. Finally, the normal probability distribution is asymptotic (meaning the tails never touch the X-axis).

continuous
μ
σ
symmetrical
0
1
z value
.6826 (or 0.68)
2 σ
3 σ

Final Self-Review Examination

First, answer all of the questions. Then check your answers against those given at the end of this chapter. Scoring: 10 problems × 10 points each = 100 possible points.

26. There are a large number of probability distributions. Of the three discussed in this chapter, which one(s) are discrete? (*a*)______ ______. Which one(s) are continuous? (*b*)______.

27. In order to construct any probability distribution, certain parameters (such as the mean) must be known. Which one(s) are needed to construct a:

    (*a*) binomial distribution______ ______ ______.

    (*b*) Poisson distribution______ ______ ______.

    (*c*) normal distribution______ ______ ______.

28. A consumer research organization has an identification project. The sponsor of the project wants to know if grocery shoppers can identify the package of certain well-known foods (Campbell's soup, Lipton's tea). Ten different packages were selected and the names deleted. The sponsor has arbitrarily decided that consumers who are able to identify 8 or more packages out of 10 are *very brand conscious*, consumers who identify 5, 6, or 7 are *somewhat brand conscious*, and so on. The consumer research organization developed a questionnaire and pilot-tested the 10 unnamed packages on 100 consumers. Out of the 100 consumers, 30 identified 8, 9, or 10 correctly. The research firm is somewhat concerned that this group (30 percent of the total) might have just guessed the correct brand name and the results are really not significant. Is it highly possible that such a large percent could have guessed the brand name correctly? Explain your decision by citing evidence. ______ ______.

29. A high-speed shearing machine has been producing about 5 percent defective parts. What is the probability that if eight sheared pieces were selected at random none would be defective? ______

30. An analysis of past records revealed that about 10 percent of the total of a mass produced part were defective. That is, 10 percent of the parts contained a burr which had to be filed off. During the past hour, several samples of 10 parts were selected at random. Most of the samples contained four defective parts. Does it appear that something is wrong with the production process, or is it reasonable to expect 4 out of 10 in a sample to be defective? Give evidence.______ ______.

31. A national grocery chain has made a large number of studies on the waiting lines at the checkout counters. They found there was an average of 1.0 shoppers waiting to be checked out. The distribution of waits appeared to follow the shape of the Poisson probability distribution. The management of the grocery chain has designed their checkout cash registers so that hardly ever will customers wait in a line of *four or more shoppers to check out*. Has management achieved its goal? Explain. ______ ______.

32. A trucking firm has found that on the average 2.0 of their earthmovers are inoperative on a given day. The distribution of the number of inoperative earthmovers follows a Poisson distribution. Out of 100 days, how many days will no earthmovers be inoperative? ______ ______.

Questions 33, 34, and 35 are based on the following problem.

Supervisors and others have rated each management trainee on a scale of 0 to 150. The ratings for each trainee were combined into a composite rating, such as 95.34. Thus, the composite ratings can be considered as being continuous data. The distribution of all the ratings approximated a normal distribution with a mean rating of 100 and a standard deviation of 20.

33. Management wants a list of the names of the top 10 percent of the trainees. The trainees with a score of __________ or more would be on the list.

34. Management has decided to dismiss those with a score of less than 85. What percent of the trainees will be dismissed? __________.

35. Those between 85 and 105 will be given additional training before deciding on their fate. What percent of the trainees will get additional training? __________.

Answers to Final Self-Review Examination

26. (*a*) binomial, Poisson
    (*b*) normal

27. (*a*) *p*(the proportion defective) and *n*(number sampled)
    (*b*) the mean μ
    (*c*) the mean μ and the standard deviation σ

28. Highly improbable that 30 percent of consumers could guess 8, 9, or 10 brand names of products correctly. It seems then that 30 percent are "very brand conscious." To solve: Probability a consumer could guess the brand name of a package correctly is 0.50. $p = 0.50$; $n = 10$. Refer to Table VII. Add 0.0429 + 0.0098 + 0.0010 = 0.0547. Only about 5 percent should have guessed 8, 9, or 10 brand names correctly. Thus 30 percent apparently can identify brand-name packages.

29. 0.6634

30. Something is wrong. Even if 10 percent of production were defective (a burr), only about 1 percent of the samples of size 10 should have contained a burr. (Refer to Table VII and $n = 10$, $p = .10$.) The probability is 0.0112 of selecting 4 out of 10 defective.

31. Yes. Only 1.8988 percent of the time should four or more persons be waiting to be checked out. Found by referring to Table VI, a μ of 1.0. Add 0.015328, 0.003066. . . . 0.000001 = 0.018988

32. 13.5335 days, found by referring to Table VI and reading the probability for a $\mu = 2.0$ and an X of 0. The probability is 0.135335.

33. 125.6, found by

    $$1.28 = \frac{X - 100}{20}$$

    To find the z of 1.28 find 0.4000 (Table IV)

34. 22.66 percent
    $z = -0.75$
    then, 0.5000 − 0.2734 = 0.2266

35. 37.21 percent, found by 0.2734 + 0.0987

An introduction to sampling

chapter

8

Data needed to make decisions can be gathered by either studying all of the items in the population (a census), or selecting a few from the population for study (a sample). The fundamental purpose of sampling is to estimate a population value, called a population parameter, based on a sample value called a sample statistic. This estimation procedure is called *statistical inference*.

Suppose that a sample of 4,000 voters in the United States revealed that 3,200, or 80 percent, were in favor of reducing the voting age to 16 years. The sample value of 80 percent is called a ____________________. If the 80 percent were used to predict the outcome of a national vote on this issue, the procedure would be called ____________________.

sample statistic

statistical inference

REASONS FOR SAMPLING

Checking each computer, each completed television set, and each automobile as it is manufactured is feasible. Contacting nearly 100 million voters one month prior to a national election in order to predict which candidate will win, or checking every fuse manufactured is not feasible. Thus, a sample is often employed because of the:

1. Destructive nature of some tests.
2. Prohibitive cost of examining the entire population.
3. Physical impossibility of studying all of the population, such as all of the fish in a lake.
4. Time limitation, such as imposed on political pollsters just prior to an election.
5. Adequacy of sample results. For example, an automotive manufacturer would probably be quite satisfied if a sample survey revealed that between 85 and 90 percent of the new car buyers would have installed an air conditioner if the price were a moderate $100.

METHODS OF PROBABILITY SAMPLING

It is essential that every item in the population has a chance of being chosen in the sample. Otherwise, the sample results might not be representative of the population. If this happens, the sample results are considered *biased*. Reasoning that they would be eminently qualified to speak for all consumers, a group of artists and designers in the Detroit, Michigan area were asked to rate certain styling features on the mock-up model of a proposed new automobile. Would this sample be biased? (yes/no) ______. Why? ____________________

yes

All consumers did not have a chance to express their opinions.

One commonly used method of assuring that all items in the population have a known chance (probability) of being chosen in the sample is called *simple random sampling*, alternately called *probability sampling*. All draft-age males prior to World War II reg istered at a local draft board, and each was assigned a number. To assure that eac male had an equal chance of being selected for service, the numbers were placed in bowl. The Secretary of War began picking numbers from the bowl and men with thos numbers were required to report to their draft board. This illustrates ____________ ____________ sampling.

simple random or probability sampling

4

Since there were a known number of draft-age males, the population is considered *finite* population. If the population is finite, instead of selecting numbers from a bow a more convenient way of selecting the items to be sampled is by using a *table of randor numbers*. For example, a sample from the 8,614 students at a university are to be su veyed. Each student has an identification number for payroll and other purposes star ing with 0001 and ending with 8,614. The first few numbers from a table of randoı numbers are shown as follows.

0694	5965	7212	5888
9121	9791	5207	9769
6970	0319	7338	8785
3426	etc.	etc.	etc.

The numbers in this table are already randomized having been emitted by an IBM com puter. Thus, student numbers can be chosen starting anywhere in the table called ____________. For illustration, the first num ber in the left column is 0694. The student with that identification number would b surveyed. Reading down the same column, 9,121 could not be used because there is n student with that identification number. The next student to be interviewed would hav the identification number ____________. Why was this method for ra domly selecting students to interview followed? ____________

table of random numbers

6,970

to prevent biased results, i.e., assure each student has a chance of being chosen

5

A simple random sample may be awkward to select in certain cases. For example, there were 1,000 invoices on file by date received to be audited on a sample basis, th invoices would have to be numbered from 0001 up to 1,000. Then a sample (say, 20 numbers) would have to be selected from a table of random numbers. The invoice t match each of the numbers would have to be located in the file.

Instead, a *systematic* sampling procedure may be used to audit the invoices. Thu if there are 1,000 invoices and 200 are to be sampled, it may be more convenient, as we as more economical, to select every fifth invoice. The number of the first invoice shoul be selected using a random device such as a table of random numbers. If the number were selected then the 4th, 9th, ________, and so on would be audited. The metho described is called ____________ sampling.

14th

systematic

6

Systematic sampling should not be used if there is a predetermined pattern to the popu lation. For example, it is desired to determine the average length of time an item stay in a warehouse. The warehouse is so arranged that the merchandise in the top bins are slow-moving items and the goods in the more accessible bins are the fast-moving items. Shown schematically:

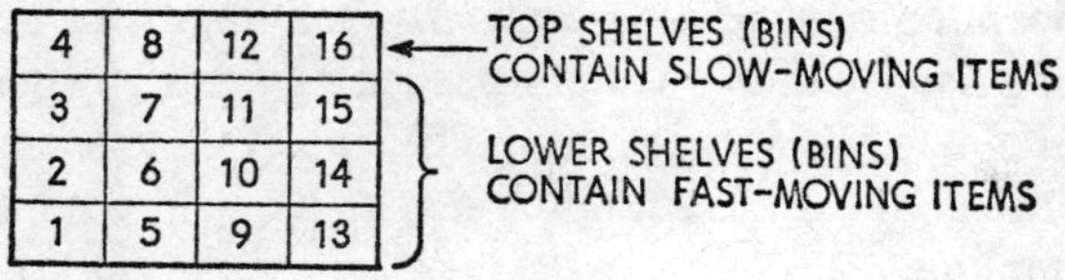

If a systematic sample of every fourth bin were to be chosen starting with bin #4, then goods in bins ____________, ____________, and ____________ would be checked. Thus, using a ________________ type sample any inference based on the sample average would be biased because ____.

#8, #12, and #16
systematic
only the slow-moving items would be chosen

7

To correct the inadequacy of the systematic selection of bins, *stratified* sampling may be used. In the previous warehouse problem, the population is actually stratified into two *subpopulations,* or *strata,* i.e., slow-moving and fast-moving items. Each strata is sampled independently. If it were decided to use a *proportional* stratified sample in the same relationship as found in the population, then for every one slow-moving item sampled ____________ fast-moving bins would be inventoried. When the items in the population are divided into subpopulations, or strata, such as in the warehouse problem, the sampling method is called ________________ sampling.

3
stratified

8

The number of items chosen in the sample need not be proportional to the proportion of items in the various strata. If the number chosen in each stratum is not proportional to their number in the subpopulations, the sampling method is called *nonproportional stratified sampling.* For example, a survey might involve interviewing presidents of firms in an industry. The firms were stratified according to the number of employees.

Size of Firm by Number of Employees	*Number of Firms*
Under 10	780
10 up to 100	210
100 and over	10
Total	1,000

If a proportional stratified sample of 100 firms were used, only (number) ____________ president of a firm with 100 or more employees would be interviewed. However, the 10 large firms in the industry probably have sales in excess of the remaining 990 firms combined. Further, the one president interviewed might not be representative of the group. Therefore, it would be more desirable to survey more presidents of large firms (possibly all 10) and fewer medium-sized and small firms. This type of sampling would be designated as ________________________ ________________________ sampling. There are other probability methods (not discussed here).

1
nonproportional stratified

9

METHODS OF NONPROBABILITY SAMPLING

There is a significant amount of *nonprobability* sampling being done in the United States. The users of nonprobability sampling, such as firms engaged in determining the market potential of newly developed products, claim that it is less expensive, not so time-consuming, more convenient, and gives results as valid as those obtained from probability type sampling.

judgment

Judgment or *purposive* sampling is one type of nonprobability sampling. As the name implies, the selection of the items in the sample is left to the ____________ of the researcher. A public opinion researcher with the problem of determining the preelection popularity of several candidates might select an area which in his judgment is typical of the voting population and concentrate his efforts in this area. This type of

judgment

nonprobability sampling called ____________ sampling generally reduces cost and can be completed in a relatively short period of time.

Convenience sampling is another type of nonprobability sampling. A nationally known bakery uses this type of sampling to test newly developed products. A small group of housewives are invited to taste and rate the pastry. Persons taking tours of automobile manufacturing plants in Detroit are often asked to rate the features of mockup models of proposed future automobiles.

Panel sampling is another nonprobability method of collecting quantitative data. Product testing firms such as National Family Opinion, Inc., and Market Facts, organize persons who have volunteered to test products or give opinions into panels. Each panel consists of about 2,000 persons. Dog owners would constitute one panel, families with children under 16 years might be another. The usual method of collecting the data is by mail questionnaire. The claimed advantages of this type of sampling are lower cost, a higher percent response because the participants are volunteers, and less time consumed because the respondents are always readily available.

Final Self-Review Examination

First, answer all of the questions. Then check your answers against those given at the end of this chapter. Scoring: 10 problems × 10 points each = 100 possible points.

10. The main purpose of sampling is to estimate a population (*a*)____________ based on a sample (*b*)____________.

11. Sampling, in contrast to a study of all items in the population, is often preferred because:
(*a*) ____________
(*b*) ____________
(*c*) ____________.

12. The two basic types of sampling are ____________ and ____________.

13. Three methods of probability sampling are ____________, ____________, ____________.

14. Three methods of nonprobability sampling are ____________, ____________, and ____________.

15. Nonprobability sampling lacks one advantage of probability sampling; namely, ____________.

16. Selected families living contiguous to a proposed shopping center were interviewed. It was found that the mean income of the sample was $9,200. Based on a systematic sample, it was

noted in the written report that "if all the families in the area were surveyed the mean income would be between $9,100 and $9,300." A (probability/nonprobability) ______________ ______________ sample was used.

Identify the method of sampling in questions 17 through 19.

17. A manufacturer of cat food wanted to package a newly developed cat food in a clear container. In order to obtain consumer reaction, he hired a consumer opinion organization to do the research. Eight different forms of the food were mailed to 1,800 cat owners who had previously volunteered to test products and give opinions. Nearly 80 percent of the respondents thought that the food labeled "Exhibit D" had the most appealing color and shape. This nonprobability sampling method is called ______________ sampling.

18. Incoming orders are given a number and filed consecutively. Every tenth order was chosen in a sample starting with number 007 and continuing with 017, 027, 037, and so on. This method is called ______________ sampling.

19. All union members have a card number. A table of random numbers was used to select numbers 1,395, 0024, 6,219, and so forth. Union members having those card numbers were surveyed regarding their political preferences. This method is called ______________ ______________ sampling.

Answers to Final Self-Review Examination

10. (*a*) parameter
    (*b*) statistic

11. (In any order) destructive nature of some tests, cost, less time consuming, adequacy of sample results, and the impossibility of studying all of the items in the population.

12. (Any order) probability, nonprobability

13. (Any order) simple random, systematic, stratified

14. (Any order) judgment, convenience, panel

15. (Any order) Using nonprobability sampling the items selected for study might not be representative of the population. Thus, the sample results might be biased.

16. probability

17. panel

18. systematic

19. simple random or probability

chapter

9

An introduction to statistical inference

1

The purpose of sampling is to draw a conclusion about some measure of the populatio (called a *parameter*) based on a sample value (called a sample *statistic*). It was note that a population might be composed of people or inanimate objects, such as automo- bile mufflers, nails, or television sets. An example of a marketing research problem might be to draw a conclusion about the arithmetic mean income of families livin contiguous to a proposed new shopping center. Suppose that a random sample of 82 families in the area were interviewed and the arithmetic mean family income compute to be $9,200. The $9,200 is called a ________________ ________________.

sample statistic

2

If one value is to be estimated, the specific estimate (such as $9,200) is called a *poin estimate*. Thus, based on the sample of 822 families, this point estimate is the bes estimate of the population mean obtainable. It should be realized that the sampl statistic of $9,200, called a ________________ estimate, may not be exactly th same as the population mean. Therefore, it may be desirable to specify a range o interval, within which the population mean might fall. For example, based on th sample mean of $9,200, the *confidence limits* might be calculated to be $9,100 an $9,300. (The necessary calculations will be examined shortly.) A probability, such a 0.90, is attached to these two numbers. It is then inferred with a probability of 0.9 that the mean income of *all* families in the proposed shopping area is in the interva from $9,100 to $9,300.

point

3

INFERENCES INVOLVING MEANS

A concept essential to the understanding of statistical inference is called the *sam pling distribution of the mean*. To illustrate, suppose that the incomes of *all* the familie in the proposed shopping center area wer known. The incomes were organized into frequency distribution and plotted as a fre quency polygon (Figure A). Is the popula tion distribution (normal/positively skewed, negatively skewed)? ________________ ________________.

FIGURE A

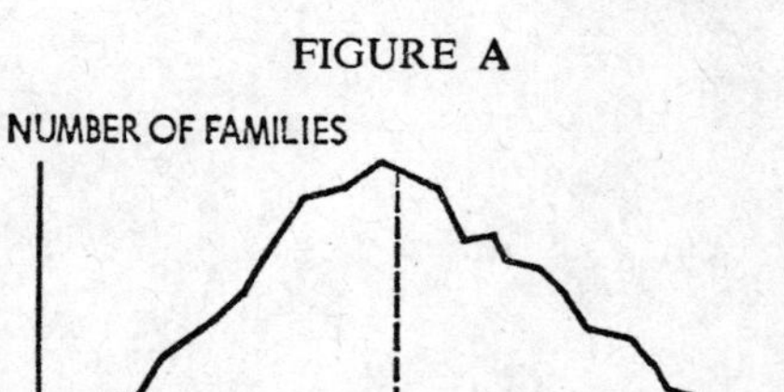

positively skewed

A sample of 100 families were selected a random from the population and their an nual incomes organized into a frequency distribution and plotted in Figure B. Another sample of 100 families (designated as Sample #2) is also plotted in Figure B. A comparison of the population distribution and sample distributions reveals (1) that the distribution of sample values tend to follow the same shape as the population values, i.e., the two sample distributions are also ____________ ____________ skewed. Make two other observations about the sample distributions (Figure B).

____
____
____
____
____
____
____.

FIGURE B

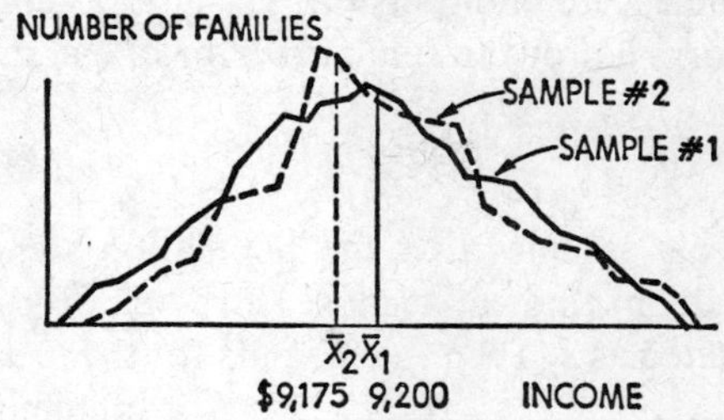

FIGURE C

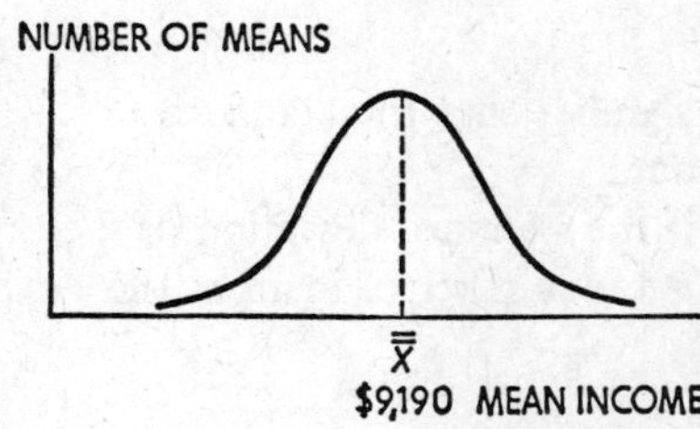

positively
(In any order.) The actual distributions of the two samples are different and the means are different.

4

The central-limit theorem

If the mean incomes of all possible samples of size 100 were plotted, the distribution of these sample means would approximate a *normal probability distribution* (Figure C in the previous illustration). Thus, if the distribution of the population values is skewed, the distributions of the sample values selected from that population will tend to be ____________________. However, the distribution of a large number of the sample means will tend to be ____________________ distributed. This distribution is called the *sampling distribution of the mean*. This concept is part of the *central-limit theorem*. A statement of the theorem is: *If a large number of random samples are chosen from any population (either normal or skewed), the means of these samples will approximate a normal probability distribution. And, the mean of these sample means (written $\bar{\bar{X}}$) will approach the population mean (written μ).*

skewed
normally

5

The standard error of the mean

The importance of the central-limit theorem will now be examined. In "real-world" sampling problems it is not feasible to take thousands of samples of, say, size 100 just to estimate the population mean. The cost and time limitations usually restrict the researcher to selecting *one* sample from the population. On the basis of this one sample he can make a point estimate and give the ____________________ limits for the population mean.

confidence

The confidence limits for the mean are based on a measure of central tendency and a measure of dispersion. The latter is designated as the *standard error of the mean.* The formula for the standard error of the mean is:

$$\sigma_{\bar{x}} = \frac{\sigma}{\sqrt{n}}$$

This assumes that the population standard deviation (σ) is known. However, σ is seldom known. It must be estimated by using the sample standard deviation, designated as s. Then the formula for the measure called the ______________ ______________ for infinite populations becomes:

standard error of the mean

$$s_{\bar{x}} = \frac{s}{\sqrt{n}}$$

Where:

$s_{\bar{x}}$ signifies that the standard error of the mean is being estimated using sample data.
s is the standard deviation of the sample.
n is the number of items in the sample.

6

To illustrate its computation, suppose that the mean tensile strength of an infinite number of steel wires is to be evaluated by selecting a random sample of 100 wires from the population and breaking them. Each wire was tested and the tensile strength recorded. The standard deviation of the sample was computed to be 500 pounds per square inch (written psi). Show the formula and compute the standard error of the mean.

$s_{\bar{x}}$ = ________ = ________ = psi

$s_{\bar{x}} = \frac{s}{\sqrt{n}} = \frac{500}{\sqrt{100}} = 50$ psi

7

The confidence interval and confidence limits

The arithmetic mean tensile strength of the 100 sample pieces was computed to be 10,000 psi. Obviously, all of the wires cannot be broken to determine the population mean (μ). The mean of the sample ($\bar{x}$) and the standard error of the mean ($s_{\bar{x}}$) are combined to set up the *confidence interval* for the population mean. In order to determine the confidence interval it is necessary to determine the two confidence limits of the sample mean. The 95 percent confidence limits (also stated as the 0.95 confidence limits) are computed by $\bar{x} \pm zs_{\bar{x}} = \bar{x} \pm 1.96s_{\bar{x}}$

Give the formula for the 95 percent confidence limits for the sample mean for the tensile strength problem, insert the appropriate numbers and solve. The 0.95 confidence limits = = = ______________ and ______________ psi.

$\bar{x} \pm 1.96s_{\bar{x}}$
$= 10,000 \pm 1.96(50)$
$=$ 9,902 and 10,098 psi

8

What are the 0.98 confidence limits for the same problem involving the tensile strengths of the steel wires? ______________ psi and ______________ psi. (If needed, refer to Chapter 7 frame #19 for a review of the procedure for determining the appro-

about 9,883.5 psi and 10-, 116.5, found by 10,000 $\pm$ 2.33(50)

riate z value.) Now interpret what these two confidence limits indicate. ________________

The probability is 0.98 that the population mean is in the interval between 9,883.5 psi and 10,116.5 psi.

/hat is the probability that the population mean tensile strength is not in the interval etween 9,883.5 psi and 10,116.5 psi? ________________.

0.02, found by 1 − 0.98

'inite populations

The formula $s/\sqrt{n}$ is applied to infinitely large populations. It is also applicable if ıe sampling is done with replacement (meaning that the item drawn at random is put ack in the population before another selection is made). In effect, sampling with ·placement is the same as an infinitely large population.

A modification is made to the formula for the standard error of the mean when the opulation is *finite* and the sample size is a large proportion of the total population. .ecall that a finite population means that the total number of persons (or inanimate bjects) are known. The modification is called the *finite population correction factor* nd is often referred to as the *finite multiplier.* The finite correction factor is:

$$\sqrt{\frac{N-n}{N-1}}$$

/here:

N is the size of the population.

n is the size of the sample.

Applying this correction factor, the standard error of the mean for a ________________ opulation is:

finite

$$s_{\bar{x}} = \frac{s}{\sqrt{n}}\sqrt{\frac{N-n}{N-1}}$$

uppose that there were 1,500 members of a union and 200 were selected at random. 'he correction factor is ________________.

0.931

0

The finite correction factor, therefore, compensates for the size of the sample in rela- .on to the size of the population. To illustrate this further, note in the following table hat the correction factor is approximately 0.997 if only 9 members out of 1,500 mem- ers of the union (about 1 ercent) were sampled. This s logical. The error in esti- ıating the mean wage of the opulation of 1,500 based on sample of 1,000 (67 percent f the population) should be ess than the error in esti- ıating the mean wage based nly on nine members.

Size of Sample	*Size of Finite Population*	*Size of Sample / Size of Population (Percent)*	*Correction Factor*
9	1,500	0.6	0.997
50	1,500	3.3	.983
200	1,500	13.3	.931
1,000	1,500	66.7	.619
1,500	1,500	100.0	0

Some statisticians do not apply the correction factor unless the size of the sample s at least 5 percent of the size of the population, and others disregard it until the ample size is at least 10 percent of the total.

In review, suppose that there are 2,001 executives in the aircraft industry. A randon sample of 400 were given a test on the principles of management. The mean test scor was computed to be 180 and the standard deviation of the scores found to be 60. Wit probability of 0.95, the mean test score of the population is in the interval betwee ______________ and ______________. Show the formula and essential work.

approximately 174.74 and 185.26 found by,

$$180 \pm 1.96 \frac{60}{\sqrt{400}} \sqrt{\frac{2{,}001 - 400}{2{,}001 - 1}}$$

Estimating the population mean for small samples

The previous frames dealt with large samples selected at random from a popula tion. If the sample size is small, the confidence limits are determined by $\bar{x} + t(s_{\bar{x}})$ Note that the only difference when working with a small sample is that a *t*-multiple i used instead of a *z*-multiple. The concept of the *t*-multiple was developed by W. S Gosset, an Irish brewmaster, writing under the name of Student. In brief, he develope a set of *t*-multiples for each sample size. These distributions are commonly referred t as *Student t* distributions (not considered here).

11

INFERENCES INVOLVING PROPORTIONS

The procedure for determining the confidence interval for the population propor tion is quite similar to that developed for a variable examined in the previous frames To illustrate, suppose a random sample of 1,000 students revealed that 800 liked revolutionary new writing pen. The point estimate of the population proportion i 0.80 found by:

$$\bar{p} = \frac{x}{n} = \frac{800}{1{,}000}$$

where x is the number in favor of the pen and n is the sample size. To find the confi dence limits for the population proportion:

$$\bar{p} \pm z s_{\bar{p}}$$

The standard error of the proportion ($s_{\bar{p}}$) is computed by:

For infinite populations	*For finite populations*
$s_{\bar{p}} = \sqrt{\frac{\bar{p}(1-\bar{p})}{n}}$	$s_{\bar{p}} = \sqrt{\frac{N-n}{N-1}} \sqrt{\frac{\bar{p}(1-\bar{p})}{n}}$

Assuming that the student population is infinite, construct the 0.95 confidence limi for the proportion of the student population who would like the revolutionary ne pen. Show essential formulas and work in the space provided. Give answers to th nearest 10th of a percent, such as 89.4 percent. ______________ and __________ percent.

77.5 and 82.5, found by

$$0.80 \pm 1.96 \sqrt{\frac{0.80(1 - 0.80)}{1{,}000}}$$

12

Sample size involving variables

A development company is considering building a shopping mall. One of the figur needed is the mean income of the residents. It would be too expensive and time-co suming to survey all residents in the area. One might ask, "How many residents should be included in a sample? 3? 50? 500? 8,000?"

Several factors have an influence on the size of the sample. The management of the development company no doubt has some idea of the precision required in the estimate of the population mean. For example, management might want the estimate of the population mean to be within $100. This would indicate that *if* the sample mean was computed to be $10,000, it would be stated that the population mean is in the interval between ______________ and ______________.

$9,900 and $10,100, found by $10,000 ± $100

13

A second factor in determining the size of the sample is the confidence coefficient. If the 0.95 confidence coefficient were selected, management would be 95 percent confident that the interval between $9,900 and $10,100 contains the population mean.

The third factor needed is an estimate of the standard deviation of the population. This can be estimated from experience, or by taking a pilot sample of, say, 30 persons. Suppose the pilot survey revealed that the standard deviation of the population is approximately $1,000. Management has specified that the sample be of sufficient size to include the population mean in the interval of ±$100 from the sample mean. Using the 0.95 confidence coefficient (and rounding 1.96 to 2 to simplify calculations), the confidence limits for the population mean are computed by:

$$\bar{x} \pm 2(s_{\bar{x}}) \quad \text{or} \quad \bar{x} \pm 2\left(\frac{s}{\sqrt{n}}\right)$$

In effect, management specified that the population mean must fall in the interval of $2s_{\bar{x}}$ or 2 ($100). Thus $s_{\bar{x}}$ = $50, found by $100/2. This concept is shown schematically.

DISTRIBUTION OF SAMPLE MEANS OF SIZE *n*

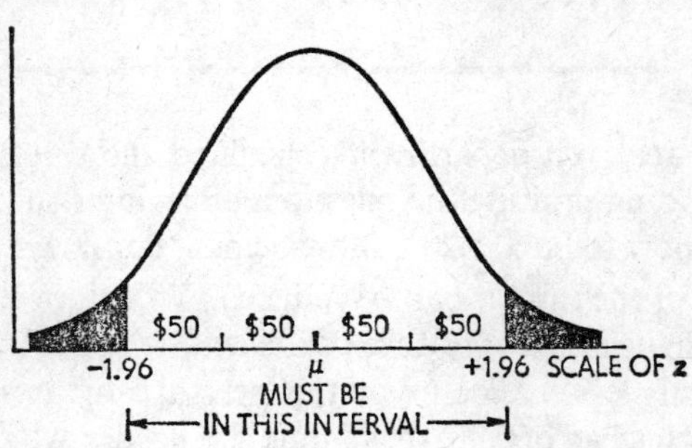

Substituting the $50 standard error specified by management and the estimated standard deviation of $1,000 from the pilot survey:

$$\$50 = \frac{\$1,000}{\sqrt{n}}$$

Solve for the size of the sample. n = ______________.

400

14

The sample size of 400 might not give the precision demanded by management (an estimate of the population mean within $100) because the population standard deviation might not be $1,000. (The $1,000 was determined from a very small pilot survey of 30 persons.) The sample of 400 persons might yield a confidence interval that is too large, too small, or exactly correct.

Suppose that the sample of 400 resulted in a sample standard deviation of $1,250. What should have been the sample size? ______________. Was the initial sample of 400 too (small/large)? ______________.

625, found by $\$50 = \dfrac{\$1,250}{\sqrt{n}}$

small, additional (225) persons must be surveyed

15

Sample size involving proportions

The procedures for estimating the sample size for problems involving proportions and variables are quite similar: (1) management must specify how precise the estimate of the population proportion is to be, (2) a confidence coefficient must be selected, and (3) the standard error of the proportion ($s_{\bar{p}}$) can be approximated from experience, or by taking a small pilot survey.

To illustrate, suppose that management wants to estimate the population proportion of homeowners in the metropolitan area who apply crabgrass killer to their lawns in the spring and fall. Management wants the estimate to be within an interval of ± 2 percent of the sample proportion. Also, the 0.98 confidence coefficient is to be used. A previous survey by the company in another metropolitan area resulted in a point estimate of the population proportion of 0.20. These three factors can be combined to determine the sample size (n). Recall that the standard error of the proportion is found by:

$$s_{\bar{p}} = \sqrt{\frac{\bar{p}(1-\bar{p})}{n}}$$

Substituting the three known values:

$$\begin{array}{r} \text{Specified by management} \rightarrow 0.02 \\ \text{The } z\text{-multiple for } 0.98 \longrightarrow 2.33 \end{array} = \sqrt{\frac{0.20(1-0.20)}{n}} \begin{array}{l} \leftarrow \text{From a previous sample} \\ \longleftarrow \text{Unknown} \end{array}$$

Solve for the size of the sample n = ______________ homeowners.

about 2,172, found by

$$\frac{0.02}{2.33} = \frac{\sqrt{0.16}}{\sqrt{n}}$$

$$0.02\sqrt{n} = 2.33\sqrt{.16}$$

$$n = (46.6)^2$$

16

The research department calculated the total cost of surveying 2,172 homeowners, including printing the questionnaires, interviewing, tabulating the results, and writing a report to be $15,204. Management considers this cost to be excessive and asks if the size of the sample can be reduced. To reduce the size of the sample, one possibility is to change the confidence coefficient from 0.98 to, say, 0.95. In effect, this would place slightly less confidence on the interval estimates. If the 0.95 confidence coefficient were used instead of 0.98, the sample size needed would be ______________.

about 1,600 if the rounded z-multiple of 2 is used; 1,537 if 1.96 is used.

Work: using $z = 2$:

$$\frac{0.02}{2} = \sqrt{\frac{0.20\,(1-0.20)}{u}}$$

$$0.02\sqrt{n} = 2\sqrt{.16}$$

$$n = (40)^2$$

17

The cost using the 0.95 confidence coefficient was found to be $11,200. Suppose that management wants to cut the cost even further, but retain the 0.95 confidence coefficient. What other concession can management make to affect a reduction in the size of the sample? (Hint: They want the population proportion to be estimated within the interval of ± 0.02 of the sample proportion.) ______________

______________.

Increase the size of the interval to, say, ±0.04.

18

Management indicated that it would be satisfactory if it were estimated that the population proportion was within ± 0.04 of the sample proportion. Now, using this revised recision figure (± 0.04), the confidence coefficient selected (0.95), and the proportion f homeowners found in another survey (0.20), determine the sample size. ________ ________________. Show work.

400 if z-multiple is rounded to 2; 384 if 1.96 is used.

$$\frac{0.04}{2} = \sqrt{\frac{0.16}{n}}$$

$$n = (20)^2$$

This number (400) would only cost $2,800 to survey. Again, because the population roportion was estimated to be 20 percent (a previous survey) the sample size might e too large or too small. Thus, the size of the sample is often a compromise between e cost of taking the sample and the preciseness desired by management.

Final Self-Review Examination

First, answer all of the questions. Then check your answers against those given at the end of this chapter. Scoring 10 problems × 10 points each = 100 possible points.

19. Explain what is meant by statistical inference. ________________ ________________ ________________.

20. In connection with sampling, explain each of the following words:
    statistic (*a*)________________.
    parameter (*b*)________________.
    population (*c*)________________.

21. State the general concept of the central-limit theorem. ________________ ________________ ________________ ________________.

22. It was found that the arithmetic mean weight of 100 items selected at random was 11,500 pounds. With a probability of 0.95, it was estimated that the population mean is between 11,400 pounds and 11,600 pounds. These two values (11,400 and 11,700) are called ________ ________________.

23. A sample of 400 executives were chosen at random and the mean age of the group computed to be 50 years. The standard deviation of the sample is 8 years. The 98 percent confidence limits for the population mean are (*a*) ________________ and ________________ years. Explain what the figures indicate. (*b*) ________________ ________________.

24. A total of 1,001 new parts were produced on the first production run. A sample of 100 revealed that the mean inside diameter is 2.0000 inches. The standard deviation of the sample was computed to be 0.0002 inches. The 0.92 confidence limits for the population mean are ________________ and ________________ inches. (Note that the population is finite.)

25. A small sample of 18 pieces of wire were selected at random and the mean tensile strength computed to be 10,000 pounds per square inch. The standard error of the mean was found to be 10 psi. The 90 percent confidence limits for the population mean are ________ ________________ psi and ________________ psi.

26. A sample public opinion poll revealed that 600 were in favor of the proposed amendment and 400 were against it. Construct the 95 percent confidence limits for the proportion of the total population in favor of the amendment. ________________ and ________ ________________.

27. The manufacturer of a foreign car is studying the possibility of introducing a new warranty. One figure needed is the arithmetic mean mileage on the odometer of their five-year-old cars. To collect this information for all cars would be expensive and time-consuming. Thus, the number to be sampled is important. Management wants to use the 0.95 confidence coefficient, and estimate the population mean within 1,000 miles. A very small pilot survey of the five-year-old cars indicated that the mean will probably be about 50,000 miles. The standard

deviation of the pilot survey was computed to be 10,000 miles. How many should be sampled? (*a*)__________. If the sample size computed for answer (*a*) is considered too large, what specifically could be done to reduce the size of the sample? Management could either (*b*)____________________
or ____________________
(or do both).

28. One large voting precinct has been traditionally Republican. The vote is usually 90 percent Republican. A pre-election poll is to be conducted to determine if there has been any change in the voting preference. The 0.95 confidence coefficient is to be used in determining the sample size and the population proportion is to be within an interval of plus and minus 3 percent of the sample proportion. What sample size is needed? ____________________.

Answers to Final Self-Review Examination

19. Statistical inference is a procedure which has been developed to describe a characteristic of a population (such as the mean income of typists) based on a sample selected from that population.
20. (*a*) A statistic refers to a sample value, such as mean of the sample is 81 pounds.
    (*b*) A parameter refers to a population value, such as the median income of all persons in the United States is $8,710.
    (*c*) A population refers to the total of either persons or inanimate objects. For example, the population might be defined as all of the students in the freshman English course at Sociable University, or all the light bulbs produced during the past month in the Schenectady plant.
21. The central-limits theorem states that (1) if a large number of random samples are selected from the population, the distribution of the sample means will approximate a normal probability distribution, (2) the mean of the sample means will approximate the population mean, and (3) the standard error of the mean of the sampling distribution is equal to $\sigma/\sqrt{n}$.
22. confidence limits
23. about 49.068 and 50.932 years, found by

$$50 \pm 2.33\left(\frac{8}{\sqrt{400}}\right)$$

The statistician is 98 percent confident that the population mean is in the interval between 49.068 and 50.932 years.

24. approximately 1.999967 inches and 2.000033 inches, found by

$$2.0000 \pm 1.75\,\frac{.0002}{\sqrt{100}}\sqrt{\frac{1{,}001 - 100}{1{,}001 - 1}}$$

25. 9,982.6 and 10,017.4 psi, found by 10,000 ± 1.740 (10)
26. about 0.57 and 0.63, found by

$$0.60 \pm 1.96\sqrt{\frac{0.60(1 - 0.60)}{1{,}000}}$$

27. (*a*) approximately 400, found by

$$\frac{1{,}000}{2} = \frac{10{,}000}{\sqrt{n}}$$

    (*b*) The confidence coefficient could be reduced from 0.95 to say 0.90 and/or the allowable error could be increased from 1,000 miles to, say, 1,500 miles.
28. about 400, found by

$$\frac{0.03}{2} = \sqrt{\frac{0.90(1 - 0.90)}{n}}$$

Statistical decision theory: tests of hypotheses

chapter

10

1

In this chapter, decision-making processes will be discussed regarding two means and two proportions. Two typical problems might be: Based on a sample of wire submitted by two suppliers, is the mean tensile strength of the wire of one company significantly higher than the mean tensile strength of the wire of the other company—or is it quite probable that the difference is due to sampling? A sample of residents living on the East Side revealed that 80 percent were in favor of Amendment No. 1, but on the West Side only 60 percent were in favor of it. One might ask, is it highly likely the difference in percents is due to sampling? Other problems might involve the difference between the mean income of two groups, or the difference between the proportion of men and women who like a new styling feature of a new automobile.

THE DECISION PROCEDURE

The decision procedure is alternatively called *rules of decision*, *tests of hypotheses*, or *tests of significance*. Six steps are usually followed in arriving at a decision.

1. State the hypothesis to be tested as well as the alternative hypothesis.
2. Select a level of significance.
3. Decide on an appropriate statistical test, examine the underlying theory and state the statistic needed.
4. Define the region of acceptance and the region of rejection.
5. Choose a random sample and compute the essential sample statistics.
6. Accept or reject the hypothesis at the level of significance selected.

Each of the six steps will now be discussed in detail.

The null hypothesis

A contractor needs a steel wire which will be woven into a cable for a bridge span. The wire must test at least 7,500 pounds per square inch (psi), or it will not be considered. Two companies, the Strongwire Company and Federal Steel, plan to submit samples for testing. First, however, a hypothesis is stated primarily to either *accept* it or to *reject* it. The hypothesis can be stated either positively or negatively. In this chapter, it has been arbitrarily decided to state it negatively, i.e., as a *null* hypothesis.

The contractor decided that if the two companies submit a sample of wires which test over 7,500 psi one of two actions will be taken—either to award the contract to one company, or to divide the contract equally between Strongwire and Federal. A general statement of the null hypothesis is that the two population means are equal; i.e., there is *no significant difference* between μ_1 and μ_2. *Thus, if this is true, any difference between the two sample means is merely due to sampling* (*chance*).

State the null hypothesis concerning the wire to be used for the bridge span. ________

____

____

"There is no significant difference between the mean of the wires from the Strongwire Company and the mean of the Federal wires."

The contractor plans to divide the contract equally if there is no significant difference between the two mean tensile strengths of the samples. If there is significant difference between the two mean tensile strengths, the contract for the wires will be given to the company submitting the stronger wires.

If the null hypothesis is *accepted* (based on the samples submitted), the contract will be (divided equally/given to one company) ______________________. If the null hypothesis is *rejected*, the difference between the two means (is/is not) ______________ significant. If the null hypothesis is *accepted*, the difference between the two means (could/could not) ______________ be due to sampling (chance).

divided equally

is

could

2

The level of significance

Three of the most commonly used levels of significance are the 0.10 level, the 0.05 level, and the 0.01 level. The 0.05 level of significance was selected for this problem. There is a 5 percent chance that the statistician will reject the null hypothesis when he should have accepted it. This is called a *Type I error*. If the null hypothesis were rejected in this tensile strength problem, explain what the level of significance indicates. "The level of significance in this problem is the probability that____."

the null hypothesis should have been accepted instead of being rejected. (This indicates that *if* in reality the two population mean tensile strengths were equal, the probability that a Type I error was made in rejecting the null hypothesis and giving the contract to just one company is 0.05.)

3

The test, the theory, and the statistic needed

In order to explain the theory underlying the ultimate decision, assume that two populations are identical. A sample is selected from one of the populations and the mean and the standard deviation of the sample are computed. Then a sample from the other population is selected, and the same two sample statistics are determined. Using these two sets of sample statistics, a measure called the *critical ratio* (designated as z) is determined. The statistic z is computed by:

$$z = \frac{\bar{X}_1 - \bar{X}_2}{\sqrt{\left(\frac{s_1}{\sqrt{n_1}}\right)^2 + \left(\frac{s_2}{\sqrt{n_2}}\right)^2}}$$

Suppose this procedure was repeated a large number of times. The sampling theory states that the large number of critical ratios which were computed will be normally distributed about a mean of 0. To put it another way, if all the critical ratios resulting from a large number of samples taken from the two populations were plotted (assuming that there is no difference between the two populations), they would approximate a normal curve. The mean of the z values would be zero. About 95 percent of the critical ratios would fall between 0 and ± 1.96.

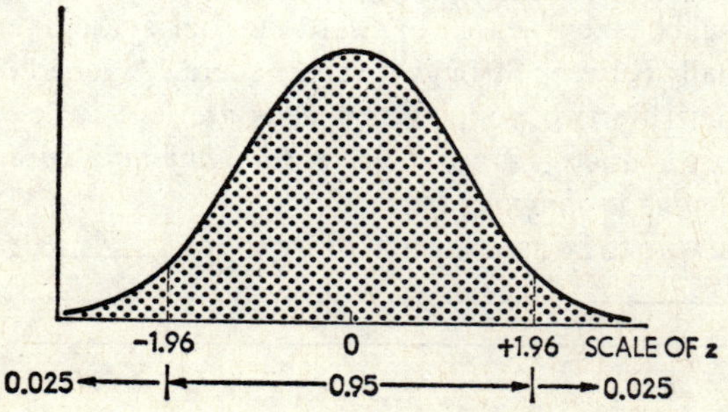

e region of acceptance and the region of rejection

Now a *decision rule* will be formulated. If a random sample is taken from the wires the Strongwire Company and another random sample is selected from the wires bmitted by Federal Steel and the z value computed, the null hypothesis will be *cepted* at the 0.05 level if the computed 'alls between 0 and +1.96, or 0 and 1.96. The null hypothesis will be *re-·ted* at the 0.05 level of significance if e computed z value does not fall in the a between +1.96 and −1.96. That is, the computed z value is 1.96 or eater, the null hypothesis is rejected. ie two areas beyond +1.96 and −1.96 e called the *tails* of the curve. This agram shows the two regions.

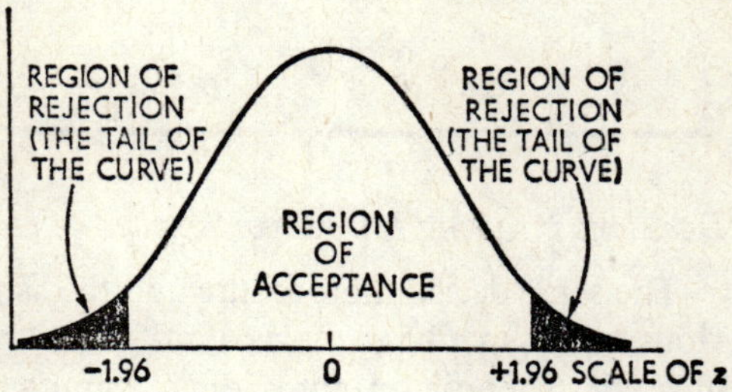

Suppose the two samples were selected and the critical ratio z was computed to be 0.82. The null hypothesis would be (accepted/rejected) ________________ at e 0.05 level of significance (previously selected). If this did happen, how would the ntract for the wires be awarded? (divided equally/awarded to company with the gher sample mean tensile strength) ________________________________ ______________. Thus, the difference between the two sample means (could/could ot) ________________ be due to chance.

accepted

divide contract equally

could

It should be noted that this is a *two-tailed test* because there is a possibility that the gn of z may be either positive or negative. If the sign of z can only be positive, or it n only be negative, it is called a one-tailed test.

---

e samples and the sample results

A sample (n) of 64 pieces of wire were selected at random from the wires of the rongwire Company and each tested for tensile strength. A sample of 100 wires were lected from the wires of Federal Steel. The mean ($\bar{X}$) and the standard deviation (s) each were computed. The results were:

Strongwire Company	*Federal Steel*
$\bar{X}_1 = 8{,}500$ psi	$\bar{X}_2 = 8{,}000$ psi
$s_1 = 120$ psi	$s_2 = 200$ psi
$n_1 = 64$	$n_2 = 100$

etermine the critical ratio:

$$z = \frac{\bar{X}_1 - \bar{X}_2}{\sqrt{\left(\frac{s_1}{\sqrt{n_1}}\right)^2 + \left(\frac{s_2}{\sqrt{n_2}}\right)^2}} = \frac{\qquad\qquad}{\sqrt{\qquad\qquad}} =$$

$z = +20$, found by $500/\sqrt{625}$

---

e decision

In this case, the null hypothesis is (accepted/rejected) ________________ be-use +20 falls ________________________________. It is highly un-

rejected

in the tail, i.e., it is greater than +1.96

chance, or sampling
Strongwire Company
95 percent certain that the wires of Strongwire have a higher tensile strength.
Type I

likely that the difference of 500 psi could be due to ______
How should the contract be awarded? ______
______. Why? ______
______

The probability is 0.05 that the null hypothesis has been rejected when it shoul have been accepted. This is called a ______ error.

6

There is no difference between the proportion of young persons and the proportion of older persons in favor of the proposed car design.
critical ratio
z

Decisions involving two proportions

The same decision procedure and the same sampling theory examined in the pre vious frames involving the means of two variables is applicable to two proportions. T illustrate, suppose an automobile manufacturer built a mock model of a propose new automobile. One of his problems is to find out whether it appeals equally t persons under 25 years and persons over 25 years of age.

State the null hypothesis. ______
______

The level of significance was arbitrarily selected as 0.01. Give the statistic needed The statistic needed is called the ______, and is designated b the letter ______.

7

accepted
rejected two-tailed
the critical ratio may be either positive or negative.

The decision rule. Recall that the level of significance is 0.01. The dividing poin between the region of acceptance and the region of rejection is 2.575. To find thi number, refer to Appendix Table IV and search for 0.4950 (which is half of 0.9900) The decision rule is: If the computed z falls between ± 2.575, the null hypothesis will b ______. If the computed z is ± 2.575 or greater, the null hypothesis will b ______. This is a (one-tailed/two-tailed) ______ test because ______.

8

The sample and sample results. Out of 2,000 younger men (under 25 years) sampled 1,600 or 80 percent were enthusiastic about the new car design. Out of 1,000 older me (over 25 years) sampled, 821 or 82.1 percent were enthusiastic about it. The basi question is whether the difference of 2.1 percent (0.80 − 0.821) is significant, o whether this difference could be due to sampling. To compute the critical ratio:

$$z = \frac{p_1 - p_2}{\sqrt{\frac{\bar{P}(1-\bar{P})}{n_1} + \frac{\bar{P}(1-\bar{P})}{n_2}}}$$

Where:

p_1 is the sample proportion of younger men
p_2 is the sample proportion of older men.
n_1 is the total number of younger men sampled

n_2 is the total number of older men sampled.
$\bar{P}$ is the weighted proportion found by

$$\frac{X_1 + X_2}{n_1 + n_2}$$

X_1 is the number of younger men enthusiastic about the car
X_2 is the number of older men enthusiastic about it.

Insert the appropriate figures in the formula and solve for the critical ratio. The critical ratio is ______________.

about −1.4(−1.374), found by

$$\bar{P} = \frac{1{,}600 + 821}{2{,}000 + 1{,}000}$$

$$\frac{0.80 - 0.821}{\sqrt{\dfrac{0.807(1 - 0.807)}{2{,}000} + \dfrac{0.807(1 - 0.807)}{1{,}000}}}$$

9

The decision. The null hypothesis should be ______________ at the ______________ level of significance. The difference of 2.1 percent (is/is not) ______________ significant. It is highly likely that the difference between the two proportions (is/is not) ______________ due to sampling (chance). Thus, if all the young men in the United States and all the older men in the United States viewed the mock model of the automobile, and the proportion of each group who were enthusiastic about it were computed, the two population proportions would probably be (equal/unequal) ______________.

accepted
0.01
is not
is

equal

10

Tests of hypotheses involving a known population mean and variance

Records have been kept by an airline on the length of life of an electronic part. It was found that the arithmetic mean length of life of the part was 200,000 miles and the standard deviation 10,000 miles. All the parts have been supplied by one manufacturer, and the airline has been satisfied with the price, delivery, and service. The Longlasting Manufacturing Company, however, claims that they have perfected the same electronic part, and its average length of life is significantly longer.

The null hypothesis is $\mu = 200{,}000$ miles, which is the same as saying that the average length of life ($\bar{X}$) of the Longlasting Company parts is not significantly different from the mean length of life determined from the long experience of the airlines with this electronic part. The level of significance chosen is 0.05. The statistic z is needed. The critical ratio z is found by:

$$z = \frac{\bar{X} - \mu}{\dfrac{\sigma}{\sqrt{n}}}$$

This is a *one-tail test* because there is only an interest in testing whether the electronic parts from Longlasting are superior, i.e., Is the mean length of life significantly more than the population mean of 200,000 miles? There would be no problem if the parts from Longlasting had a mean life-span of less than 200,000. (The airline would continue buying from the present supplier.) Thus, the critical value for the decision rule is 1.645 (instead of 1.96), found by finding the critical value for 0.4500 in Appendix Table IV. Shown schematically:

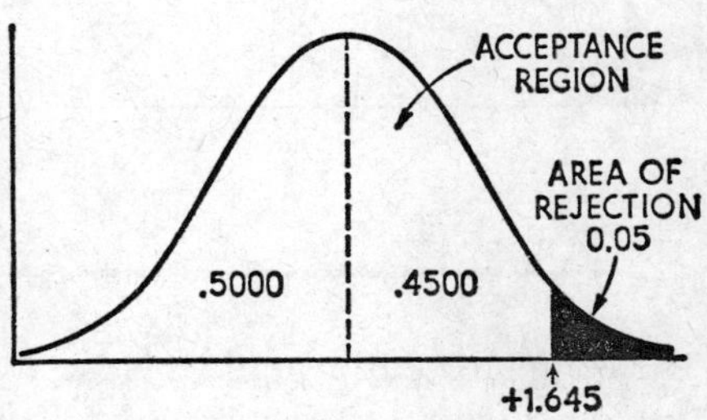

Thus, the decision rule states that if the computed critical ratio z is less than $+1.645$ the null hypothesis should be (accepted/rejected) ______________.

accepted

A sample of 2,500 parts were selected from the production line of Longlasting Manufacturing and the parts tested under an accelerated life testing program. The mean life was 215,000 miles. (The dispersion about the mean was quite satisfactory.) The question is, could this large a difference between the population mean (200,000 miles) and this sample mean be due to chance (sampling)? Find the critical ratio z ______________.

+75, found by 15,000/200

At the 0.05 level of significance the null hypothesis is ______________. Is it likely that the difference between the two means is due to chance? (yes/no) ______________ Recommend a course of action for the airline. ______________

rejected

no

Price and other factors being equal, buy from Longlasting. Their electronic parts do last longer on the average.

There is a ______________ percent chance that the hypothesis has been rejected when it should have been accepted.

5

11

Tests of hypothesis involving a known population proportion

Past records of a soup company reveal that 40 percent of the test group must indicate a newly developed soup is excellent or the soup will not be successful (if marketed). A new soup called "Beefy" is given the usual testing, and 600 out of the 2,000 sampled, or 30 percent, rated it excellent. One might ask, could this large a difference (0.10, found by 0.40 − 0.30) be due to sampling? The null hypothesis to be tested is ______________. The level of significance selected is 0.01. This is a one-tail test. Why? ______________.

the difference between the sample proportion and the known population proportion is not significant.

The soup company only has a problem when the sample proportion is less than the population percent of 0.40.

The critical ratio z is computed by:

$$z = \frac{p - P}{\sqrt{\frac{P(1-P)}{n}}}$$

where small letter p is the sample proportion, capital P is the known population proportion, and n is the number in the sample.

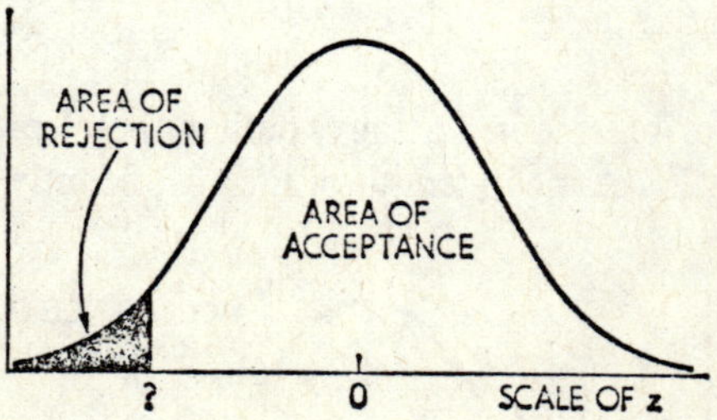

The decision rule is shown schematically. Thus, the decision rule is: accept the null hypothesis if the computed critical ratio z falls in the area to the right of ______________, but reject it if z falls in the tail of the normal curve i.e., ______________ or beyond.

−2.33

−2.33

12

The computed critical ratio z is ______________. Based on the value of the computed z and the decision rule formulated in the previous frame, make a deci-

about −9.1, found by $-.10/\sqrt{.00012}$

ion and explain what it indicates. ____

____

____.

The −9.1 falls in the region of rejection and the null hypothesis is rejected. The difference of 10 percent (0.40 − 0.30) is significant at the 0.01 level. It is highly unlikely that this large a difference could be due to sampling (chance) errors. The new soup, Beefy, would probably not be successful, if marketed.

3 ____

ype I and Type II errors

In sampling, there is always a risk that a wrong decision has been made. The alpha isk, or the Type I error, is usually specified before the sampling is done. The probbility of making a Type I error corresponds to the area in the tails of a normal curve. hese areas are designated as the area of ______________. The Type I rror, such as 0.05, is *the probability that the null hypothesis will be rejected when it hould have been accepted.*

rejection

A Type II error, called the beta risk, is *the probability of accepting a hypothesis when should have been rejected.* These probabilities are the basis for operating characteristic curves used extensively in quality control work. (Computations not examined ere.)

Final Self-Review Examination

First, answer all of the questions. Then check your answers against those given at the end of this chapter. Scoring: 10 problems × 10 points each = 100 possible points.

14. The engineering department has the project of increasing the tensile strength of a wire. First, 100 pieces of the wire were tested for tensile strength. The mean tensile strength was computed to be 1,000 pounds per square inch, and the standard deviation of the 100 pieces was 20 psi. As an experiment, some of the wire was treated with zonodium. A sample of 81 wires was tested. The mean tensile strength was found to be 1,200 pounds, and the standard deviation of the sample was 27 psi. Did the zonodium treatment significantly increase the mean tensile strength, or is the difference between the two means due to sampling? Use the 0.05 level of significance. The null hypothesis to be tested is ______________________

______________________________.

15. (Refer to the problem in frame #14.) Follow the usual six steps and arrive at a decision. The decision is (*a*) ______________________

______________________________. Explain. (*b*) ______________________

______________________________.

16. Two different methods of stamping out a small part are being used. Each method produces some defective parts. The problem is to determine whether one method is producing a significantly larger percent defective. A sample of 300 pieces was selected at random from the pieces produced using Method A, and it was found that 18 were defective. Out of a sample of 200 pieces produced using Method B, 10 were defective. Test the hypothesis at the 0.01 level. The decision rule is ______________________

______________________________.

17. (Refer to the problem in frame #16.) Follow the usual six steps and arrive at a decision. At the 0.01 level of significance, is it reasonable to assume that the difference between the two percent defectives is due to chance? (*a*) ______. Explain. (*b*) ______________________

______________________________.

18. Records of the scores on a scholastic aptitude test taken by prospective college freshmen revealed that the arithmetic mean score is 110 and the standard deviation is 10. These thou-

sands of scores can be considered the population. A new group just took the test, and a random sample of 400 revealed that the mean score was 106. Select one of the more commonly used levels of significance (*a*) ________ and indicate whether the mean of this latest group of prospective freshmen is significantly lower than the mean of past groups. The decision is (*b*) ____.

19. (Refer to the problem in frame #18.) Was a one-tail or two-tail test used? (*a*) ____________. Explain. (*b*) ____.

20. Past records indicate that a drug is 75 percent effective in minimizing the aftereffects of an operation. That is, 75 percent of the patients only had slight aftereffects. The manufacturer of a new drug claims that it is as effective, or even more effective, than the one now being used. His new drug was administered to a sample of 200 patients and 120 had slight aftereffects. Accept or refute his claim at the 0.10 level of significance. Answer. ____.

21. (Refer to the problem in frame #20.) The critical value used in the drug problem is ____________.

22. Explain what is meant by a Type I error. ____.

23. Explain what is meant by a Type II error. ____.

swers to Final Self-Review Examination

4. There is no significant difference between the mean tensile strength of the treated wire and the mean tensile strength of the untreated wire.

5. (*a*) Reject the null hypothesis at the 0.05 level. It is highly unlikely that the difference of 200 psi could be due to sampling.
   (*b*) The decision rule was to accept the null hypothesis if the critical ratio was found to be between 0 and +1.96 or 0 and −1.96, but reject if ±1.96 or greater. The critical ratio z was found to be approximately −55 found by:

$$z = \frac{1{,}000 - 1{,}200}{\sqrt{\left(\frac{20}{\sqrt{100}}\right)^2 + \left(\frac{27}{\sqrt{81}}\right)^2}}$$

   so the null hypothesis was rejected at the 0.05 level.

6. Accept null hypothesis if the computed critical ratio z is between 0 and ±2.575, reject if it falls outside those limits.

7. (*a*) yes
   (*b*) The critical ratio z was computed to be 0.5.

$$z = \frac{0.06 - 0.05}{\sqrt{\frac{0.056(0.944)}{300} + \frac{0.056(0.944)}{200}}}$$

   The 0.5 falls in the region of acceptance. The difference of 0.01 could be due to chance (sampling).

8. (*a*) Either 0.10, 0.05, or 0.01 are most common.
   (*b*) The difference of 4 points between the average of all prospective freshmen and the average of the latest group to take the test is significant at any of the three levels selected. The computed z is −8 found by:

$$z = \frac{106 - 110}{\frac{10}{\sqrt{400}}}$$

   The computed z falls in the area of rejection (outside −1.28 for the 0.10 level, or outside −1.645 for the 0.05 level, or outside −2.33 for the 0.01 level of significance).

19. (*a*) One-tail test used
    (*b*) Only interested in whether the latest group had mean test score significantly less than prior prospective freshmen.

20. Refute. The critical ratio z is about −5 found by:

$$z = \frac{0.60 - 0.75}{\sqrt{\frac{0.75(1 - 0.75)}{200}}}$$

    The computed z falls in the area of rejection (beyond −1.28) so the null hypothesis is rejected. It is highly unlikely that this new drug is as effective as the one currently being used.

21. −1.28 (This is a one-tail test so look for 0.4000 in Appendix Table IV and read the approximate critical value found in the left column.)

22. A Type I error is the probability that the null hypothesis will be rejected when in fact it is true.

23. A Type II error is the probability of accepting a hypothesis when it should have been rejected.

chapter

11

An introduction to decision making under uncertanity

1

The approach to making a decision in the previous two chapters was to set up a null hypothesis, establish a decision rule, take a sample, and on the basis of the sample results make a decision. That approach might be characterized as being objective in nature and based on probability theory. In this chapter, a relatively new and different approach to decision making will be examined.

Business firms, state and local governments, the federal government, hospitals, universities, and others make numerous decisions every day. A personal decision may be to wear the brown shoes instead of the tan ones; another decision might be to buy IBM stock instead of taking a vacation. A businessman may decide to purchase modern Danish instead of early American furniture for his office.

Some decisions are made under conditions of *certainty*, but others must be made under conditions of *uncertainty*. Quotations on a new Plymouth automobile were made by two reputable dealers. One quotation was $2,795, the other $2,995 for the identical model and accessories. The decision to buy it from the dealer submitting the quotation of $2,795 would be made under conditions of (certainty/uncertainty) ____________ because all the facts were known. Another decision maker bought a home at 811 Norcross Lane instead of the one located at 19270 Valley View Drive, reasoning that the home on Norcross Lane will appreciate in value more than the one on Valley View. However, because he is not absolutely sure that this will happen, the decision was made under conditions of ____________.

certainty

uncertainty

2

Manufacturers of automobiles, drill presses, bolts, refrigerators, and so forth are dependent upon the demand of other manufacturers, wholesalers, retailers, or consumers. The demand for their output is called an *event*. Future demand for their products is uncertain. It is said that the *state of nature* (the future) is uncertain. If the manufacturer does not know whether he will sell 1,000, 2,000, or 10,000 gross next month, it is said that the ____________ is uncertain.

state of nature

3

The manufacturer (the decision maker) is not sure which state of nature (the event) will actually occur. He must produce the bolts now, however, in anticipation of next month's orders which must be filled immediately upon receipt. Under conditions of uncertainty it is said that he has a choice among several alternative *acts*. For each of these acts there are numerous possible results called *payoffs*, *consequences*, or *outcomes*. If the decision maker decided to produce 27,000 gross now (called the ____________), the result (called the ____________) might be a profit of $24,000, or even a loss.

act

outcome, payoff or consequence

4

he main parts of the decision problem under conditions of uncertainty are summarized as follows. Insert the correct word (either outcome, event, or act) opposite ach group of explanatory statements.

n ________ characterized by:	Uncertainty regarding future demand. An unknown state of nature. A decision maker who has no control over future demand.	event
n ________ characterized by:	Two or more courses of action which are open to the decision maker. A decision maker who must evaluate various alternatives. A decision maker who selects a course of action based on certain criteria.	act
he ________ night be:	Profit Break-even Loss	consequence, payoff, or outcome

5

Case of decision making under uncertainty

This case examines the decision-making process further with the objective of eveloping a procedure which will suggest the most profitable consequence of an act. The business fraternity on campus wants to earn money and get business experience y starting and operating a small business. One which seems to hold promise is a ports car rental agency similar to one operated by Sociable University. Plans are to ent a car to a student for $200 a week, including gas, oil, and all expenses, starting on Friday. However, the fraternity does not have a sufficient amount of capital to buy number of sports cars. They have been investigating an arrangement with Sports Cars, Ltd. to secure sports cars from them at $150 a week. Thus, the fraternity would arn a profit of ________ a week for each sports car rented.

$50

6

There is one problem. Sports Cars, Ltd. has other customers and must know by Wednesday of each week how many cars the fraternity wants on Friday. Thus, for the raternity there is an element of uncertainty. If, for example, the fraternity reserves six ars on Wednesday and only four students want them on Friday, they would sustain n outright loss of ________. If they reserved four cars and four students wanted them, the total profit would be ________. Finally, if the fraternity eserved four cars and six students wanted to rent them on Friday, the total profit would be ________, but the fraternity would have lost the opportunity to make an additional ________ because the supply of cars would have been inadequate.

$100
$200
$200
$100

7

THE PAYOFF TABLE

The various combinations of demand by the students (the event) and the supply o sports cars on hand (the act) determined in the previous frame are organized into a table called a *payoff table*. In this case, to keep the computations at a minimum onl events and acts of 4, 5, and 6 are considered.

Complete the payoff table. Note that each number to be inserted in the blanks i the outcome, or consequence, of a particular act and event.

$200 $200
50 250 250
100

ACT (Number of Sports Cars Available)	*EVENT (Number of Cars Demanded by Students)* 4	5	6
	OUTCOME (PAYOFF)		
4	$______	$______	$200
5	______	______	___
6	−100	______	300

8

payoff table

$200
$250
$300

If the previous table, called a __________ _______, was the only information avail able, the decision maker might consider reserving four cars from Sports Cars, Ltd every week and be assured of earning a profit of __________. However, he migh want to consider reserving five cars and hope to make a maximum of __________ instead of only $200. By reserving six cars he might earn a maximum of __________

9

The payoff table in frame #7 ignores the valuable experience Sociable University ha had with sports car rentals. In order to explore the problem further, the fraternit contacted SU regarding their experience. They have had the rental agency for 20 weeks and reported their demand as follows (complete the table by inserting the correc probabilities in the spaces).

.10
.70
.20
.00
1.00

Number of Sports Cars Demanded	*Number of Weeks*	*Percent of the Total (Probability)*
3	0	0.00
4	20	__
5	140	__
6	40	__
7	0	__
Total	200	__.__

10

If the information in the previous table were the only data available, the decision make (the fraternity) might decide to reserve four sports cars every week from Sports Car

Ltd. reasoning that four would always be demanded. However, more than four were demanded ______________ percent of the weeks. If only four were reserved, the fraternity would be foregoing additional profit by not having a sufficient number available. A possible alternative would be to order six sports cars on Wednesday thus assuring that there would always be a sufficient number of cars available. Note, however, that in ______________ percent of the weeks, the fraternity would have an excess number of cars. Another possible act might be to order the most frequent number of cars demanded, or ______________ (number).

90

80

5

11

EXPECTED PAYOFF

Assuming that the two universities are similar, the payoff table and the experience at Sociable University are combined to arrive at the *expected payoff* of an act. This is alternatively called *expected profit* or *expected monetary value.*

Some of the calculations for the expected payoff for the act of reserving five sports cars every week from Sports Cars, Ltd. follow (complete the table).

CALCULATIONS FOR THE EXPECTED PAYOFF ON THE ACT OF RESERVING FIVE SPORTS CARS EVERY WEEK FROM SPORTS CARS, LTD.

Event (Demand) (*Col. 1*) *X*	*Probability of Outcome Occurring** (*Col. 2*) *P(X)*	*Payoff†* (*Col. 3*) *Y*	*Expected Profit* (*Col. 4*) (*Col. 2 × Col. 3*) *P(X)Y*
4	0.10	$ 50	$ 5
5	.70	250	175
6	.20	___	___
		Total	___

Source: * Frame 9; † frame 7.

$250 $50
Total, $230

12

The total expected profit on five sports cars was found to be $230. This means that based on the experience at Sociable University, and the various payoffs from the payoff table, the fraternity could expect a profit of $230 *in the long run* if they automatically reserved five sports cars every week from Sports Cars, Ltd.

EXPECTED WEEKLY PROFIT IN THE LONG RUN FOR THE RESERVATION OF 4, 5, AND 6 SPORTS CARS FROM SPORTS CARS, LTD.

Demand *X*	*Expected Profit* $\Sigma[P(X)Y]$
4	$___
5	230
6	___

$200

$120

The reservation of five sports cars from Sports Cars, Ltd. is only one possibility. The $230 expected profit for five cars may not result in the maximum profit in the long run. Determine the expected weekly profit for four and for six sports cars and insert the amounts in the table.

13

An analysis of the various expected profits in the foregoing table indicates that the reservation of (number)______________ sports cars will in the long run yield the

five

$230

greatest expected profit. This profit of ______________ is based on the experience at Sociable University, a student rental of $200 and a reservation fee of $150 payable to Sports Cars, Ltd.

14

OPPORTUNITY LOSS

Another way of deciding on the number of sports cars to reserve from Sports Cars, Ltd. is to determine the amount of profit which might be lost because the state of nature (demand on Friday) was not known at the time the reservation was sent in on Wednesday. This potential loss is called *opportunity loss* or *regret*.

To illustrate, suppose the fraternity reserved six sports cars on Wednesday, but only four students wanted them on Friday. The fraternity would be earning no profit on the two excess cars, and the opportunity loss would be $300, found by 2 cars × $150 paid to Sports Cars, Ltd. Conversely, if the fraternity had four cars on hand and five students wanted them, not having the one additional car on hand would cost the fraternity the opportunity to make an extra $50. The $50 is the opportunity loss.

Complete the following opportunity loss table. Note that each number to be inserted is the outcome (opportunity loss) of a particular act and event.

Margin answers:

$ 50 $100
150 0 50
150 0

ACT (Number of Sports Cars Available)	*EVENT (Number of Cars Demanded by Students)* 4	5	6
	OUTCOME (OR CONSEQUENCE)		
4	$ 0	$___	$___
5	___	___	___
6	$300	___	___

15

EXPECTED OPPORTUNITY LOSS

The opportunity losses in the previous table for various levels of supply and demand again ignore the past experience of Sociable University. This past experience is used to compute the *expected opportunity loss* for one possible level of supply—five sports

COMPUTATIONS FOR THE EXPECTED OPPORTUNITY LOSS FOR THE RESERVATION OF FIVE SPORTS CARS

Demand (Col. 1) X	*Probability* (Col. 2) P(X)*	*Opportunity Loss† (Col. 3) OL*	*Expected Opportunity Loss (Col. 4) (Col. 2 × Col. 3) P(X)OL*
4	0.10	$150	$15
5	.70	0	0
6	.20	50	10
			$25

Source: * Frame #9; † frame #14.

ars. The expected opportunity loss in the long run was found to be $25 a week. (See ne previous computations.) This means that based on the experience at SU, the business fraternity would lose $25 a week in lost opportunities if they reserved five cars very week. Some weeks they would have the exact number on hand (5) to meet emand (5), but other weeks they would either have an excess or a shortage of rental ars. The average loss (expected opportunity loss) of $25 would result due to the inbility of the fraternity to predict future demand.

The $25 may not be the lowest expected opportunity loss. Compute the expected opportunity loss for the supply of four and six sports cars respectively and insert the mounts in the following summary table.

EXPECTED OPPORTUNITY LOSS FOR 4, 5, AND 6 SPORTS CARS

	ACT (Number of Sports Cars Available)		
	4	*5*	*6*
Expected opportunity loss.......	$_____	$25	$_____

The complete table is:
$55 $25 $135

6

n analysis of the findings indicates that the lowest expected opportunity loss is ____ ________. The fraternity would experience the smallest level of lost opportunity if ey reserved (number) ________________ sports cars every week from Sports Cars, Ltd. To put it another way, they would have the least regret if they reserved five ars every week. The minimum opportunity loss ($25) is also called *minimax regret.*

$25

5

This reinforces the decision made previously that five sports cars would give the ighest level of profit ($230) in the long run. Thus, there are two ways to approach the ecision, either compute the ________________ profit or compute the ________ ______ ________________________ loss. Both methods will suggest the same most rofitable course of action.

expected
expected opportunity

7

ALUE OF PERFECT INFORMATION

Before entering into a long-term agreement with Sports Cars, Ltd. to reserve five ports cars weekly, the fraternity might want to consider ways to determine the exact emand every week. If the fraternity knew on Wednesday that exactly four, five, or six udents would want a car on Friday, it could maximize its profit by reserving the orrect number. What is this advance information worth to the fraternity? That is, hat is the *value of perfect information?*

The value of perfect information can be computed by subtracting the maximum rofit under conditions of uncertainty from the maximum profit under conditions of ertainty. The maximum profit under conditions of uncertainty was found to be $230. Now compute the expected profit under conditions of certainty. (In practice this would mean that the fraternity would know on Wednesday *exactly* how many students would emand a sports car on Friday and would reserve the cars accordingly.) If four cars were reserved and four students demanded them, the total profit would be $200, found by 4 × $50 for each car. But based on the experience at Sociable University, this demand (4) only happens 10 percent of the weeks. The average expected profit, if perfect knowledge of demand were known, would be $20, found by 0.10 × $200. These calculations are shown on the first line of the following table.

Complete the table and find the total expected profit under conditions of certainty

CALCULATIONS OF EXPECTED PROFIT UNDER CONDITIONS OF CERTAINTY

Event (Col. 1)	Profit* Each Unit (Col. 2)	Total Profit (Col. 3) Col. 1 × Col. 2	Probability of Event† (Col. 4)	Expected Profit (Col. 5) Col. 3 × Col. 4
4	$50	$200	0.10	$20
5	50	______	.70	______
6	50	______	.20	______
			Total	______

* Based on $200 rental to students and a $150 reservation fee.
† From frame #9.

$250	$175
300	60
Total	$255

18

To compute the value of perfect information:

$255 | $______ profit under conditions of certainty (from frame #17)

$230 | − ______ profit under conditions of uncertainty (from frame #11)

$25 | = ______ value of perfect information

Note again that the value of perfect information is also the same as minimax regret. Thus, the least amount of opportunity loss ($25 in this case) can be described by the terms "minimum expected opportunity loss," "minimax regret," and the "value of perfect information."

The fraternity should only pay up to $25 a week for perfect prediction of demand. This might be the pay for a student whose job it would be to secure advance commitments for sports cars prior to the reservation deadline on Wednesday. If the student wanted payment of more than $25 a week, the fraternity would be advised to order five cars every week because in the long run they would be assured of a profit of ______ ______ a week.

$230

Final Self-Review Examination

First, answer all of the questions. Then check your answers against those given at the end of this chapter. Scoring: 10 problems × 10 points each = 100 possible points.

19. There are three main parts to a decision problem under conditions of uncertainty. Insert the correct word opposite each group of explanatory statements. The words are: *event, act, outcome.*

(*a*) ______ Uncertainty regarding future demand. Decision maker has no control over future demand.

(*b*) ______ Two or more courses of action open to decision maker. Decision maker selects a course of action based on experience and other criteria.

(*c*) ______ Profit
Break-even
Loss

20. It is said that the state of nature is unknown. What does this mean to the decision maker?

____

______________________________.

Questions 21 through 28 are based on the following problem:

Two partners are considering starting an electronic repair service for manufacturers, wholesalers, and retailers. Plans include starting with a force of between six and nine electronic experts. Hourly pay would be \$10 regardless of whether the repairman was on call or sitting in the office awaiting a call. The charge to the clients would be \$20 an hour. A similar service in Pittsburgh, which has been operating for about 10,000 hours (approximately 5 years), revealed that:

Number of Men Demanded	*Number of Hours*
5	0
6	2,000
7	4,000
8	3,000
9	1,000
10	0
Total	10,000

21. Assist the partners in making a decision by determining the maximum hourly profit which would result from hiring 6, 7, 8, or 9 men. The first step is to set up a payoff table. Insert essential figures and identify the parts of the table.

22. Based on the Pittsburgh experience, set up a table of probabilities showing the event and the probability of the event.

23. Compute the expected hourly profit for 6, 7, 8, and 9 employees.

24. Based on the previous calculations, the most profitable number of men to hire is ______________. The hourly profit in the long run for this number is ______________.

25. Another way to arrive at a decision is to determine the expected opportunity loss of certain actions. First, set up an opportunity loss table.

26. The next step is to determine the expected opportunity loss per hour for 6, 7, 8, and 9 employees.

27. The least hourly opportunity loss amounts to (*a*) ______________ which indicates that (number) (*b*) ______________ of employees would be the most profitable number to hire.
Now compute the value of perfect information. (*c*) ______________ answer. It should agree with the minimum opportunity loss. Does it? (yes/no) (*d*) ______________.

28. Briefly summarize the case and the findings.

____

____

____

____

____

____

____

______________________________.

Answers to Final Self-Review Examination

19. (*a*) event
(*b*) act
(*c*) outcome, consequence or payoff

20. It means that the future demand is unknown.

21.

ACT	*EVENT* 6	7	8	9
	OUTCOME (Payoff)			
6	$60	$60	$60	$60
7	50	70	70	70
8	40	60	80	80
9	30	50	70	90

22.

Event	*Probability*
6	0.20
7	.40
8	.30
9	.10

23.

Event	*Expected Profit*
6	$60
7	66
8	64
9	56

24. 7
$66

25.

ACT	*EVENT* 6	7	8	9
	OUTCOME (Opportunity Loss)			
6	$ 0	$10	$20	$30
7	10	0	10	20
8	20	10	0	10
9	30	20	10	0

26.

Event	*Expected Opportunity Loss*
6	$13
7	7
8	9
9	17

27. (*a*) $7
(*b*) 7 employees
(*c*) COMPUTATION OF PROFIT UNDER CERTAINTY

Event	*Profit Each Unit*	*Total*	*Probability*	*Expected Profit*
6	$10	$60	0.20	$12
7	10	70	.40	28
8	10	80	.30	24
9	10	90	.10	9
Total				$73

Then:

$73 (profit under certainty)
−66 (profit under uncertainty)
$ 7 value of perfect information

(*d*) Yes, it agrees with the minimum opportunity loss.

28. The partners are attempting to determine the most profitable course of action. Should they hire 6, 7, 8, or 9 employees? Based on the experience at Pittsburgh, hourly wages of $10 and an hourly fee to clients ($20), the maximum hourly expected profit was computed to be $66 for 7 employees. This was reinforced by computing the minimum expected loss ($7 an hour) for 7 employees. This was also the value of perfect information. The partners might be satisfied with less profit, such as $56 for 9 employees, and always have men available for electronics service.

3ayes' Theorem and decision making

chapter

12

'homas Bayes (1702–1761), an English clergyman, made a significant contribution to ıe area of decision making. It is called the Bayes' Theorem, or the Bayes' Rule. The ule appeared in a paper entitled "An Essay Solving a Problem in the Doctrine of :hances" published shortly after his death.

In order to illustrate the rule, suppose that a machine operator grinds a very thin isk the size of a dime plain on one side and mills a slot on the other side. Then the isks are wrapped for shipment. The operator suddenly realized that he did not ıachine the slot in one of the last four pieces he made, but cannot recall which one vas missed. One might ask, what is the probability that one of the four pieces selected t random (say the one on the extreme right) is defective? There is (number) ______ hance out of (total number) ______. That is, the probability P = (fraction) ______ = 0.____. This is called a *prior* probability because it can be deterıined before any sampling is done or before an experiment is conducted.

one
four
1/4 = 0.25

---

uppose the same machined piece is unwrapped and tossed into the air. If it lands with slot showing face up, the machine operator would know it (was/was not) ______ ıe defective one. That is, P = ______.

was not
0.00

Iowever, if the piece landed with the plain face up, what is the probability that it is ıe defective piece? To answer this, consider what would happen (theoretically) in the ong-run if each machined piece were tossed in the air 250 times. If the piece were ıachined correctly, out of the 250 tosses a plain face would appear about (number) ______ times. But out of 250 tosses, the defective piece which has two lain sides, the plain face would appear (number) ______ times.

125
250

'hus, if each piece were tossed 250 times, theoretically the following would result. 'ill in the blanks. (Assume that the defective piece is on extreme right.)

:OSSES:	250	250	250	250	= 1,000 total
	○	○	○	○	
'IECE IS:	perfect	perfect	perfect	defective	
'LAIN:	____	____	____	____	= ____ total

125
125
125
250
625

5

625
250
250/625 = 0.40

Thus, out of a total of 1,000 tosses, __________ plain faces would appear. And, ou of the 625 plain faces, __________ would be attributed to the defective piece wit two plain faces. P = (fraction) __________ = 0.__________. This probabilit is called the *posterior* probability because it was determined *after* an experiment wa conducted.

6

BAYES' RULE

posterior

The probability of 0.40 (frame #5), called a __________ probability will now be determined using Bayes' Rule. In the general form, $B_1, B_2 \ldots . B_n$ ar mutually exclusive events which include every possible outcome in the sample spac Suppose that A is another event in the sample space. Then $P(B|A)$ can be determine from the equation:

$$P(B|A) = \frac{P(B)P(A|B)}{\sum_i P(B)P(A|B)}$$

To put it another way, Bayes' Rule can be used to determine the probability that ou come B will occur given the additional information that outcome A has been observe

In order to associate the letters in the general form with those being used in th problem, *Def* was arbitrarily chosen to represent a defective piece and *OK* a perfe piece. The equation then becomes:

$$P(\text{Def}|A) = \frac{P(\text{Def})P(A|\text{Def})}{P(\text{Def})P(A|\text{Def}) + P(\text{OK})P(A|\text{OK})}$$

where:

$P(\text{Def}|A)$ is the posterior probability to be determined. In this problem, it is tl probability that the piece on the extreme right is defective, given a experiment or sample results A. (*The experimental result was a pla face appearing after the piece was tossed in the air.*)

¼ or 0.25

$P(\text{Def})$ is the probability of choosing one of the four pieces *prior* to the exper ment and finding it defective. $P(\text{Def})$ = __________.

1

$P(A|\text{Def})$ is the probability that experimental or sample results A (a plain fac will appear, *assuming that a defective piece is being tossed into the a* It is P = __________.

¾ or 0.75

$P(\text{OK})$ is the probability of choosing one piece *prior* to the experiment ar finding it perfect (one side plain, the other side slotted). $P(\text{OK})$ __________.

½ or 0.50

$P(A|\text{OK})$ is the probability that outcome A (a plain face) will result—*assuming perfect piece is being tossed into the air.* It is P = __________

7

Now, using Bayes' Rule determine the posterior probability that the machined piece on the extreme right is defective, i.e., after it was tossed in the air and it landed plain side up. (Note that the answer is the same as you found intuitively in frame #5.)

$P(\text{Def}|A) =$ ________________ $= 0.$____

$$\frac{(0.25)(1.0)}{(0.25)(1.0) + (0.75)(0.50)} = 0.40$$

8

CASE ILLUSTRATION—A PROBLEM OF SALES FORECASTING

In June the management of a department store chain requested that a forecast be made of the probable economic conditions in the area during the forthcoming Christmas selling season. The chief forecaster studied a number of economic indicators, such as the GNP, department store sales, and so on. His report to management was in the form of probabilities.

Economic Condition	*Probability*
Excellent	0.3
Very Good	.4
Good	.2
Poor	.1
	1.0

The forecasts are to be revised in July or August if any *additional information* becomes available. One possible source of additional information might be the dollar volume of Christmas merchandise ordered by the many departmental buyers during the summer months. The departmental buyers working independently place orders for toys, ornaments, and other Christmas gifts in quantities they believe will sell.

In order to explore total dollar volume of Christmas orders as a reliable source of additional information, the forecaster reviewed his past forecasts and the level of Christmas orders placed by the buyers during the same years. He found that when he forecasted *excellent* economic conditions for the Christmas selling season, the buyers had placed a *high* level of orders 70 percent of the years. However, 25 percent of the years their orders were of *average* size, and 5 percent of the time their orders were *low*. (The buyers worked independently of each other and were not aware of the June forecast to management.) These three probabilities can be found on the first row in the table. Fill in the remaining blanks.

Economic Forecast in June	*Probability of Level of Orders During the Summer*			
	High	*Average*	*Low*	*Sum*
Excellent	0.70	0.25	0.05	1.00
Very Good	.50	.30	.20	____
Good	.20	.30	____	1.00
Poor	.10	.40	.50	1.00

1.00
.50

9

The Bayes' Theorem can be used to revise the prior probabilities in order to determine the posterior probabilities. The $P(O_1|\text{Exc})$ of 0.70 found in the upper left corner of the following table indicates the probability is 0.70 there will be a high level of orders (O_1) given that (|) the June forecast of the economic conditions at Christmas is excellent

The probability is 0.50 a low level of orders will be placed, given a June economic forecast of poor.

(Exc). What does the [$0.50P(O_3|\text{Poor})$] in the lower right corner of the table mean?

____

____

Complete the table.

$P(O_2|\text{Exc})$
$P(O_2|\text{VG})$
$P(O_2|\text{G})$
$P(O_2|\text{Poor})$

Economic Forecast by Forecaster	*Level of Orders from Buyers*		
	High O_1	*Average* O_2	*Low* O_3
Excellent (Exc)	0.70 $P(O_1|\text{Exc})$	0.25 ________	0.05 $P(O_3|\text{Exc})$
Very Good (VG)	.50 $P(O_1|\text{VG})$	.30 ________	.20 $P(O_3|\text{VG})$
Good (G)	.20 $P(O_1|\text{G})$	.30 ________	.50 $P(O_3|\text{G})$
Poor (Poor)	.10 $P(O_1|\text{Poor})$	.40 ________	.50 $P(O_3|\text{Poor})$

10

Recall that in June the forecaster gave management a forecast in terms of probabilities for the coming Christmas selling season, i.e., $P(\text{Exc}) = 0.30$, $P(\text{VG}) = 0.40$, $P(\text{G}) = 0.20$, and $P(\text{Poor}) = 0.10$.

Suppose the total dollar volume of orders from the buyers for Christmas merchandise has just been released. It is a *high* level of orders. Should the prior probabilities given management in June be revised upward, or downward based on this additional information?

First using Bayes' Rule, the prior probability of 0.30 (Excellent) will be revised given this recently released high level of orders.

$$P(\text{Exc}|O_1) = \frac{P(\text{Exc})P(O_1|\text{Exc})}{P(\text{Exc})P(O_1|\text{Exc}) + P(\text{VG})P(O_1|\text{VG}) + P(G)P(O_1|G) + P(\text{Poor})P(O_1|\text{Poor})}$$

$$= \frac{(0.30)(0.70)}{(0.30)(0.70) + (0.40)(0.50) + (0.20)(0.20) + (0.10)(0.10)}$$

$$= \frac{0.21}{0.46} = 0.4565$$

prior
upward
high
posterior
.4565

Thus, the probability of 0.30 sent to management in June, called the ________ ________ probability, indicating that economic conditions at Christmas would be excellent should be revised (upward/downward) ________. This revision is based on the additional information that the buyers had ordered a ________ level of Christmas merchandise. The revised probability is called the ________ probability. The prior probability of 0.30 would be revised upward to 0.________.

11

.evise the remaining prior probabilities in the following table based on the additional ıformation (*high* level of orders) just released.

Economic Forecast	*Prior Probabilities*	*Final Calculations for Posterior Probabilities*		*Posterior Probabilities*
Excellent	0.30	0.21/0.46	=	0.4565
Very Good	.40	______	=	____
Good	.20	______	=	____
Poor	.10	______	=	____
Total	.	______		.

.20/.46 = 0.4348
.04/.46 = 0.0870
.01/.46 = 0.0217
1.00 .46/.46 1.0000

12

'hus, the prior probability for poor economic conditions during the Christmas selling eason should be revised (downward/upward) ______________ from ____________ ɔ ______________ based on the ______________ level of summer orders.

downward from .10
.0217 high

13

ı summary, this decision problem illustrates the importance of additional informa-ion. The chief forecaster for the department store chain makes an economic forecast ɔ management regarding the Christmas selling season in the form of probabilities, alled ______________ probabilities, as early as June. The importance of any new ata, called ______________ ______________, which will allow the initial fore-ast to be revised is self-evident. Based on past experience, a relationship between the rior probabilities and the level orders of the buyers during the summer was dis-overed. This additional information allowed the prior probabilities to be revised. 'he revised probabilities, called ______________ probabilities, will better assist ıanagement in hiring for the Christmas selling season and deciding on an advertising trategy, and they may even result in a cancellation of some orders.

prior
additional information

posterior

One weakness in the approach could be in the assigned prior probabilities. In this 'ecision problem, they were assigned by the chief forecaster and represent his judg-ıent. If the assistant chief forecaster had been given the job, his set of prior prob-.bilities could have been different. The probabilities arrived at by the assistant to the ssistant chief forecaster would, no doubt, be different from those of his two superiors.

There is a considerable amount of discussion in current literature regarding the ole of this subjective judgment. Some argue that the statistician should not be con-erned with decision problems involving subjective probabilities because by their 'ery nature they have built-in errors. The more accepted philosophy is that Bayes' Theorem allows the decision maker to revise the initial probabilities in an orderly vay when additional information becomes available.

Final Self-Review Examination

First, answer all of the questions. Then check your answers against those given at the end of this chapter. Scoring: 10 problems × 10 points each = 100 possible points.

14. There are five coins on the desk all with heads showing face up. It is known, however, that one of the coins is not a true coin and has a head on both sides. What is the probability of choosing one of the coins at random and finding it to be the imperfect coin? (*a*)____________________. This probability was determined before any experiment was conducted. Thus, it is called the (*b*)__________ probability.

15. One of the coins was then tossed in the air, and it landed with a head face up. Now what is the probability that it is the two-headed coin? (*a*)__________________. This probability is called the (*b*)______________ probability.

Questions 16 through 23 are based on the following decision problem.

Before each new product is marketed nationally, a manufacturer of soaps, waxes, and other products has a panel of executives indicate its probable success. Toujour L'Amour, a newly developed soap, was rated by the executives and the composite ratings converted to probabilities.

Composite Rating	*Prior Probability*
Highly Successful	0.60
Moderately Successful	.30
Failure	.10
	1.00

The newly developed product is then test-marketed and the sales in the test market classified as being *above average* or *below average*.

In order that the prior probabilities of the executives and the test market results be combined to make a decision to market or not to market Toujour L'Amour, a study of the experience regarding new products within the past few years was made. It revealed that when the executive panel indicated that the product would probably be highly successful, 80 percent of those products had above average sales and 20 percent had below average sales in the test market. These percents and the other results of the study are:

When Executives Indicated Product Would Be:	*Sales in Test Market Were:*	*Percent*
Highly Successful (Hi)	Above Average (AB)	80
	Below Average (BL)	20
Moderately Successful (Mod)	Above Average (AB)	60
	Below Average (BL)	40
Failure (Fail)	Above Average (AB)	10
	Below Average (BL)	90

16. In order to use the rule of Bayes, the first step is to organize the data into a table complete with abbreviations. Fill in the blanks.

Prior Opinion of Executives	*Test Market Sales* Above Average (*AB*)		Below Average (*BL*)	
Highly Successful (Hi)	0.80	$P(AB\|Hi)$	0.20	$P(BL\|Hi)$
Moderately Successful (Mod)	__	____	__	____
Failure (Fail)	__	____	__	____

17. Explain what the figures and designations in the upper right corner [0.20 $P(BL|Hi)$] mean.
____
____
____
____________________________________.

18. The soap Toujour L'Amour has just been test marketed in Illinois and sales in the test market were *below average*. Now the (*a*)________ probabilities can be revised using this fact called the (*b*)________________ to arrive at the (*c*)____________ probabilities.

19. Using the additional information gathered from the Illinois test market (question 18), namely, sales were *below average*, revise the initial probability of the executive panel that Toujour L'Amour will be highly successful. The answer is (*a*)__________________. An OPTIONAL problem is to revise the prior probability that the soap will fail (again as-

suming below average sales in the Illinois test market). The answer is (*b*)________________.

20. Thus, the prior probability of highly successful, (*a*)____________, should be revised (upward/downward) (*b*)______________ based on the additional information that sales of the soap were below average in the test market. The posterior probability was found to be (*c*)______.

21. Suppose that instead of Toujour L'Amour having below average sales in the Illinois test market they were *above average*. The posterior probability for Highly Successful would have been (*a*)______________.

22. Explain what the posterior probability computed in question 21 means. ____.

23. What is the major purpose (or advantage) of using the rule of Bayes in decision problems? (*a*)____.

What is a weakness to this approach to decision making? (*b*)____.

Answers to Final Self-Review Examination

14. (*a*) $1/5 = 0.20$
    (*b*) prior
15. (*a*) 0.3333
    (*b*) posterior
16. $0.60\,P(\text{AB}|\text{Mod})$ $0.40\,P(\text{BL}|\text{Mod})$
    $.10\,P(\text{AB}|\text{Fail})$ $.90\,P(\text{BL}|\text{Fail})$
17. The probability is 0.20 that sales in the test market area will be below average, given an initial rating of highly successful by the panel of executives.
18. (*a*) prior
    (*b*) additional information
    (*c*) posterior
19. (*a*) .364
    (*b*) .272
20. (*a*) .60
    (*b*) downward
    (*c*) .364
21. .716
22. It means that based on above average sales in the Illinois test market, the prior probability of 0.60 for Highly Successful would be revised upward to about 0.72.
23. (*a*) The advantage of this approach is that the rule of Bayes allows the initial forecasts in the form of probabilities to be revised upward or downward as related additional information becomes available.
    (*b*) The weakness in this problem is that the prior probabilities represent the opinions of a panel of executives. Another panel would probably have given a different set of initial probabilities. That is, there is subjective judgment involved in determining the prior probabilities.

chapter 13

Chi-square

1

The chi-square test is another hypothesis-testing technique used to test (1) a set of observed frequencies with a set of hypothetical frequencies, (2) two or more sets of observed frequencies with the objective of finding out if the differences among the sets are significant. Since frequencies are the result of counting, *the chi-square test is applicable to data in discrete form.*

GOODNESS OF FIT

To illustrate the use of the chi-square test involving a set of *observed* frequencies and a set of hypothetical, or *expected*, frequencies, suppose there is some suspicion that one die being used in a dice game is loaded. The application of the chi-square test in problems of this nature is often referred to as tests of *goodness of fit*. In order to test whether the die is true, a general procedure similar to that used in testing hypotheses is followed. The usual six steps are:

Step 1. A hypothesis is stated. Again, it will be stated as a *null* hypothesis. The null hypothesis to be tested in this problem is that *the die is not loaded.* To put it another way, if the die is not loaded, and if it is thrown a large number of times, any difference between the set of observed frequencies and the set of ________________ frequencies could be due to chance.

expected

2

Step 2. A level of significance is stated. The 0.05 level was arbitrarily decided on for this test. As noted previously, other commonly used levels of significance are the 0.01 and the 0.10 levels.

Step 3. The statistic needed is identified. The statistic needed in this problem is chi-square (χ^2). It is computed by:

$$\chi^2 = \sum \frac{(f_o - f_e)^2}{f_e}$$

where:

f_o is the frequency observed.
f_e is the frequency expected.

Step 4. A critical value is determined from the table of the distribution of chi-square (Appendix Table V). The critical value of χ^2 read from the table will be the dividing point between the area of acceptance and the area of rejection. In this chi-square test, called a test of ________________ ____ ____________, involving a set of expected frequencies and a set of ________________________ frequencies, the degrees of freedom are determined by $n - 1$. There are six faces on a die called *cells*, so $n = 6$. There are 5 degrees of freedom found by $6 - 1$. Referring to Appendix Table V, the critical value of chi-square for 5 d.f. and the 0.05 level of significance is ________________.

goodness of fit
observed
11.1

3

[T]his critical value (11.1) is the dividing point between the area of acceptance and the [a]rea of rejection. If the computed value of χ^2 is less than 11.1, it falls within the area [o]f acceptance, and the null hypothesis will be *accepted.* However, if the computed [v]alue of χ^2 is 11.1 or greater, it falls within the area of rejection, and the null hypothesis [w]ill be *rejected.*

Step 5. A sample is selected. In this case, [t]he die was tossed 180 times. Even if the [d]ie is not loaded, it is not expected that the [s]ample of 180 tosses would yield an equal [n]umber for each face of the die. However, it [d]oes seem that 3 spots and 5 spots appear [m]ore frequently and 4 and 6 spots less fre[q]uently than should be expected if the die [w]ere true.

RESULTS OF TOSSING ONE DIE 180 TIMES

Face of Die	*Number of Times Face Appeared* f_o
1	25
2	26
3	48
4	16
5	50
6	15
Total	180

Theoretically, if the die were not loaded, [o]ut of 180 tosses each face (1, 2, 3, 4, 5, and 6) would appear an equal number of [t]imes, or ______ times each. This number is the expected frequency (f_e). 30

4

[S]tep 6. Compute χ^2. Accept the null hypothesis if the computed chi-square falls [w]ithin the region of acceptance but reject it if the computed χ^2 is (less than/equal to or [g]reater than) ______________________ [t]he critical value of 11.1.

equal to or greater than

Complete the table and determine the value of chi-square.

CALCULATIONS FOR CHI- SQUARE

Face of Die	f_o	f_e	$f_o - f_e$	$(f_o - f_e)^2$	$\frac{(f_o - f_e)^2}{f_e}$
1	25	30	−5	25	25/30 = 0.83
2	26	30	___	___	______
3	48	30	___	___	______
4	16	30	___	___	______
5	50	30	___	___	______
6	15	30	___	___	______
Total	180	180	0		______

−4	16	16/30 =	0.53
+18	324	324/30 =	10.80
−14	196	196/30 =	6.53
+20	400	400/30 =	13.33
−15	225	225/30 =	7.50
			39.52

The computed value of chi-square is approximately ______________. 39.52

5

[T]he computed value of chi-square (39.52) is (less than/equal to or greater than) ______________________ the critical value of ______________. There[f]ore, the null hypothesis is (accepted/rejected) ______________ at the 0.05 [l]evel of significance. This indicates that it is highly probable that the die (is/is not) __________ loaded.

equal to or greater than
11.1
rejected
is

6

.05
would not

To put it another way, by rejecting the null hypothesis at the ______ level, it indi cates that the pattern of observed frequencies probably (would/would not) ______ ______ occur by chance.

7

There has been *no* significant change in preference.
chi-square (χ^2)
2, found by 3 − 1

One of the assumptions underlying the foregoing use of chi-square is that the sampl data was collected using probability methods. Specifically, in this die-tossing experi ment it means that each time the die was tossed, there was an equal chance of 1, 2, 3 4, 5, and 6 appearing face up. Also, only one face can appear each toss, i.e., the out come is *mutually exclusive*. And, each toss is *independent* of the previous tosses.

All of the expected frequencies (f_e) in the previous illustration were equal (30) However, the expected frequencies need not be equal. Suppose that repeated poll revealed that 65 percent of the teen-age population are highly enthusiastic about a certain type of popular music, 10 percent have no opinion, and 25 percent dislike it These percentages are assumed to be the population preferences. A sample of teen agers is to be selected at random to determine if there has been any change in prefer ence. Before any sampling is done, however, the null hypothesis must be stated. It i ______ ______. The 0.01 level of significance is to be used The statistic to be computed is called ______ desig nated by the Greek ______. In order to locate the critical value o chi-square, the number of degrees of freedom must be determined. The d.f. ar ______, found by ______.

8

9.21
9.21
accepted
9.21
rejected

Referring to Appendix Table V, the critical value of chi-square is ______ This means that if the computed statistic χ^2 using sample results is less than ______ the null hypothesis will be (accepted/rejected) ______. Howeve if the computed value of chi-square is equal to or greater than ______ th null hypothesis will be ______.

9

260, found by 65% × 400
40, found by 10% × 400
100, found by 25% × 400
expected (f_e)

Recall that past records indicate that 65 percent of the teen-agers are highly enthusi astic, 10 percent have no opinion, and 25 percent dislike a certain type of popula music. Suppose the sample results were *exactly* as expected. How many teen-agers ou of the 400 sampled would be highly enthusiastic about the music? ______ How many would be expected to have no opinion? ______, and how man (theoretically) would dislike the music? ______. These three number are called the ______ frequencies.

10

These expected frequencies and the actual sample (observed) results are shown in th following table.

Teen-Age Preference	*Sample Results* f_o	*Expected Results* f_e
Highly Enthusiastic	252	260
No opinion	50	40
Dislike	98	100

Does $\Sigma f_o = \Sigma f_e$? (yes/no)__________. What is the approximate computed value of chi-square? __________.

yes (400)
about 2.79, found by
0.25 + 2.50 + 0.04

11

Should the null hypothesis be accepted or rejected at the 0.05 level?__________. Reasoning? ____. Does this mean that there probably has been a significant change in teen-age reaction to the music? __________.

accepted
computed χ^2 value of 2.79 is less than the critical value of 9.21.
no

12

CONTINGENCY TABLES

Data may be classified in two ways. If the opinions of the males and females were recorded separately, the table containing these two classifications (sex and opinion) would be called a two-way classification table, or a *contingency table.* (See the left table which follows.) The table containing the music preference, by sex, has three rows (enthusiastic, no opinion, and dislike) and two columns (male, female). It is called a 3 × 2 contingency table.

MUSIC PREFERENCE, BY SEX

Opinion	*Sex* *Male*	*Female*	*Total*
Enthusiastic	120	132	252
No opinion	24	26	50
Dislike	40	58	98
Total	184	216	400

SALES, BY MARITAL STATUS OF SALESMEN

Sales	*Marital Status* *Married*	*Single*	*Other*	*Total*
High	213	73	18	304
Average	87	64	87	238
Low	16	99	97	212
None	1	185	158	244

The ____________________ table (on right) containing sales, by marital status of salesmen is a __________ × __________ table. If Jim Simpson is single and had low sales during the year, he would be one of the 99 observed frequencies shown in the table. William Hook is married and had high sales during the year. He would be one of __________ observed frequencies in the contingency table.

contingency
4 × 3

213

13

A study of middle-management personnel is to be conducted. One of the objectives of the study is to determine what effect, if any, adjustment to marriage has on income.

Plans are to select 500 married men at random and give each one a Marital Adjustment Test (MAT). It was arbitrarily decided to subdivide the MAT scores into four classes. Incomes are to be classified into three groups.

There is *no* relationship between marital adjustment and the level of income.
acceptance (or rejection)
rejection (or acceptance)

Before any sampling is done or tests given, a null hypothesis must be formulated. It is: ____ ____________________. The 0.10 level of significance is to be used. As before, the statistic χ^2 is needed. To find the critical value, which is the dividing point between the area of ____________________ and the area of ____________________, the degrees of freedom must first be determined. A convenient method of finding the degrees of freedom for a contingency table is: (rows − 1) (columns − 1). In this problem there are __________ rows and __________ columns. The degrees of freedom are __________.

4 rows and 3
6

14

A sample of 500 middle-management personnel were selected at random and each given the Marriage Adjustment Test. The score and the level of income of each man was recorded and then tallied in the appropriate cell. For example, John J. Jordon had a MAT of 510 and an income of $55,000. Thus, he is one of the 100 in the cell "over 500 MAT, income $50,000 and over." The observed frequencies are in the following table called a ____________________.

contingency table

Marital Adjustment	*Under $10,000*	*Income $10,000–$49,999*	*Income $50,000 and Over*	*Total*
Very well (500 and over)	10	40	100	150
Fairly well (300–499)	15	20	15	50
Below average (100–299)	40	50	10	100
Poor (under 100)	125	60	15	200
	190	170	140	500

Does there seem to be any relationship between marital adjustment and income? (yes/no) ____________________. Explain ____ ____ ____________________. The counts in the various cells in the table are called the ____________________ frequencies.

yes
Most of the men who are very well adjusted to marriage have incomes of $50,000 and over. Conversely, most of the men who are poorly adjusted have low incomes.
observed

15

Now to determine the expected frequencies (f_e). Note in the preceding contingency table that 150 out of the 500 married men (30 percent) are very well adjusted to marriage. If there is *no relationship whatsoever* between marital adjustment and income, it can be expected that 30 percent of the 190 men who had incomes under $10,000 would be *very well* adjusted to marriage. The expected frequency (f_e) for that cell would be 57, found by 30 percent × 190. (This f_e of 57 is placed beside the f_o of 10 in the following table.) Again, if there is no relationship between marital adjustment and income, it can be expected that 30 percent of the 170 married men who had incomes in the $10,000–$49,999 range would be well adjusted. The expected frequency for that cell is ____________________. Further, if there is no relationship, it can be expected that 50

51

out of the 500, or 10 percent of the married men in any income group would be expected to be *fairly well* adjusted to marriage. For example, it would be expected that 10 percent of the 190 men (or 19 men) who had incomes under $10,000 would be fairly well adjusted to marriage.

Determine the remaining expected frequencies and insert them in the table.

Marital Adjustment	Under $10,000		Income $10,000–$49,999		Income $50,000 and over		Total
	f_o	f_e	f_o	f_e	f_o	f_e	
Very well (500 and over)	10	(57)	40	(51)	100	( )	150
Fairly well (300–499)	15	( )	20	( )	15	( )	50
Below average (100–299)	40	( )	50	( )	10	( )	100
Poor (under 100)	125	( )	60	( )	15	( )	200
Total	190	( )	170	( )	140	( )	500

		42
19	17	14
38	34	28
76	68	56
190	170	140

Due to rounding, the total of the expected frequencies for a column may not be equal to the total of the observed frequencies for that column. If this does happen, the totals should be forced to be equal by adjusting one or more of the expected frequencies in the column.

16

Recall that

$$x^2 = \sum \frac{(f_o - f_e)^2}{f_e}$$

In this problem, and starting with the upper left cell:

$$= \frac{(10 - 57)^2}{57} + \frac{(40 - 51)^2}{51} + \cdots$$

Compute chi-square. Chi-square = ________. Arrive at a decision. The decision is to ________ the null hypothesis at the ________ level of significance. The reason is that the computed value of chi-square is ________ the critical table value of ________.

approximately 204.42
reject
0.10
more than 10.6

17

Thus, it is highly (likely/unlikely) ________ that the computed chi-square value of 204.42 is due to chance. Therefore, it is highly probable that there (is/is not) ________ a relationship between marital adjustment (as measured by the MAT) and the level of income.

unlikely
is

Certain limitations in the use of chi-square should be noted: (1) The number of cells should be 5 or more. (2) The expected number of frequencies in a cell should be 5 or more (some suggest 10). If the number of cells must be less than 5, the expected frequencies in each of the cells should be greater than 5 (some suggest 10).

The chi-square test has other uses. It can be used to determine whether or not a frequency distribution obtained from a sample follows a normal distribution. Also, it is applicable in testing whether a sampling distribution can be considered a Poisson distribution.

Final Self-Review Examination

First, answer all of the questions. Then check your answers against those given at the end of this chapter. Scoring: 10 problems × 10 points each = 100 possible points.

18. Chi-square is particularly applicable when the data are in (continuous/discrete) ________ form.

19. The use of chi-square in goodness-of-fit tests implies that there is (one/more than one) (*a*)________________ set of observed frequencies and one set of (*b*)________________ frequencies.

Questions 20 through 23 are based on the following:

Past records revealed that 10 percent of the radio sets purchased had only the AM broadcast band, 70 percent had both AM and FM, and 20 percent FM only. A recent sample of 200 purchases revealed that 15 sets had AM only, 140 sets had AM and FM, and 45 radio sets had FM only. Has there been a significant change in the pattern of purchases?

20. The null hypothesis is ________________
____
____.

21. The 0.10 level of significance is to be used. The critical value of chi-square is ____________.

22. The computed χ^2 is ________________.

23. Should the null hypothesis be accepted or rejected at the 0.10 level? (*a*)____________. Has there been a significant change in the pattern of purchase? (yes/no) (*b*)____________.

Questions 24 through 27 are based on the following.

Artin Corporation, a manufacturer of major appliances, wants to find out if there is any significant difference between the reasons given by former Artin owners and non-Artin owners for buying a new Artin Appliance. A random sample of 200 recent purchasers were asked to indicate the major reason why they purchased an Artin.

24. The results of the survey follow.

	Previous Ownership	
Major Reason for Purchase	*Owned an Artin*	*Did not own an Artin*
Style....................	19	21
Price....................	34	26
Reputation of manufacturer...........	57	43

Is there a significant difference between the set of reasons given by former Artin owners and the set of reasons given by non-Artin owners? The hypothesis is to be tested at the 0.05 (5 percent) level.

The previous table is a (*a*)________ × ________ table, called a (*b*)________________ table.

25. How many degrees of freedom are there? (*a*)__________. The critical value is (*b*)________.

26. The computed chi-square value is (*a*)________. The null hypothesis is (accepted/rejected) (*b*)________________.

27. Explain what either accepting or rejecting the null hypothesis indicates. ________________
____
____
____
____
____.

Answers to Final Self-Review Examination

18. discrete
19. (*a*) one
    (*b*) expected
20. There has been no change in the pattern of purchases.
21. 4.61
22. about 1.88, found by: $25/20 + 0 + 25/40$
23. (*a*) accepted
    (*b*) no
24. (*a*) 3×2
    (*b*) contingency
25. (*a*) 2
    (*b*) 5.99
26. (*a*) about 1.1, found by: $9/22 + 1/33 + 4/55 + 9/18 + 1/27 + 4/45$
    (*b*) accepted
27. Accepting the null hypothesis indicates that there is no relationship between the previous ownership pattern (owned an Artin or did not own one) and major reasons given for purchasing the appliance.

chapter

14

Statistical quality control

1

Statistical quality control is another area in which the decision rules introduced in Chapter 10 are applied. *Statistical* quality control is a relatively recent innovation. During the 17th, 18th, and 19th centuries, American industry was largely characterized by small shops making such simple hand-crafted products as candles, spoons, chairs, plows, and shoes. The individual craftsman was responsible for the "quality" of his work. The Industrial Revolution brought changes. Unskilled workers were organized into production lines with a worker performing only one operation, such as sewing on only the sole of the shoe.

The concepts of statistical quality control were developed in the 1930's by Dr. Walter Shewhart of the Bell Telephone Laboratories. His ideas were adopted by many firms mass-producing guns, bombsights, radar, and other intricate instruments during World War II. Basically, instead of inspecting every part produced (which would have been costly and very time-consuming), decisions were made based on statistical sampling techniques. For the purpose of controlling the quality, the *Shewhart Control Chart Technique* was developed for in-process manufacturing operations.

CONTROL CHARTS

Fundamental to all production is that there is no such thing as two identical parts. The difference in outside diameter from one valve stem to the next is minute (perhaps a billionth of an inch), but it is different. That is, if a more precise measuring instrument was available, a difference would be discernible.

The variation in a manufacturing process is either a *chance* cause or an *assignable* cause. Chance causes are large in number, random in nature, and cannot be entirely eliminated. For example, in making glass bottles the temperature of the mold, composition of the batch of glass, temperature of the molten glass, and so on are controlled to produce a bottle to weigh 2.0000 ounces. However, weights of 45 bottles selected at random revealed that there was variation in the weights ranging from 1.9997 ounces to 2.0003 ounces.

Weight (In Ounces)	*Number of Bottles*
1.9997	OO
1.9998	OOOOOO
1.9999	OOOOOOOOO
2.0000	OOOOOOOOOOOOOO
2.0001	OOOOOOOO
2.0002	OOOOO
2.0003	O

Assuming that all of the bottles fell within the acceptable tolerances, the differences in weight were due to slight differences in the temperature of the molten glass, and other factors which were difficult, if not impossible, to identify or correct.

Assignable causes can be identified. For example, a drill is found to be dull. In another operation it was discovered that the operator was not feeding the piece of steel into the shearing machine correctly. Thus, management is mostly concerned with (chance/assignable) ______________ causes. Why? ______________

____

____

assignable. Can't do much about chance causes, but can sharpen drill, etc.

herefore, the basic purpose of statistical quality control charts is to identify *when* ssignable causes of variation have entered the production system. It is important, for xample, to know when the drill has become dull so that remedial action can be taken nmediately. Using terms common to quality control, it is important to know when roduction is *in control* or *out of control.* If the inside diameter of the holes falls within e specified tolerances, production is said to be *in control.* However, if the drill becomes dull and the inside diameter exceeds the specified tolerance (and production is nacceptable), the process is said to be ________ ________ ________.

out of control

One group of quality control charts has been developed for *variables* (measurable ata), such as outside diameter, weights, and lengths. A second group of charts is for *ttributes.* A bulb lights or it does not, there are imperfections in a panel or there are ot, a part will fit or it will not. These are examples of problems requiring attribute harts.

Charts for variables

Bar X charts. As the name implies, bar X charts (also called *mean charts* and *X-bar harts*) are designed to portray variations in the process average. To set up a bar X hart, it is essential that the process average and standard deviation be known or stimated.

It is the usual practice in the United States to use the 99.7 percent confidence limits n quality control work. In quality control the two confidence limits are called the *pper control limits* and the *lower control limits.*

A new process is set to mass-produce a 30-ounce container, but as previously noted, ariation in weight is expected because of variation in temperature of the molten glass, tc. In order to design a control chart for the process average, a sample of five conainers were selected every half hour and each weighed. (See the following table.) After he 9 A.M. sample, it was decided to set up a bar X chart. The mean of the four sample neans is 29.95 ounces found by 119.8/4.

WEIGHTS OF FIVE GLASS CONTAINERS SELECTED AT RANDOM EVERY HALF HOUR

	Weights of Sample Number							
Time	*1*	*2*	*3*	*4*	*5*	*Sum*	*Mean*	*Range*
7:30 A.M.	30	31	30	30	31	152	30.4	1
8:00 A.M.	29	30	28	29	30	146	29.2	2
8:30 A.M.	31	30	29	30	31	151	30.2	4
9:00 A.M.	32	28	30	30	30	150	30.0	2
							119.8	9

The centerline, or $\bar{\bar{X}}$, is 29.95 and the upper control limit and the lower control limit an be found by $\bar{\bar{X}} \pm 3\sigma_{\bar{x}}$. However, a much shorter method has been discovered using constant A_2 and the average range $\bar{R}$. The UCL and LCL can be computed by $\bar{\bar{X}} \pm$

$A_2\bar{R}$. The average range for the four samples is 2.25, found by 9/4. The factor A_2 is found in Appendix Table II for a sample size n of 5. It is 0.577. Then:

$$\text{UCL and LCL} = \bar{\bar{X}} \pm A_2\bar{R} = 29.95 \pm 0.577(2.25) = 28.65 \text{ and } 31.25 \text{ ounces}$$

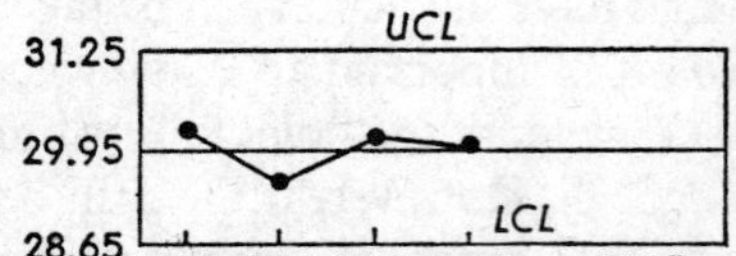

The completed bar X chart, including the means for the first four samples, is shown.

A new high-speed shearing machine is set to cut steel bars to 10.65 inches. Six pieces are selected at random every hour and the length of each checked. Construct a bar X chart based on the first three hours of operation. Show essential figures, such as the UCL, and plot the means for the first three hours. (Note: To facilitate computations, the whole number 10 has been omitted from all the readings. Thus, the first observation at 1 P.M. should really be 10.6.)

LENGTHS OF SIX BARS SELECTED AT RANDOM EVERY HOUR

	Lengths of Sample Number					
Time	*1*	*2*	*3*	*4*	*5*	*6*
1 P.M.	6	7	7	8	6	8
2 P.M.	10	7	7	8	9	7
3 P.M.	8	7	7	8	7	8

Based on this initial experience, about ________ percent of the means of samples of size six should fall between ________ and ________ inches.

Time	*Means*	*Range*
1 P.M.	7	2
2 P.M.	8	3
3 P.M.	7.5	1
	22.5	6

$\bar{\bar{X}} = 22.5/3 = 7.5$

$\bar{R} = 6/3 = 2$

$\bar{\bar{X}} \pm A_2\bar{R} =$
$7.5 \pm 0.483(2)$

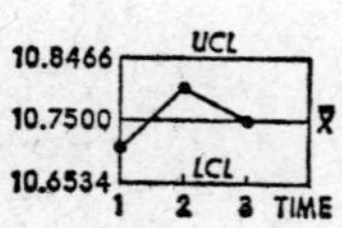

99.7

10.6534 inches and 10.8466 inches

4

A control chart for the mean may be misleading, if there is extreme variation in the weight. For example, note the extreme weights of the glass containers in the following table.

	Weights of Sample Number					
Time	*1*	*2*	*3*	*4*	*5*	*Mean*
7:30 A.M.	58	2	58	30	2	30
8:00 A.M.	45	1	1	45	58	30
8:30 A.M.	59	28	2	60	1	30
9:00 A.M.	3	48	4	2	93	30

Although $\bar{\bar{X}} = 30$ as specified (and the mean weight of each sample was exactly 30 ounces), the extreme weights of the glass containers would no doubt result in a shutdown of the machines. What is needed then is another chart to show the variation in the ranges.

Range charts. The upper and lower control limits for a range chart are found by

$\bar{R} \pm 3\sigma_{\bar{R}}$. Instead of doing these extensive calculations, the upper control limit can be estimated by $D_4\bar{R}$ and the lower control limit by $D_3\bar{R}$.

The average range $\bar{R}$ in the glass container problem (frame #3) is 2.25, and the factor D_4 for a sample size n of 5 is 2.115 (from Appendix Table II). And, $D_3 = 0$. Then, UCL $= D_4\bar{R} = 2.115\,(2.25) = 4.75875$. The LCL $= D_3\bar{R} = 0\,(2.25) = 0$. The complete range chart, including the four ranges computed for the 7:30 A.M., 8:00 A.M., 8:30 A.M., and 9:00 A.M. samples, follows.

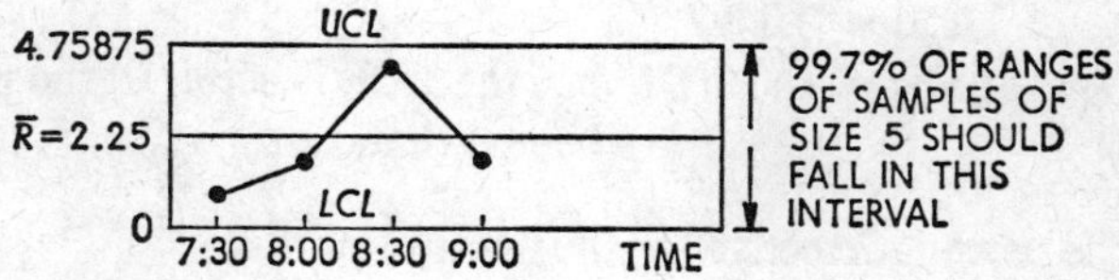

Now, using the same sample data on the length of sheared steel bars from frame #3 construct a range chart in the space provided. Show essential work and plot the ranges for the 1:00 P.M., 2:00 P.M. and 3:00 P.M. samples.

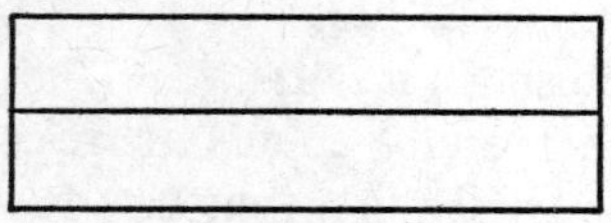

UCL $= D_4\bar{R} = 2.004(2)$
$= 4.008$
LCL $= D_3\bar{R} = 0(2) = 0$

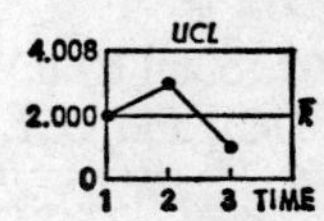

5

Charts for attributes

Percent defective charts. These charts are also called fraction defective charts, p charts, and $\bar{p}$ charts (pronounced p-bar charts). As the name implies, the percent defective chart portrays graphically the percent of the production which is not acceptable.

Suppose that a roll of steel exactly 200 inches long and 1 inch wide is fed into an automatic machine which cuts off a 1-inch piece and at the same time punches a hole in the center of the piece. The 200 square pieces are then moved to the assembly line. If for any reason a piece cannot be used, the worker puts it aside. The record of the first five production runs follows.

Production Number	*Number of Pieces Produced*	*Number of Pieces Defective*	*Percent Defective*
1	200	4	0.02
2	200	3	.015
3	200	5	.025
4	200	6	.03
5	200	2	.01
			0.10

The average percent defective ($\bar{p}$) is .02, found by:

$$\bar{p} = \frac{\Sigma \text{ of the percent defective}}{\text{Number of samples}} = \frac{0.10}{5} = 0.02 \text{ (this is the centerline on the } p \text{ chart)}$$

The upper and lower control limits are determined by:

$$\bar{p} \pm 3\sigma_{\bar{p}} = \bar{p} \pm 3\sqrt{\frac{\bar{p}(1-\bar{p})}{n}} = 0.02 \pm 3\sqrt{\frac{0.02(0.98)}{200}} = 0.02 \pm 3(0.0099)$$
$$= 0.02 \pm 0.0297$$

Thus, the

UCL = 0.0497
LCL = −0.0097, but the LCL is set at 0 (the percent defective cannot be less than zero)

The percent defective for the first five production runs is plotted on the percent defective chart.

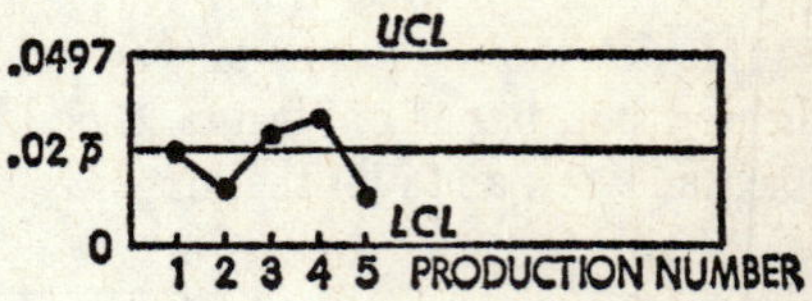

A new high-speed shearing machine is designed to cut off 400 pieces from a long bar. The sheared pieces travel over several holes, and if a piece is too long or too short, it falls into a reject box. The machine operator counts the rejects after each 400 pieces are sheared. The number of rejects for the first four bars is shown in the following table.

Bar Number	*Number Produced*	*Number of Rejects*
1	400	12
2	400	8
3	400	12
4	400	16

Set up a percent defective chart and plot the percent defective for the first four bars sheared.

If management was satisfied with the machine's performance, then any production over 0. __________ percent defective would be considered "out of control."

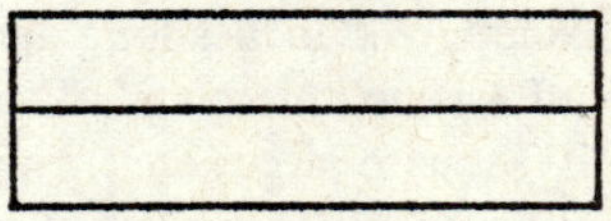

p = 0.03 found by 0.12/4. Then UCL and LCL = $0.03 \pm 3\sqrt{\frac{(0.03)(.97)}{400}}$
UCL = .05559; LCL = .00441

.05559 (or 5.559 percent defective)

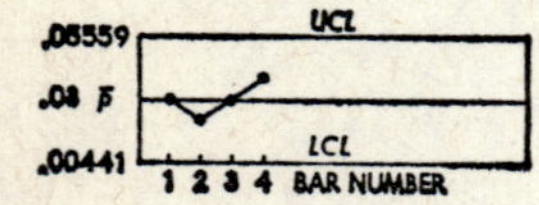

6

c̄ chart. The $\bar{c}$ chart is designed to control the *number of defects per unit.* An example might be the number of defects in a radio set just assembled. It might require that three solder joints be resoldered, one missing wire be inserted, and the inoperative dial light replaced. Thus, there was a total of five defects for the unit. On an automobile door three spots had to be touched up and a screw inserted in the window.

Its construction and interpretation is similar to the $\bar{p}$ chart. The UCL and LCL can be found by $\bar{c} \pm 3\sigma_{\bar{c}}$ where $\bar{c}$ is the arithmetic mean number of defects per unit. However, instead of calculating $\sigma_{\bar{c}}$ it can be approximated by $\sqrt{\bar{c}}$. Thus, the UCL and LCL = $\bar{c} \pm 3\sqrt{\bar{c}}$.

To illustrate the construction of a $\bar{c}$ chart, suppose that the number of defects per television chassis for the first 10 produced was: 4, 5, 3, 6, 0, 4, 5, 0, 7, and 6. The average number of defects per unit is: $\bar{c}$ = __________, found by __________ __________. The upper control limit is __________ and the lower control limit is __________. Now, insert these figures on the following control chart and plot the number of defects per unit for the first 10 chassis checked.

4, found by 40/10
10, found by $4 + 3\sqrt{4}$
0 (− 2 is not realistic)

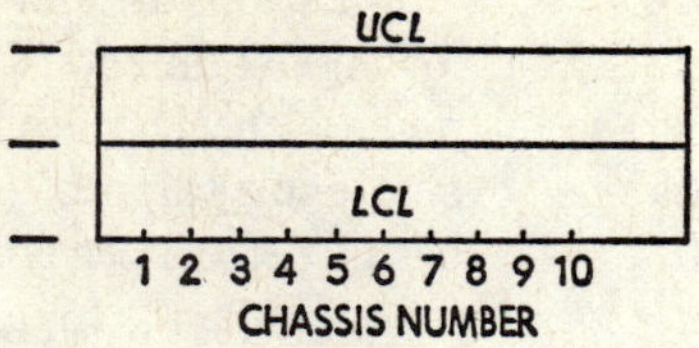

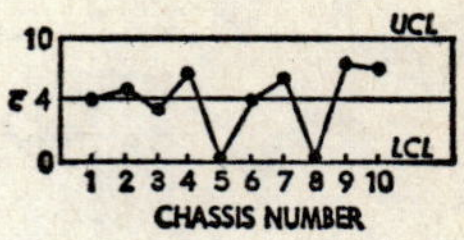

ased on this initial production of television chassis, the average number of defects per ıassis is ____________. About ____________ percent of the chassis will have ɛtween ____________ and ____________ defects. The control chart, called ____________ chart, merely portrays the actual situation. Management must ɛcide whether an average of four and a range of from 0 to 10 defects per unit is satis-ctory. No doubt the chart would be revised after more chassis are produced.

Statistical quality control charts are utilized by most manufacturers emphasizing ass production. However, a statistical quality control department usually has other sponsibilities including deciding whether to accept or reject an incoming shipment parts. They do this based on a technique called *acceptance sampling*. Briefly, it is the chnique of selecting a sample from the incoming shipment and deciding whether to cept or reject it, based on the number of defective items found in the sample.

4. About 99.7
0 and 10
$\bar{c}$

Final Self-Review Examination

First, answer all of the questions. Then check your answers against those given at the end of this chapter. Use the tables in the appendix, if necessary. Scoring: 10 problems × 10 points each = 100 possible points.

8. There are two general types of statistical quality control charts; namely, charts for ____________ and charts for ____________.

Questions 9, 10, and 11 are based on the following. A new process has just been started. The quality control inspector measures the length of four pieces every hour and records the length of each.

	Sample Piece			
	1	*2*	*3*	*4*
TIME	*Measurements*			
9 A.M.	1	4	5	2
10 A.M.	2	3	2	1
11 A.M.	4	4	4	4

9. Design a bar X chart and plot the essential data for the first three hours.

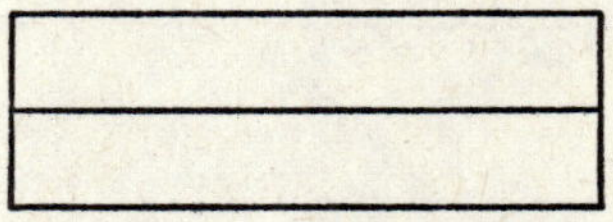

10. Design a range chart and plot the essential data for the first three hours.

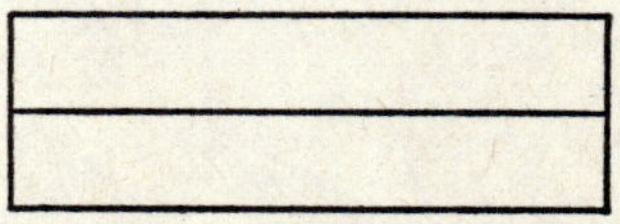

11. Now briefly interpret the two charts. ____________

Questions 12 and 13 are based on the following. An automatic machine mills a slot in flat piece of steel. If the slot is not positioned correctly, or not the correct width, it will not fit into an assembly. In order to control the percent defective, the first batch of pieces is stamped automatically with a 1, the second batch with a 2, and so forth. A batch is 200 pieces. The number of defectives per batch are as shown in the following table.

Batch Number	*Number in Batch*	*Number Defective*
1	200	8
2	200	6
3	200	12
4	200	10
5	200	4

12. Construct a percent defective chart. Plot the appropriate figures, including the percent defectives for the first five batches.

13. Briefly, interpret the chart. ______

Questions 14 and 15 are based on the following. At the end of the assembly line, a computer is checked out and the defects corrected before it is shipped to the customer. The number of defects per computer were recorded as follows: 18, 14, 15, and 17.

14. Set up a $\bar{c}$ chart based on the first four computers off the assembly line. Plot the essential data for the four computers.

15. Briefly, interpret the chart. ______

16. Plots which fall between the upper control limit and the lower control limit indicate that the process is ______ ______.

17. Explain what is meant by acceptance sampling. ______

Answers to Final Self-Review Examination

8. variables and attributes

9.

Means	*Range*
3	4
2	2
4	0

$\bar{X} = 3 \quad \bar{R} = 2$

Then: UCL, LCL $= 3 \pm A_2\bar{R}$
$= 3 \pm 0.729(2)$

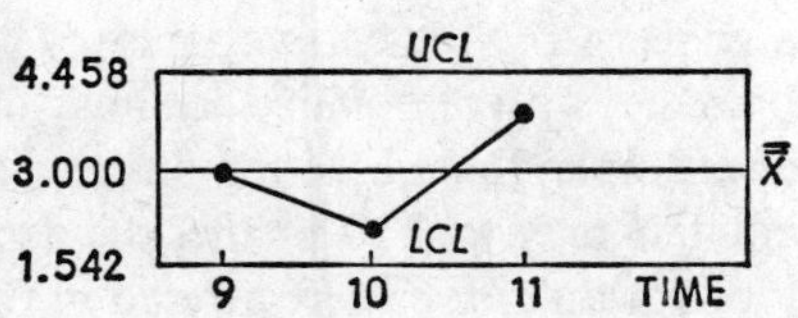

10. UCL $= D_4\bar{R} = 2.282(2)$
LCL $= D_3\bar{R} = 0(2)$

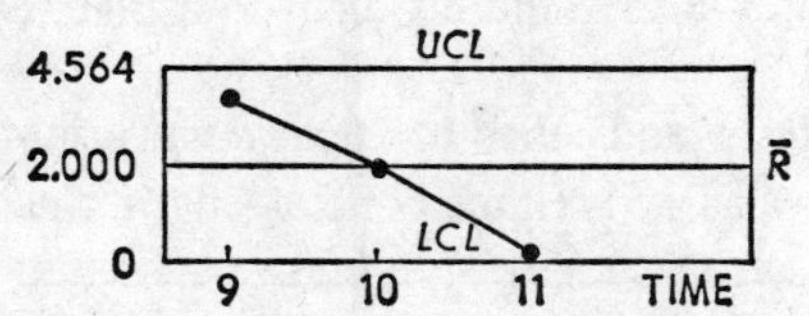

11. About 99.7 percent of the average lengths of four pieces selected at random will vary between 1.542 and 4.458. The range of the four pieces will vary between 0 and 4.564 about 99.7 percent of the time.

12. $\bar{p} = 0.04$

Then UCL and LCL $= p \pm 3\sqrt{\dfrac{\bar{p}(1-\bar{p})}{n}}$
$0.04 \pm 3\sqrt{0.000192} = 0.04 \pm 3(0.0139)$

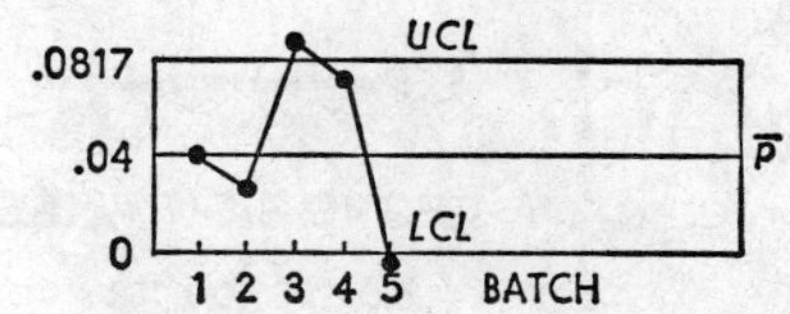

13. Based on this initial experience, 99.7 percent of the batches should be between zero percent and 8.17 percent defective with an average of 4 percent defective.

14. $\bar{c} = 16$. Then $\bar{c} \pm 3\sqrt{\bar{c}} = 16 \pm 3\sqrt{16} = 4, 28$

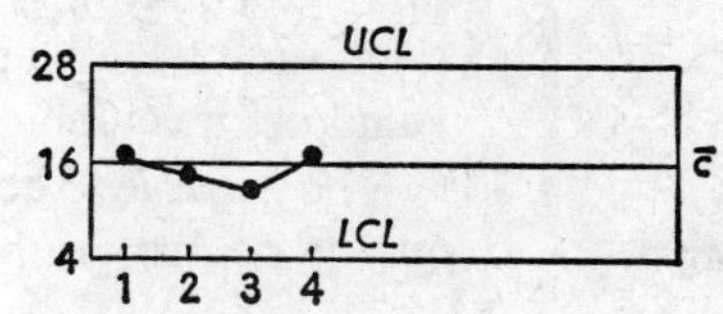

15. Based on this initial experience, 99.7 percent of the computers will have between 4 and 28 defects. The average is 16.

16. in control

17. It is a technique whereby a sample is taken from an incoming shipment and the shipment is accepted or rejected based on the number of defectives in the sample.

chapter

15

Simple regression and correlation

1

REGRESSION ANALYSIS

Regression and correlation analysis is concerned with two variables. The fundamental purpose of regression analysis is to predict with reasonable accuracy one of the variables based on the other variable. For example, the marketing director of a firm manufacturing replacement automobile mufflers may wish to predict the demand for the mufflers in a region based on the number of automobiles registered in the region over four years old. A perfume manufacturer may wish to predict the sales of his perfumes based on advertising expenditures. The quality control department of a steel fabricator may wish to predict the knee bend strength of a steel plate based on the thickness of the plate. (Knee bend strength is the amount of bend a plate can withstand before cracking.)

The variable to be predicted is designated *Y* and called the *dependent* variable. In the quality control problem, the dependent variable is (knee bend strength/thickness)____________________. Prediction of the ____________________ variable is based on an *independent* variable designated as *X*. In this problem, the independent variable is ______________________________.

knee bend strength
dependent
thickness

2

The quality control engineer selected several steel plates of varying thicknesses at random and determined the knee bend strength of each. The results of the experiment are shown in the following table.

A cursory examination of the paired data, i.e., thickness and knee bend strength for each steel plate, reveals that the knee bend strength of a steel plate of, say, 4.5 inches thick (could/could not) ____________________ be predicted with some degree of precision. The predicted knee bend strength for the 4.5-inch plate would be *about* ________. ______ thousand pounds per square inch (psi).

could
9.5 or 9,500 psi

Thickness of Plate (In Inches) *X*	*Knee Bend Strength (000 Pounds per Square Inch)* *Y*
3	7
1	3
4	8
3	6
5	11

---

o further emphasize the relationship beveen X and Y, the paired data can be porayed graphically in a *scatter diagram.* To lot the paired data, the dependent variable nee bend strength in this problem) is ways plotted on the Y-axis. Thus, the dependent variable is always plotted on e ________________. For exmple, the paired data for the first plot rom the previous table) is 3 inches on the -axis and 7,000 pounds on the Y-axis. omplete the graph called a ______________________.

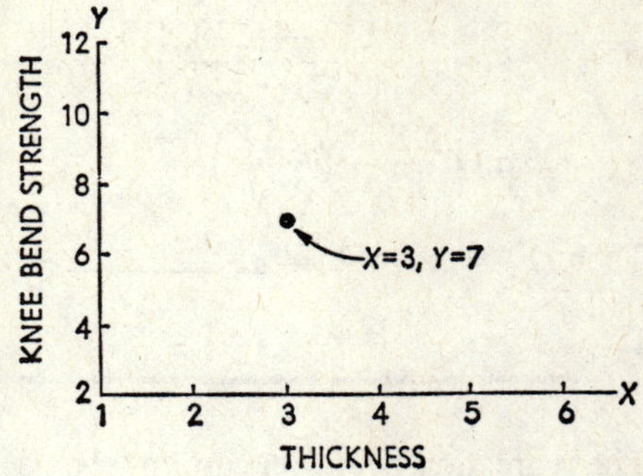

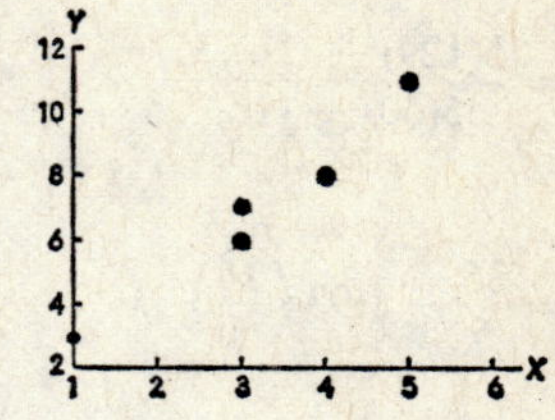

X-axis

scatter diagram

---

he scatter diagram shows: (1) As the thickness of the steel plate increases so does ________ ________ ________. (2) A straight line seems to best escribe the average path of the points. (3) Any prediction of knee bend strength canot be 100 percent accurate but can be fairly precise.

knee bend strength

HE LEAST SQUARES METHOD OF DETERMINING THE REGRESSION QUATION

A linear equation, therefore, will be used as the *regression* equation. The regression quation is also called an *estimating* equation. The equation for the regression line is $_p = a + bX$.

Using the least squares method, the computation of a and b in the equation, called ________________ or ________________ equation, sums and other ssential figures are needed. Complete the following table.

Thickness X	Knee Bend Strength Y	XY	X^2	Y^2
3	7	21	9	49
1	3	—	—	—
4	8	—	—	—
3	6	—	—	—
5	11	—	—	—
Total —	—	—	—	—

regression or estimating

			3	1	9
			32	16	64
			18	9	36
			55	25	121
Total	16	35	129	60	279

---

he equation for the regression line can be determined by two methods. The first ethod involves solving two equations simultaneously.

The second method of arriving at the regression does not require that the two equa tions be solved simultaneously. a and b can be found directly by using the followin formulas. Using the same problem (thickness and knee bend strengths), insert th appropriate figures from frame #5 in the formulas and solve for a and b.

$$b = \frac{n(\Sigma XY) - (\Sigma X)(\Sigma Y)}{n(\Sigma X^2) - (\Sigma X)^2} = \_\_\_\_\_\_\_\_\_\_ =$$

$$a = \frac{\Sigma Y}{n} - b\left(\frac{\Sigma X}{n}\right) = \_\_\_\_\_\_\_\_\_\_ =$$

Then, $\bar{Y}_p = a + bX =$ ______ + ______ X

$$b = \frac{5(129) - (16)(35)}{5(60) - (16)^2} =$$

1.93

$$a = \frac{35}{5} - 1.93\left(\frac{16}{5}\right) =$$

0.82

$\bar{Y}_p = 0.82 + 1.93X$

7

The regression equation can now be used to determine the points on the straight lin by substituting various values for X into the equation. For example, when the thick ness of a steel plate (X) is 2 inches, $\bar{Y}_p$ is 4.68, found by: $\bar{Y}_p = 0.82 + 1.93(2)$ ir thousands of pounds per square inch.

This indicates that when th thickness of a steel plate is 2 inches the knee bend strength of that plat is estimated to be 4,680 pounds Complete the following table by de termining the estimated knee benc strengths for various thicknesses

Thickness (Inches) X	*Knee Bend Strengths* Y
1	___,___
2	4,680
3	___,___
4	___,___
5	___,___
6	___,___

Note that for each increase of inch in thickness (X), the estimatec or predicted knee bend strengt ($\bar{Y}_p$) increases by ________

The complete table is:
2,750
4,680
6,610
8,540
10,470
12,400

1,930

Thus, b is defined as the average change in Y_p for each change of one (either increase o decrease) in X. $\bar{Y}_p$ is the average predicted value of the Y variable for a selected X value. The letter a in the equation is the value of Y when $\bar{X} = 0$. Another way to put i is: a is the estimated value of Y where the regression line crosses the Y-axis when X i 0. X in the regression equation is any value of X that is selected (such as 3 inches)

8

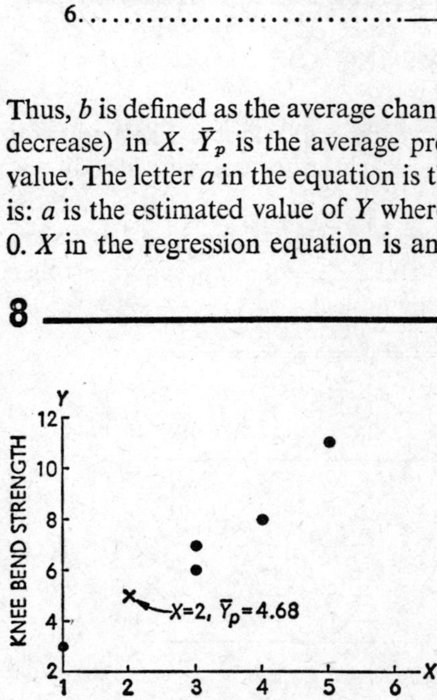

Now, using the paired points ($\bar{Y}_p$ and X), th linear regression line can be plotted on th following graph called a ________ ________. One plot on the straigh line is shown ($\bar{Y}_p = 4.68$, $X = 2$). Plot th remaining points. Then connect the point with a straight line.

Determine the following from the scatte diagram. If a steel plate was 3.5 inches thick what is the approximate knee bend strength ____.____ thousand pounds. No check this approximation by using the regression equation.

$\bar{Y}_p = 0.82 + 1.93X =$ ____.____ thousand pounds.

scatter diagram

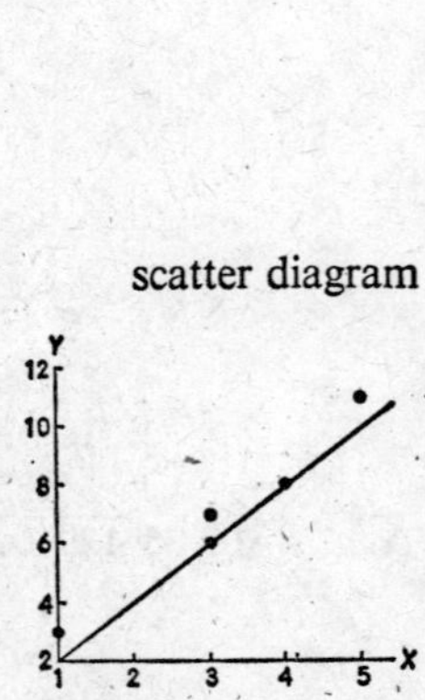

7.5 (or 7,500 pounds)

7.575

9

ERROR IN PREDICTING

Note in the preceding scatter diagram that all of the points do not fall on the regression line. If all of the plots had fallen on the straight line, and if the number of observations had been sufficiently large, there would be no error in predicting knee bend strength. That is, knee bend strength could be predicted with 100 percent accuracy. Perfect prediction in problems involving economics and business is practically nonexistent. Even in this problem the thickness of the steel is not a perfect predictor of knee bend strength, probably due to slight differences in the composition of the steel.

What is needed, then, is a measure which would indicate how precise the prediction of Y is, based on X, or conversely, how inaccurate the prediction might be. This measure is called the *standard error of estimate*. One formula is:

$$s_{y \cdot x} = \sqrt{\frac{\Sigma(Y - \bar{Y}_p)^2}{n - 2}}$$

The symbol for the standard error of estimate ($s_{y \cdot x}$) represents the standard deviation of the Y's based on the X's. This measure of error, called the ____, is similar in concept to the standard deviation discussed in Chapter 5. The standard deviation measures the dispersion about an average, the standard error of estimate measures the dispersion about an average line, called the __________________ line.

standard error of estimate

regression (or estimating)

10

To compute $s_{y \cdot x}$, the deviations $(Y - \bar{Y}_p)$ are needed. These are the vertical deviations from the regression line.

Complete the table.

Thickness (Inches) X	Knee Bend Strength (000) Y	Estimated Strength* (000) $\bar{Y}_p$	$Y - \bar{Y}_p$†	$(Y - \bar{Y}_p)^2$
3	7	6.61	+0.39	0.1521
1	3	2.75	___	___
4	8	8.54	___	___
3	6	6.61	___	___
5	11	10.47	___	___
Total				___

* From frame #7.
† The sum of the deviations should be 0. (Slight discrepancy due to the rounding of a and b.)

Give the formula, insert the essential figures, and find the standard error of estimate.

$s_{y \cdot x} =$ ________ = ________ = ________ pounds

+0.25	0.0625
− .54	.2916
− .61	.3721
+ .53	.2809
	1.1592

$$s_{y \cdot x} = \sqrt{\frac{\Sigma(Y - \bar{Y}_p)^2}{n - 2}} = \sqrt{\frac{1.1592}{5 - 2}} = 0.62 \text{ or } 620 \text{ pounds}$$

11

CONFIDENCE LIMITS FOR PREDICTIONS

Theoretically, the standard error of estimate is a valid measure to use in setting *confidence limits* about a predicted value of $\bar{Y}_p$, if the size of the sample is large, say,

2,000 and the points on the scatter diagram are normally distributed about the regression line. If these conditions did exist in this knee bend strength problem, then the statistician would be 95 percent confident that, for a given thickness (X), the predicted knee bend strength would be somewhere between $\bar{Y}_p \pm z(s_{y \cdot x})$ or $\bar{Y}_p \pm 2s_{y \cdot x}$. Recall that the regression equation was computed to be $\bar{Y}_p = 0.82 + 1.93X$ (in thousands of pounds per square inch). The standard error of the estimate was found to be 620 psi. For a steel plate 4 inches thick, the predicted knee bend strength would be 8,540 psi, found by $\bar{Y}_p = 0.82 + 1.93(4)$. The 95 percent confidence limits would be 7,300 psi and 9,780 psi, found by 8,540 psi $\pm$ 2(620 psi).

Other z values can be found in Appendix Table IV. The procedure to find the z value was explained in Chapter 5. For the 92 percent confidence limits, it is approximately 1.75 (determined by locating 0.4600 and reading the z value in the left margin).

The 90 percent confidence limits for the predicted value of $\bar{Y}_p$ given a steel plate 5 inches thick are __________ and __________ psi. Interpret these limits__________

9.45 and 11.49 (in thousands of pounds) found by $10.47 \pm 1.645(0.62)$

The statistician is 90 percent confident that if a steel plate 5 inches thick were selected at random, the knee bend strength would be between 9,450 pounds and 11,490 pounds.

It should be recognized that the two assumptions (normality and a large sample) are not met in this knee bend problem. The sample size was kept small to facilitate computations. If a small sample were essential, however, a small correction factor would have to be introduced. (This correction factor will not be considered here.) Of major importance is the concept of confidence limits about the regression line.

12

CORRELATION ANALYSIS

In the previous section, a regression line was fitted to paired data consisting of a dependent variable Y (knee bend strength) and an independent variable X (thickness). The objective was to predict knee bend strength based on the thickness of the steel plate. The error of the prediction is measured by the standard error of the estimate. If the standard error of the estimate is 0, there is no error in the prediction. All of the dots on the scatter diagram would fall on the regression line, as shown in Figure A. However, in the knee bend problem $s_{y \cdot x}$ is 620 psi indicating an error in the prediction. This is evidenced by the scatter about the regression line in Figure B.

FIGURE A

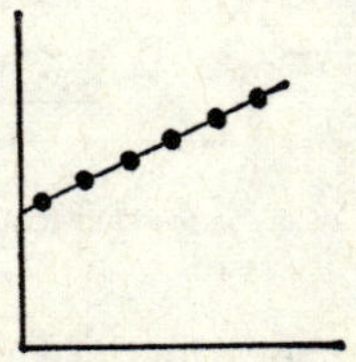

$s_{y \cdot x} = 0$

FIGURE B

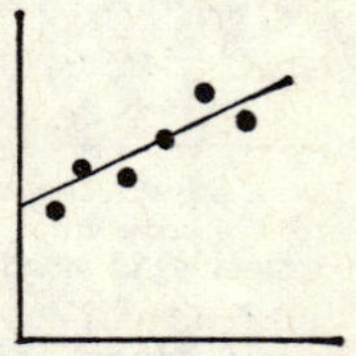

$s_{y \cdot x} = 620$ psi

The 620 pounds per square inch represents the variation in knee bend strength *not* explained by the thickness of the steel. The 620 psi is difficult to interpret. Is the unexplained variation (620 psi) large or small? Further, if 620 psi is the amount not explained, what is the variation in knee bend strength explained by the thickness of the steel?

A more meaningful way of expressing the variation in Y explained and not explained by the independent variable X is in terms of percents. The proportion of the variation

Y *explained* by X is called the *coefficient of determination* (r^2). The variation in the dependent variable Y not explained by the independent variable X is called the *coefficient of nondetermination*, found by $1 - r^2$. It is designated by either $1 - r^2$, or k^2.

The value of either coefficient may vary from 0 to 1. A coefficient of determination of 0 indicates that none of the variation in Y is explained by the X variable. A coefficient of determination of 1 indicates that ____________________ . An r^2 of 0.91 would suggest that a large part of the variation in the Y variable is determined by the variable. (The computation of the coefficient of determination will be shown shortly.)

all, or 100 percent, of the variation in Y is explained by X.

3

The square root of the coefficient of determination is called the *correlation coefficient r*. A convenient formula for computing the correlation coefficient follows. Note that the numerator in the formula is the same as used in determining b in the regression equation. All the essential numbers were computed in frame #5. Find the correlation coefficient, coefficient of determination, and the coefficient of nondetermination.

$$r = \frac{n(\Sigma XY) - (\Sigma X)(\Sigma Y)}{\sqrt{[n(\Sigma X^2) - (\Sigma X)^2][n(\Sigma Y^2) - (\Sigma Y)^2]}}$$

$=$ __________ $= 0.$________

.98, found by

$$\frac{5(129) - (16)(35)}{\sqrt{[5(60) - (16)^2][5(279) - (35)^2]}}$$

The coefficient of determination (r^2) is 0.________ and the coefficient of nondetermination 0.________.

.96
.04

4

How interpret the coefficient of determination ____________________ and the coefficient of nondetermination (which is often called the coefficient of alienation). ____________________

96 percent of the variation in knee bend strength is explained by the thickness of the steel.
4 percent of the variation in knee bend strength is not attributable to the thickness.

The coefficient of correlation (r) is 0.98. It is defined as the degree of relationship, or the degree of correlation, between knee bend strength and the thickness of the steel plates. The meaning of the coefficient of correlation is not as explicit as that of the coefficient of determination. In a problem such as the one involving knee bend strength and thickness, Y increases as X increases. Thus, the correlation coefficient can have a value from 0 to +1 with zero indicating no relationship and +1 indicating perfect relationship between the two variables. In this problem, 0.98 indicates ____________________

0.98 indicates a high degree of relationship between knee bend strength and thickness.

5

In the knee bend problem, there is a *positive* relationship, i.e., as X (thickness) increases Y (strength) (increases/decreases) __________. However, the correlation coefficient can be *negative*. For example, note in Figure A that as the price (X) of the commodity increased, the sales __________.

increases

decreased

FIGURE A

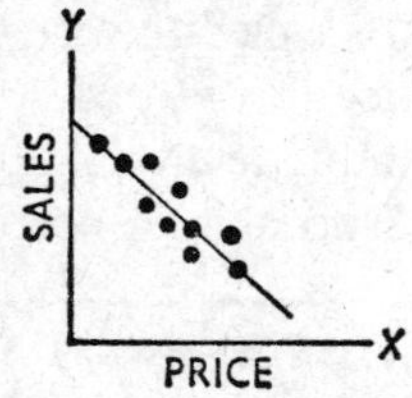

FIGURE B

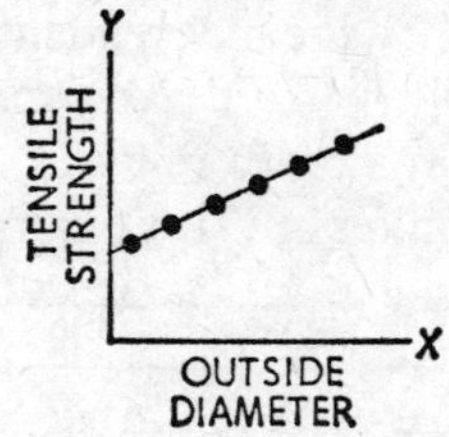

FIGURE C

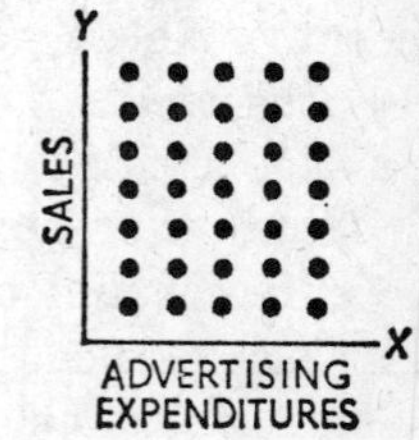

−1
+1
Diameter is a perfect predictor of strength.
About 0. There is practically no relationship.

Thus, the correlation coefficient can have a value between +1 and ______ inclusive. Refer to Figure B. What is the approximate coefficient of correlation? ______ ______. What does the coefficient indicate? ______ ______. Refer to Figure C. What is the approximate coefficient of correlation? ______. What does this indicate? ______.

Final Self-Review Examination

First, answer all of the questions. Then check your answers against those given at the end of this chapter. Scoring: 10 problems × 10 points each = 100 possible points.

All of the questions are based on the following problem.

A personnel director has the responsibility of selecting new salesmen. In order to make the best selection possible from a group of job applicants, he designed a placement test which he called the DOT test. His objective is to predict the level of sales of an individual based on his DOT test score. However, in order to determine whether there is any relationship between his DOT test and sales he asked several veteran salesmen to take the test. Their test scores and their average weekly sales are shown in the following table. (In practice, many more paired observations would be needed.)

Salesmen	*DOT Test Score*	*Weekly Sales ($000)*
Sam Jones	3	$5
Bob Patten	4	7
Jim Farmer	2	4

16. Does it appear that the personnel director will be able to predict the sales of an applicant based on his DOT test score? (yes/no) (*a*)______ ______. Which variable is the dependent variable? (*b*)______.

17. In order to portray this relationship graphically, plot the paired data in a graph called a (*a*)______ ______. The DOT test scores, which are the (dependent/independent) (*b*)______ variable, must be plotted on the (*c*)______ axis. (Label the axes.)

18. Determine the equation for the straight line which will pass through the paired points. The line is called a (*a*)______ or ______ line. The equation is (*b*) $\bar{Y}_p$ = ______ = ______ (Carry calculations to the nearest hundredth, such as 1.68.)

19. Plot the line on the scatter diagram in frame #17. Give the calculations for one point on the straight line. (*a*)______ ______

Mr. James Coffman is an applicant for a position as salesman. He scored 6 on the DOT test. Based on the regression equation (frame #18), what is his predicted average weekly sales? (*b*)$______.

20. Assume that the standard error of estimate was computed to be $.1, i.e., $100. What is the 98 percent confidence limit for Mr. James Coffman's predicted weekly sales (from frame #19)? (*a*)$______ and $______.

Interpret the confidence limits (*b*)________________

____

21. The coefficient of determination is (*a*)________
Interpret (*b*)________________________

____

22. The coefficient of nondetermination is (*a*)______.
Interpret (*b*)________________________

____

23. The coefficient of correlation is (*a*)________.
Interpret (*b*)________________________

____

24. The proportion of the explained variation is called the (*a*)____________________.
The degree of relationship between *X* and *Y* is measured by the (*b*)__________________.

25. Briefly summarize the problem, the measures of regression and correlation used to solve the problem, and draw some observations based on the measures computed.____________

____

____

____

____

Answers to Final Self-Review Examination

16. (*a*) yes
(*b*) sales

17. (*a*) scatter diagram
(*b*) independent
(*c*) *X*-axis

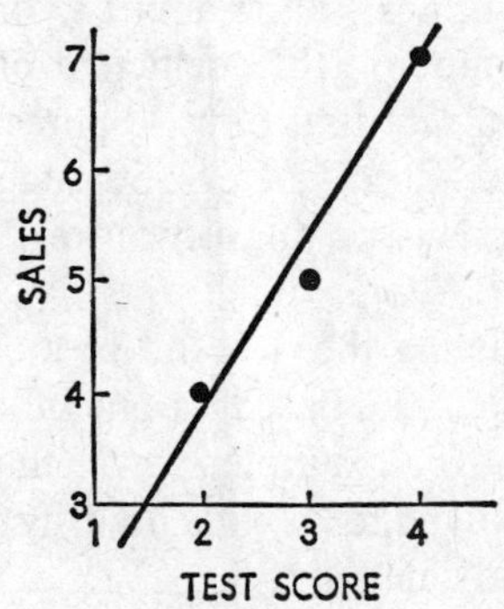

18. (*a*) regression or estimating
(*b*) $\bar{Y}_p = a + bX = 0.83 + 1.50X$

19. (*a*) When $X = 2$, $\bar{Y}_p = 3.83$ (found by $\bar{Y}_p = 0.83 + 1.5(2)$)
When $X = 3$, $\bar{Y}_p = 5.33$, and when $X = 4$, $\bar{Y}_p = 6.83$
(*b*) \$9.83 or \$9,830

20. (*a*) \$9,597 and \$10,063, found by \$9,830 ± 2.33 (\$100)
(*b*) The personnel manager would be 98 percent confident that if an applicant scored 6 on the DOT test he would sell between \$9,597 and \$10,063 a week. To put it another way, 98 out of 100 weeks an applicant with a test score of 6 should sell between \$9,597 and \$10,063.

21. (*a*) 0.96
(*b*) 96 percent of the variation in sales are explained by the test score.

22. (*a*) 0.04
(*b*) 4 percent of the variation in weekly sales of an individual are not accounted for by the DOT test.

23. (*a*) 0.98
(*b*) There is an extremely high degree of relationship between the test score and sales.

24. (*a*) the coefficient of determination
(*b*) the coefficient of correlation

25. The personnel manager wanted to predict with reasonable accuracy the weekly sales of a salesman based on a test score. If there were a high correlation between his DOT test score and sales, the test would be very useful in hiring new salesmen. A small group of veteran salesmen took the test, and the test score of each paired with his sales. The relationship between the two variables is excellent ($r = 0.98$). About 96 percent of the variation in sales is explained by the test score. The regression equation $\bar{Y}_p = 0.83 + 1.50X$ can be used to predict the sales of a salesman. The error in the prediction is measured by the standard error of estimate (\$100).

chapter
16

Multiple correlation and regression

1

The simple linear regression and correlation analysis in the previous chapter dealt with *two* variables. The basic objectives were to determine the degree of association between the two variables and to arrive at an equation which might be used to predict one variable (Y) designated as the (dependent/independent) ______________ variable, based on an independent variable (X). Recall that one measure of the degree of association is called the coefficient of ______________. It may have a numerical value between 0 and ______________. The linear predicting equation (called a regression equation) is in the form of $\bar{Y}_p =$ ______________.

dependent

determination, or correlation; 1

$\bar{Y}_p = a + bX$

2

Although useful, simple regression and correlation considers only the relationship between *one* independent variable and the dependent variable and ignores the possible effect of any other independent variable which might be related. To illustrate the point, the tensile strength of steel wire might appear at the outset to only be based on the outside diameter of the wire. However, suppose the coefficient of determination (r^2) was computed to be 0.90. This would indicate that only 90 percent of the variation in tensile strength is attributable to outside diameter and suggests that other factors contributed to tensile strength, such as the composition of the wire and the temperature of the furnace.

The same logic might be applied to predicting the demand of a consumer go such as new color television sets. Predicting demand based on one independent variable, such as the number of new consumers (for example, newly married couples), might not fully explain all the variation in demand as indicated by a coefficient of determination of 0.74. What does the 0.74 indicate? ______________. Replacement of old black-and-white sets, and the purchases of a second or third set for the home are other factors which might also be contributing to demand.

74 percent of the variation in the demand for new color television sets is attributable to new consumers.

3

Because of the large number of calculations needed, hand calculations or electronic calculators are seldom used now to solve real-world multiple correlation and regression problems. Instead, a number of computer programs are available.

As an illustration of the use of multiple correlation and regression techniques, and the use of a computer, suppose that the sales analyst of a large firm which manufactures and distributes automotive parts wants to make an annual sales forecast for each of the 10 sales territories. There are several factors which he thinks are related to the annual level of sales in a territory: (1) The number of retail outlets in the territory carrying their parts. (2) The average number of new automobiles sold per month ı the territory. (3) The total personal income in the territory. The number of new ıtomobiles sold is published every month by the state registrar of motor vehicles, nd the federal government releases the personal income figures by state for the first ıarter of the year in April.

Thus, if there is found to be a relationship between the three variables and sales, ıe analyst could gather the figures for each territory in April and predict the sales for ıe entire year. In order to determine whether there is a relationship, the analyst colcted the annual sales, called the (dependent/independent) ________________ ıriable, the number of outlets, new automobile registrations, and the first-quarter ersonal income for each territory for last year.

dependent

rritory	*Annual Sales* Y *or* X_1	*Retail Outlets* X_2	*New Cars* X_3	*Personal Income* X_4
1	17702.	1535.	8717.	2127.
2	21139.	674.	13248.	2490.
3	18969.	570.	11011.	3205.
4	15890.	630.	9737.	2528.
5	26247.	984.	15488.	4233.
6	20680.	888.	10219.	3998.
7	14081.	874.	8592.	2794.
8	20080.	708.	12802.	2696.
9	28420.	1740.	16002.	4879.
10	10134.	536.	6029.	847.

The analyst arbitrarily decided to record the sales (Y) to the nearest million dollars. For example, the sales in territory #1 for last year were actually $17,702,000. (See the accompanying printout.) There were 1,535 retail outlets (X_2), and a monthly average of 8,717 new cars registered (X_2) in the territory. Five zeros have been omitted from the X_4 dependent variable, so the first-quarter personal income was 212,700,000 for territory #1. Briefly, from left to right, interpret the four figures for rritory #2. ____

____.

annual sales (Y) $21,139,-000
674 retail outlets (X_2)
13,248 average monthly new car registrations (X_3)
$249,000,000 first-quarter personal income (X_4)

ULTIPLE CORRELATION

he correlation matrix

In order to arrive at statistical measures which might be of value in predicting anıal sales, the *IBM 360 Stepwise Multiple Regression Program* was used. The simple ›rrelation coefficients between X_1 and X_2, between X_1 and X_3, and so on were emitted st. This set of simple correlation coefficients is called the *correlation matrix*.

CCRRELATICN MATRIX

	Annual Sales X_1	*Retail Outlets* X_2	*New Cars* X_3	*Personal Income* X_4
ROW 1	1.C0000	C.55811	0.95200	C.88C49
RCW 2	0.55811	1.0000C	0.38018	0.49970
ROW 3	0.95200	0.38018	1.CCCCC	C.79195
ROW 4	0.88049	C.49970	0.79195	1.COCCC

0.55811
a rather low relationship
scatter diagrams

Note, for example, that the correlation between X_1 (annual sales) and X_4 (person income) is 0.88049, indicating a very high correlation between these two variable Further, the correlation between annual sales and the number of retail outlets in territory is 0.__________, indicating ______________________________

These two relationships are portrayed in the form of ______________

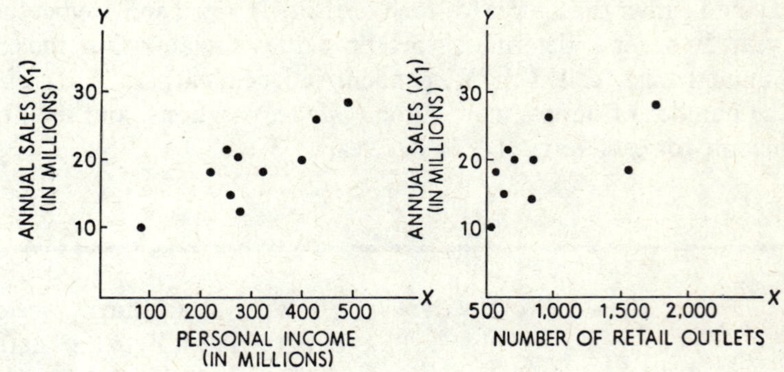

6

The computer then searches for the independent variable most highly correlat with the dependent variable (annual sales). It is X_3 (new cars registered in the ter tory), because the highest simple correlation coefficient in the correlation matrix 0.95200.

As a first step (identified as STEP 1 in the following printout), various statistic measures are computed. Most of these measures will be examined in the followi frames.

```
STEP   1

VARIABLE ENTERED..... 3

SUM OF SQUARES REDUCED IN THIS STEP....238232288.000
PROPORTION REDUCED IN THIS STEP........          0.906

CUMULATIVE SUM OF SQUARES REDUCED......238232288.000
CUMULATIVE PROPORTION REDUCED..........          0.906

FOR  1 VARIABLES ENTERED
  MULTIPLE CORRELATION COEFFICIENT...      0.952
       (ADJUSTED FOR D.F.)...........      0.952
  F-VALUE FOR ANALYSIS OF VARIANCE...     77.378
  STANDARD ERROR OF ESTIMATE......... 1754.659
       (ADJUSTED FOR D.F.)........... 1754.659

  VARIABLE      REGRESSION      STD. ERROR OF      COMPUTED
   NUMBER       COEFFICIENT     REG. COEFF.        T-VALUE
     3             1.61757         0.18389           8.796
  INTERCEPT     1242.51172
```

The coefficient of determination and nondetermination

Recall from the previous chapter that the percent of variation in Y explained by t dependent variable X is called the *coefficient of determination*. In multiple correlati and regression analysis, it is symbolized by R^2 and can assume a value betwe 0 and +1.

coefficient of determination

In the foregoing printout, R^2 is designated as the CUMULATIVE PROPORTIO REDUCED, or 0.906. The 0.906, called the ______________________ indicates in this problem that __________ percent of the variation in the __________________ of a territory is explained by the __________ __________.

90.6
annual sales
number of new cars registered

The coefficient of nondetermination, $1 - R^2$, logically is the percent of the variation in annual sales not explained by X_3 (new car registrations). It is 0. ______, indicating that ______________________________.

0.094, found by $1 - 0.906$
only 9.4 percent of the variation is not explained by new car registration

7

The multiple correlation coefficient

Referring to the printout for STEP 1 note that the *multiple correlation coefficient* is 0.952. It is the square root of the coefficient of determination, and it is designated as R. Multiple R is interpreted the same as the simple correlation coefficient, i.e., it indicates the degree of relationship or association between Y (the dependent variable) and the independent variables. However, unlike the simple correlation coefficient, the multiple correlation coefficient cannot be negative. Its value is between 0 and +1. Interpret the multiple R in this problem. ______________________________ ______________________________.

It is very close to +1 and therefore indicates near-perfect relationship between sales and the number of new cars registered

8

Next, using partial correlation coefficients and the remaining variables, the computer in STEP 2 enters the variable having the highest partial correlation coefficient. It was found to be X_2 (number of retail outlets). In brief, this partial correlation coefficient, written $r_{21 \cdot 4}$, measures the relationship between the number of retail outlets in the territory (X_2) and sales in the territory (X_1), but in the calculations the other remaining independent variables, though taken into account, are *held constant*. In contrast, r_{21} is a simple correlation coefficient. Here the other independent variables are not taken into account but instead are *completely ignored*.

```
STEP   2

VARIAELE ENTERED..... 2

SUM CF SGUARES RECUCED IN THIS STEP.... 11825974.CC0
PRCPCRTICN RECUCED IN THIS STEP........        0.045

CUMULATIVE SUM OF SQUARES REDUCED......25005E256.CC0
CUMULATIVE PROPORTION REDUCED..........        0.951

FOR  2 VARIABLES ENTERED
  MULTIFLE CORRELATION COEFFICIENT...     C.975
       (ADJUSTED FOR D.F.)...........     C.972
  F-VALUE FOR ANALYSIS OF VARIANCE...    68.35C
  STANCARD ERROR OF ESTIMATE......... 1352.492
       (ADJUSTED FOR D.F.)........... 1434.534

  VARIAELE      REGRESSION     STD. ERRCR CF      COMPUTED
   NUMBER       COEFFICIENT     REG. COEFF.        T-VALUE
     3            1.46943        0.15325            9.589
     2            3.01873        1.18725            2.543
  INTERCEPT     140.56226
```

Note that, logically, the multiple correlation coefficient R increased from 0.952 for just one independent variable to 0. __________ for the two independent variables. And the coefficient of determination increased from 0.906 for one inde-

0.975 (or 0.972)

0.951

pendent variable to ______________ for the two independent variables. (To repeat, this is designated as the CUMULATIVE PROPORTION REDUCED in the printout.)

9

personal income
0.986 (or 0.981)
0.971
2.9

In STEP 3, the remaining independent variable, namely, ______________ ______________, is included. Thus, the following printout includes all of the three independent variables. Logically, R increased from 0.975 for two variables to ______________ for all three. Likewise, the coefficient of determination increased from 0.951 for two independent variables to ______________ for all three. Including all three independent variables, only ______________ percent of the variation in annual sales is not explained.

```
STEP  3

VARIABLE ENTERED..... 4

SUM OF SQUARES REDUCED IN THIS STEP....  5280771.000
PROPORTION REDUCED IN THIS STEP........        0.020

CUMULATIVE SUM OF SQUARES REDUCED......255339024.000
CUMULATIVE PROPORTION REDUCED..........        0.971

FOR  3 VARIABLES ENTERED
  MULTIPLE CORRELATION COEFFICIENT...       0.986
        (ADJUSTED FOR D.F.)..........       0.981
  F-VALUE FOR ANALYSIS OF VARIANCE...      67.874
  STANDARD ERROR OF ESTIMATE.........    1119.813
        (ADJUSTED FOR D.F.)..........    1269.748

  VARIABLE      REGRESSION       STD. ERROR OF     COMPUTED
   NUMBER       COEFFICIENT       REG. COEFF.       T-VALUE
     3             1.17294          0.19228          6.100
     2             2.26089          1.05008          2.153
     4             1.15578          0.56321          2.052
  INTERCEPT      705.35986
```

10

MULTIPLE REGRESSION

The multiple regression equation

The simple linear regression equation $\bar{Y}_p = a + bX$ portrays the *average* regression between two variables. The multiple regression equation merely extends the simple regression equation to include the many independent variables being used to predict the one dependent variable. Complete the general form of the multiple regression equation applicable to this problem.

b_4X_4

$$\bar{Y}_p = a + b_2X_2 + b_3X_3 + \text{______________}$$

11

In the multiple regression equation, a is called the *intercept* and is a constant. The various b values (b_2, b_3, b_4) are also constants. They are alternatively called *b coefficients, beta coefficients,* or *net regression coefficients*. In the computer printout they are designated as just *regression coefficients*. These are shown for STEP 3.

```
VARIABLE      REGRESSION
 NUMBER       COEFFICIENT
   3             1.17294
   2             2.26089
   4             1.15578
INTERCEPT      705.35986
```

'he regression coefficient of 2.26089 indicates that if the number of retail outlets in he territory increased by 1, annual sales would increase by $2,260.89. (The other ariables are assumed to remain constant.) Interpret the meaning of the b_3 coefficient.

____

______________. The complete equation, called the ______________ ______________ ______________, for this problem is (insert actual umbers in the equation):

$\bar{Y}_p =$ ______________________________

For each increase of one new automobile registration, annual sales will increase $1,172.94. (This assumes that the other variables remain constant.)

multiple regression equation

$\bar{Y}_p = 705.35986 + 2.26089X_2 + 1.17294X_3 + 1.15578X_4$

2

'o illustrate its use, suppose that in some future year the analyst wanted to predict ie annual sales in a certain territory. There were 900 retail outlets in the territory, ie average monthly new car registrations were 11,000, and the federal government's stimate of first-quarter personal income was $300 million. So $X_2 = 900, X_3 = 11{,}000$, nd $X_4 = 3{,}000$ (because five zeros have been omitted). The predicted annual sales or the territory would be $19,089,360, found by (some digits omitted to facilitate omputations):

$$\bar{Y}_p = \underset{\text{constant } a}{705.36} + \underset{b_2 \text{ (firms)}}{2.26(900)} + \underset{b_3 \text{ (new cars)}}{1.17(11{,}000)} + \underset{b_4 \text{ (personal income)}}{1.16(3000)}$$

Suppose that the analyst wanted to use the multiple regression equation in another territory to estimate annual sales. There were 800 retail outlets, a monthly average of 10,000 new cars registered, and the first-quarter personal income estimate was 250 million. Predicted annual sales for the territory is ______________.

$17,113,360, found by $705.36 + 1,808 + 11,700 + 2,900 (in thousands of dollars)

3

Multiple standard error of estimate

The multiple regression equation gives an *average* predicted value of Y for selected alues of $X_2, X_3 \ldots X_n$. It means in this case that unless the relationship is perfect, ie actual sales at the end of the year will not always be *exactly* the same as the sales ediction made in April. Thus, in practical business problems, there is usually some screpancy between the predicted value and the actual value. This error in prediction in be measured by the *multiple standard error of estimate.*

In the previous chapter (simple correlation), the standard error of estimate was ased on the squared deviations from the regression line. It measured the dispersion scatter about the linear regression line. In multiple regression, it measures the disersion or scatter about the multiple regression plane. That is, the standard error of timate measures the deviations of the actual Y values from the predicted values $\bar{Y}_p$). The formula is quite similar to the one used in simple regression. In this case, is the standard deviation of Y (sales), based on X_2 (retail outlets), X_3 (new cars), and (personal income). It was computed to be $1,119,813.

The multiple standard error of estimate is used in the same manner as the standard ror of estimate was used in the two-variable simple regression case. Assuming at there are a large number of territories and that the values of Y (sales) are mewhat normally distributed around the regression plane, then:

$\bar{Y}_p \pm 1(S_{y \cdot 234})$ encompasses about 68 percent of the actual Y values (sales) around the regression plane.

Using the predicted sales of $19,089,360 from frame #12 [given 900 firms (X_2), 11,00 new cars (X_3), and $300 million personal income (X_4)] the two limits are about $18. million and $20.2 million, found by:

$19,089,360 ± 1 ($1,119,813) = $17,969,547 and $20,209,173 (or rounded, $18.0 million and $20.2 million)

To put it another way, if there were a large number of territories with the same thre combinations (900, 11,000, and $300 million), it could be expected that in abo
68 ________________ percent of the territories the actual annual sales would be b
$20.2 tween approximately $18.0 million and ________.________ million, with the ave
$19,089,360 age sales being about ________________. And, 95 percent of the annual sal would be between $\bar{Y}_p \pm 2S_{y \cdot 234}$, and so forth.

Finally, it should be noted that, as expected, when the multiple coefficient of co relation increased as each dependent variable was entered, the multiple standa error of estimate decreased.

Step	*Enter Variable*	*Multiple Correlation Coefficient*	*Standard Error of Estimate*
1	3	0.952	$1,754,659
2	2	0.975	1,352,492
3	4	0.986	1,119,813

14

In summary of this multiple correlation and regression analysis, the objective was
dependent predict the annual sales of a territory, designated as the ________________ vari ble, as early as April, on the basis of the number of retail outlets in the territo (X_2), new car registrations (X_3), and personal income (X_4). In order to determine t relationship between the dependent variable and the three independent variabl the annual sales and the figures for the three independent variables as of April we gathered for each of the ten marketing territories of the company.

Using the *IBM Stepwise Multiple Regression Program*, in STEP 1 the comput selected the independent variable which was most highly correlated with sales. It w new car registrations ($R = 0.952$). Then, step by step, the independent variables we entered. In STEP 2, the new car registrations and the number of retail outlets co bined to give a better relationship ($R = 0.975$). Finally, in STEP 3, the inclusion all three independent variables raised the correlation coefficient to 0.986. And each independent variable was entered, the error associated with any predicti logically decreased.

In each step the computer also determined the multiple regression equation computing the b values (called the regression coefficients). Based on the regressi equation, the annual sales of a territory could be predicted as early as April by kno ing the number of retail outlets, the number of new cars registered, and the fir quarter personal income in the territory. The error in the prediction is measured the multiple standard error of estimate.

inal Self-Review Examination

irst, answer all of the questions. Then check your nswers against those given at the end of this chapter. coring: 10 problems × 10 points each = 100 possi-le points.

3. Discuss the advantages of multiple correlation and regression analysis compared with simple regression and correlation. ______

4. The general form of the multiple regression equation is: ______

5. Suppose that a multiple regression equation is: $\bar{Y}_p = 16.18 + 0.06X_2 + 21.01X_3 + 2.14X_4 + 3.4X_5 - .87X_6$. The b_5 of 3.4 indicates ______.

6. The error in predicting using the multiple regression equation is measured by the ______.

17. Interpret a coefficient of determination of 0.81. ______

18. If the coefficient of determination is 0.81, what is the correlation coefficient? (*a*)______ Interpret (*b*)______

19. If the coefficient of determination is 0.81, what is the coefficient of nondetermination? (*a*)______ Interpret (*b*)______

20. In multiple correlation and regression analysis the value of the coefficient of determination, the coefficient of nondetermination, and the correlation coefficient may be between 0 and +1. (true/false) (*a*)______. If false, explain (*b*)______

21. The variable to be predicted in a multiple regression problem is called the ______ ______ variable.

Answers to Final Self-Review Examination

13. The use of simple correlation in real business problems usually indicates that, say, only 70 percent of the variation in Y is based on the one independent variable (X). This indicates that there are other variables which must be affecting the dependent variable Y. Multiple correlation and regression analysis includes the possible effect of many variables on the dependent variable.
14. $\bar{Y}_p = a + b_2X_2 + b_3X_3 + \ldots b_nX_n$
15. For each increase of 1 in the variable X_5, $\bar{Y}_p$ will increase by 3.4 (assuming that the other variables remain constant).
16. standard error of the estimate
17. 81 percent of the variation in $\bar{Y}_p$ is attributable to the independent variables (X_2, X_3, and so on)
18. (*a*) 0.90, found by $\sqrt{0.81}$; (*b*) There is a high degree of association (+1 is perfect correlation).
19. (*a*) 0.19; (*b*) 19 percent of the variation in $\bar{Y}_p$ is not attributable to the independent variables.
20. true
21. dependent

chapter

17

ime series analysis

1

\ time series is a set of data taken periodically, usually yearly, quarterly, monthly, or ʋeekly. Examples of a time series are the annual sales of the IBM Corporation since 952, and the monthly production of automobiles since 1949.

One purpose of analyzing data over a period of time is to make long-term or hort-term forecasts. Long-term forecasts of sales, production, or imports might be or 5, 10, 15, or 20 years. These forecasts are made to assist management in develop-ng a strategy and alternative strategies. For example, the United States Forest Serv-ce revealed that in 1960 ten billion board feet of lumber were used, but by 2000 the emand will be 21 billion board feet. (The strategy of Georgia-Pacific to meet this emand is to plant five trees for every one cut down.)

Short-term forecasts, usually of under one year, are common. Examples are pre-ictions of the level of Christmas sales, third-quarter employment, and the following tatement which appeared in *Business Week:* "Gross national product rose at an nnual rate of 7.5% in the first quarter. It moderated to 6.2% in the second, 5.1% in e third, and, estimates are that the rise will be 3.8% in the fourth." (*Business Veek*, April 3, 1978, p. 20.)

OMPONENTS OF A TIME SERIES

Using the classical approach to time eries analysis, data over a period of ime has four components: namely, 1) long-term or secular trend, (2) cycli-al variation, (3) seasonal variation, and 4) irregular or random variation.

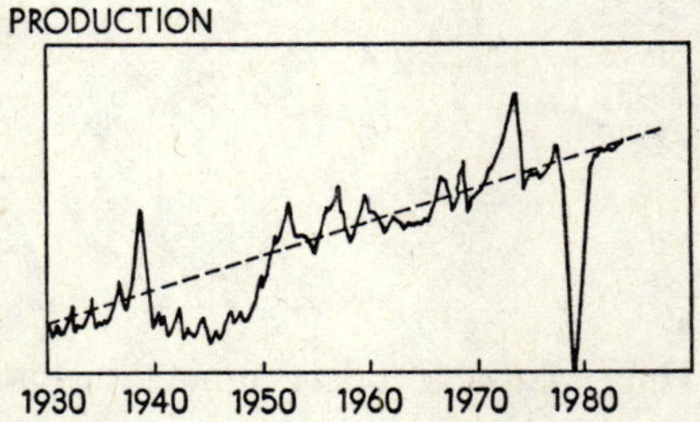

The production series shown at ight contains monthly data since 1930. The dashed line characterizes the aver-ge upward movement, or the long-term secular trend, of production since 1930. It is alled the *secular trend* line. Note that there is considerable cyclical variation above nd below ____________ ____________ line.

secular trend

3

ECULAR TREND

There are many types of growth curves which can describe the long-term move-nent of a business and economic series. The dashed line drawn through the sales eries in Figure A typifies the growth in sales from 1957. Describe the growth. _____

____

Sales had an initial period of slow growth followed by a period of rapid growth. In recent years sales have leveled off.

The straight line drawn through the production series in Figure B best describes th trend in production since 1958.

FIGURE A

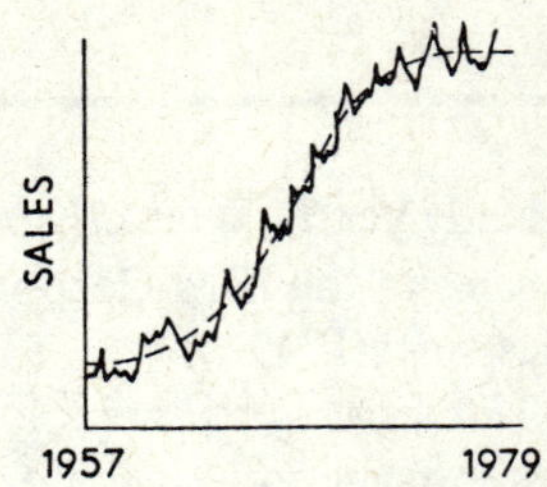

FIGURE B

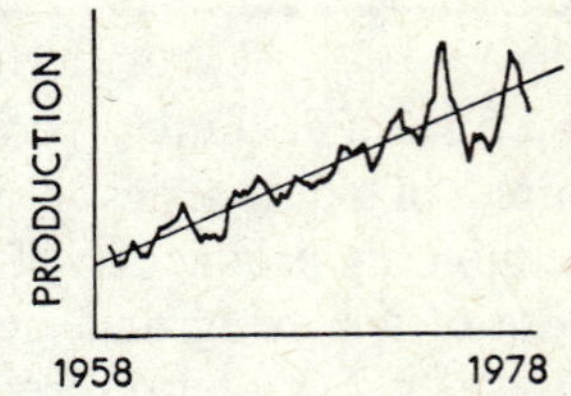

4

STRAIGHT-LINE (LINEAR) TRENDS

Arithmetic straight-line trend

If the long-term trend pattern tends to follow a straight line when plotted on arithmetic graph paper, it indicates that the trend line is increasing (or decreasing) at a constant absolute amount. The imports of an item is an illustration. (The number of time periods have been kept at a minimum to facilitate computations.)

Year	*Imports (\$ Billions)*
1974	\$3
1975	5
1976	4
1977	7
1978	9

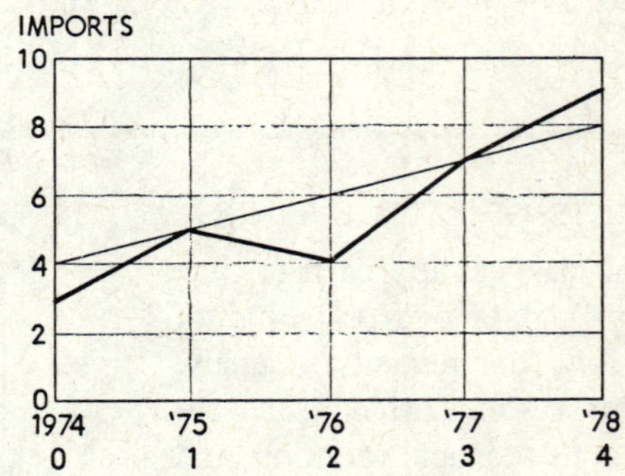

Three methods of determining the linear-trend equation will be examined: namely, th *freehand* method, the *semiaverage* method, and the method of *least squares.*

The freehand method. A straight line has been drawn through the data shown in th preceding graph. The year 1974 is designated as the origin, or zero year. The year 197 is coded 1; 1976 is coded 2; . . . and 1978 is coded 4. Note that the line intercepts th
4 *Y*-axis in the zero year (1974) at \$________ billion. This is *a* in the linea equation $\bar{Y}_p = a + bX$. Also note on the straight line representing imports that th
8 imports increased from about \$4 billion in 1974 to about \$________ billion i 1978. Imports increased on the average \$4 billion (\$8 − \$4) in the four-year perioc
1 or \$________ billion a year. This is *b*. Thus, the straight-line equatio
freehand using the ________ method is:

$\bar{Y}_p = 4 + 1X$

$$\bar{Y}_p = \_\_\_\_ + \_\_\_\_ X$$

where: imports are in billions, the origin (or zero year) is 1974, and *X* increases by unit for each year (i.e., 0, 1, 2, etc.).

5

Plot the following production data. Connect the points by straight lines. Then, using the freehand method draw a straight line through the plots.

Years	*Production (000 Units)*
1974	5
1975	9
1976	7
1977	8
1978	10
1979	9

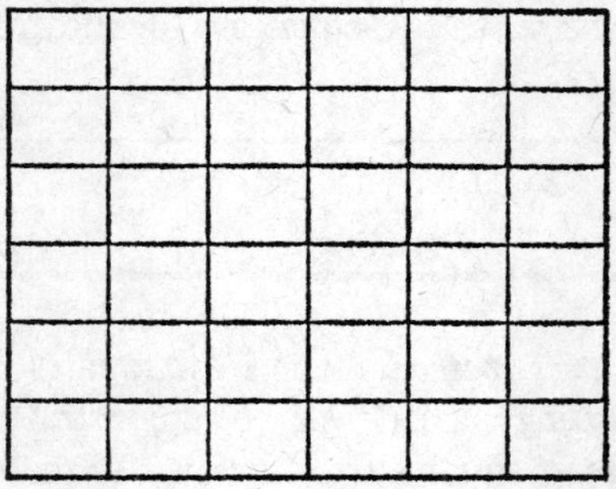

The ________________ method was used to estimate the straight-line trend.

The linear-trend equation is (approximately) $\bar{Y}_p =$ ________________

Based on the linear-trend equation, estimated production for 1981 is ________________ units.

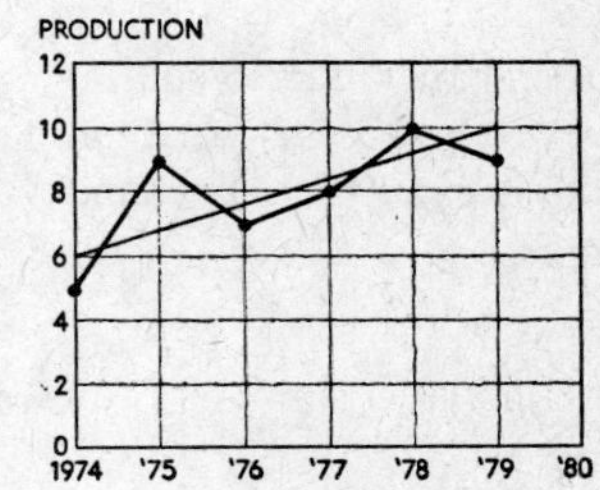

freehand

$\bar{Y}_p = 6 + 0.8X$

11.6 thousand

6

The semiaverage method. Two averages are determined in order to find the trend line. Using the following data on imports, the average of the first half is \$4 billion computed by (\$3 + \$5 + \$4)/3. The average of the other half is \$6.66 billion, computed by (\$4 + \$7 + \$9)/3. (There is an *odd* number of years, and it was arbitrarily decided to include the \$4 billion for 1976 in both averages.)

Year	*Imports (\$ Billions)*	
1974	\$3	
1975	5	$\frac{\$12}{3}$ = \$4 average
1976	4	
1977	7	$\frac{\$20}{3}$ = \$6.66 average
1978	9	

Note that imports rose from the average of \$4 billion in 1975 to \$6.66 billion in 1977, or a \$2.66 billion increase in two years. Thus, the average annual increase is \$1.33 billion, found by \$2.66/2. This (\$1.33 billion) is *b*. The trend line value of \$5.33 billion for 1976 was found by adding \$1.33 billion to the 1975 trend line value of \$4 billion. Then, the average increase in imports (\$1.33 billion) was added to \$5.33 billion to arrive at the 1977 trend value. What is the trend equation? ________________ X

$\bar{Y}_p = 2.67 + 1.33X$

7

The linear-trend equations determined using the freehand method ($\bar{Y}_p = 4 + 1X$) from frame #4 and the semiaverage method ($\bar{Y}_p = 2.67 + 1.33X$) are not identical. The discrepancy is caused by the subjective judgment involved in drawing the freehand line. Four different individuals might arrive at four different equations for the data on imports. However, the freehand method can be used when a quick approximation of the trend equation is needed.

If there are an *even* number of years, the averages for the two halves can be computed directly. Compute the linear-trend equation using the semiaverage method for the production data from frame #5 (repeated as follows):

Year	*Production (000 Units)*
1974	5
1975	9
1976	7
1977	8
1978	10
1979	9

semiaverage

$\bar{Y}_p = 6.34 + 0.66X$

$\bar{Y}_p = 6 + 0.8X$

no

Discrepancy due to subjective judgment used in drawing the freehand line.

The equation using the __________ __________ method is:

$\bar{Y}_p =$ ____________________

The equation using the freehand method from frame #5 is ____________ ____________ Are the two equations identical? (yes/no) ____________

If not, why not? ____

____

8

The least squares method. The least squares method of finding the straight line gives the "best fitting" line. (It can be demonstrated that the sum of the squared deviations from the least squares trend line is less than the sum of the squared deviations from the line determined using either the freehand method or the semiaverage method.)

Using the least squares method, and the import data given previously, the trend equation will be computed. To arrive at the equation, the sums, squares, and other figures needed are shown in the following table: n is the number of years. In this problem there are five years.

Year	*Imports (\$ Billions)* *Y*	*X*	*XY*	*X*²	*Y*²
1974	\$ 3	0	0	0	9
1975	5	1	5	1	25
1976	4	2	8	4	16
1977	7	3	21	9	49
1978	9	4	36	16	81
	\$28	10	70	30	180

Two equations are solved simultaneously. They are:

$$\text{I:}\quad \Sigma Y = na + b\Sigma X$$
$$\text{II:}\quad \Sigma XY = a\Sigma X + b\Sigma X^2$$

$$28 = 5a + 10b$$
$$70 = 10a + 30b$$

Equation I can be multiplied by 10, and Equation II by 5 to eliminate a:

$$(10\times)\,280 = 50a + 100b$$
$$(5\times)\,350 = 50a + 150b$$

Subtracting Equation II from Equation I:

$$\text{I: } 280 = 50a + 100b$$
$$\text{II: } 350 = 50a + 150b$$
$$-70 = -50b$$
$$b = 1.4$$

The b value of 1.4 can be substituted in Equation I or Equation II to solve for a.

$$\text{Equation I:}\quad 28 = 5a + 10b$$
$$28 = 5a + 10(1.4)$$
$$14 = 5a$$
$$a = 2.8$$

'he equation is $\bar{Y}_p = 2.8 + 1.4X$ where imports are in billions of dollars and 1974 is he origin or zero year.

Using the same production figures (frame #5), plot the data. Then determine the inear trend equation using the least squares ethod. The equation is ______________ ______________ where production is in ______________ ______________ and the origin is ______________. The ______________ ______________ method was used.

The two equations are:
$48 = 6a + 15b$
$132 = 15a + 55b$

$\bar{Y}_p = 6.25 + 0.7X$

thousands of units
1974
least squares

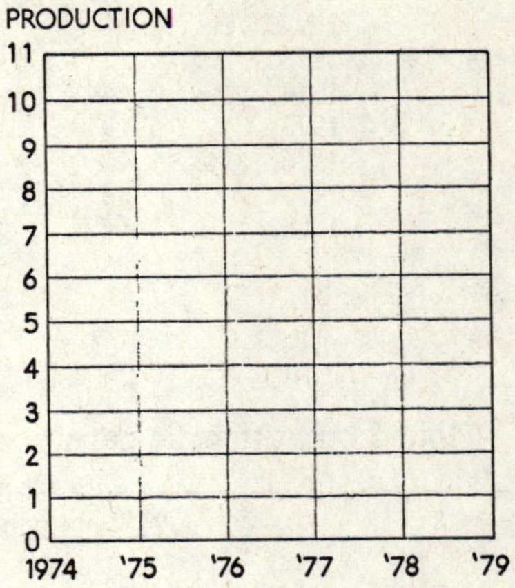

Determine the coordinates for the straight line and lot the line. Two coordinates are:

$X = 0,\ \bar{Y}_p =$ ______________, and
$X = 4,\ \bar{Y}_p =$ ______________

6.25
9.05

Using the equation, the projected production for 985 is ______________ units.

13.95 (13,950 units)

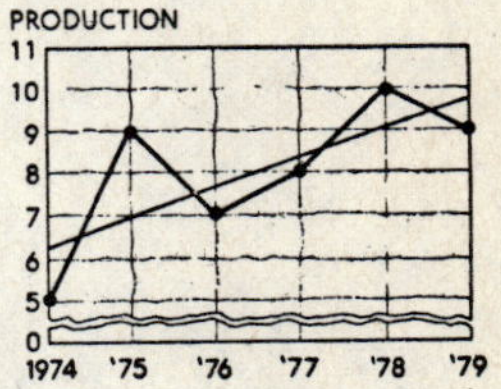

Semilogarithmic straight-line trend

A semilogarithmic straight-line trend is appropriate when the series of sales, production, and so forth is considered to be increasing or decreasing at a somewhat constant *rate*. Thus, an arithmetic straight-line equation should be used if overall the data s increasing (or decreasing) at a somewhat constant (amount/rate) ______________ ______________ and a semilogarithmic straight-line equation should be used if the data s changing at a somewhat constant ______________.

amount
rate

0 ---

The differences in the two series are shown in Figure A and Figure B.

FIGURE A

Year	Sales ($000)
1972	$10
1973	20
1974	17
1975	25
1976	34
1977	31
1978	40

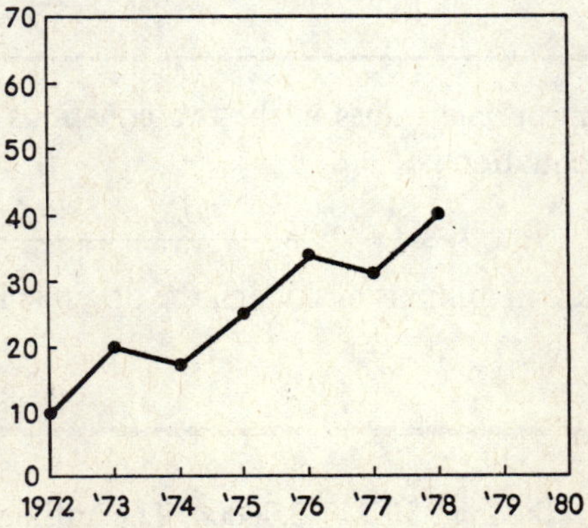

Plotted on arithmetic paper, sales on the average are increasing at (approximately) constant ______________, but the rate of increase is ______________ ver the period of time.

amount decreasing

FIGURE B

Year	*Exports (Millions)*
1972	1
1973	2
1974	4
1975	9
1976	16
1977	33
1978	64

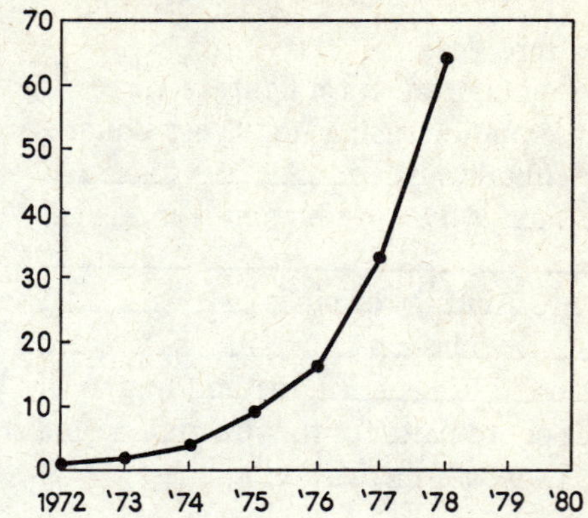

Plotted on arithmetic paper, exports are increasing at (approximately) a constant

rate ____________ but the amount of increase is ____________

increasing ____________ over the period of time.

11

The semilogarithmic trend equation can be found using the least squares method. The two equations to be solved simultaneously are:

$$\text{I:}\quad \Sigma \log Y = na + b\Sigma X$$
$$\text{II:}\quad \Sigma X \log Y = a\Sigma X + b\Sigma X^2$$

Sales in the following table appear to be increasing at a somewhat constant rate (about 50 percent). The sums and other figures needed to find the trend line equation follow.

Year	*Sales (\$ Millions)*	*X*	*log Y*	*X log Y*	*X²*
1973	\$1.00	0	0.0000	0.0000	0
1974	1.50	1	.1761	0.1761	1
1975	2.25	2	.3522	0.7044	4
1976	3.38	3	.5289	1.5867	9
1977	5.06	4	.742	2.8168	16
		10	1.7614	5.2840	30

Insert the appropriate values in the two equations and solve for b and a. The semilogarithmic equation is:

$\log \bar{Y}_p = .00004 + .1761X$

$$\log \bar{Y}_p = \underline{\qquad\qquad\qquad}$$

where sales are in millions of dollars, the origin is 1973, and X increases one unit eac year.

12

When $X = 0$, the log of $\bar{Y}_p = 0.00004$. The antilog of 0.00004 is approximately 1.0C Thus, one of the coordinates on the line is $X = 0$, $\bar{Y}_p = 1.00$. Determine the $\bar{Y}_p$ valu

approximately 5.07 when $X = 4$ ____________. The forecast of sales for th

approximately 25.7 year 1981 is ____________.

13

Now plot the three points on the semilogarithmic graph paper.

The straight-line trend is (arithmetic/semilogarithmic) ______________. Being semilogarithmic, b represents a *percent* change in Y for each increase of one in X. The logarithm of b is 0.1761 and the antilog of that number is ______________. This indicates that sales have been increasing about 50 percent on the average from 1973 to 1977. The forecast for 1981 of \$25.7 million is based on an average annual increase of ______________ percent.

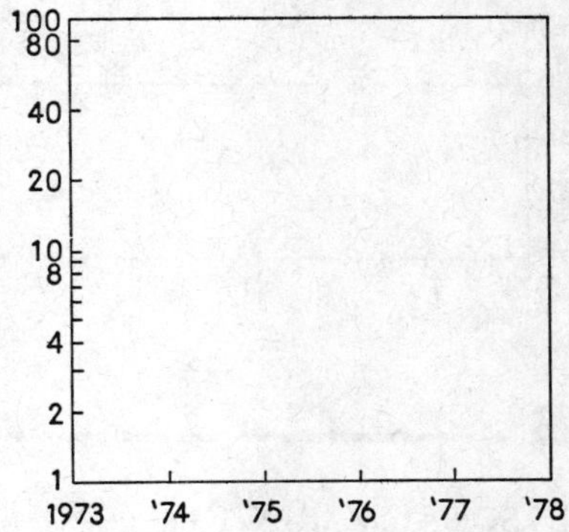

semilogarithmic
1.50
50

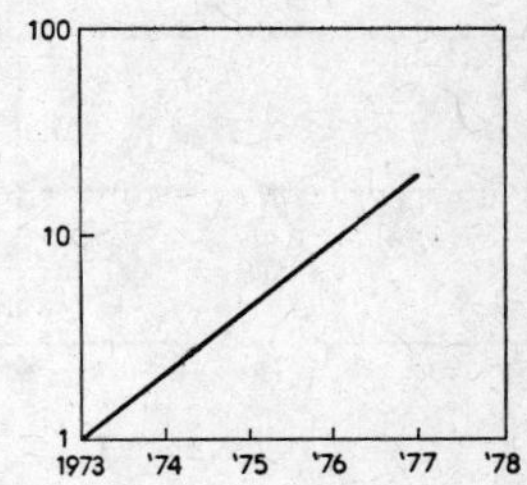

14

The price of an electronic part increased as follows:

Determine the semilogarithmic straight-line trend equation using the least squares method: $\log \bar{Y}_p =$ ______________. Price increased about ______________ percent on the average per year.

Years	*Price*
1976	\$1.92
1977	2.40
1978	2.89
1979	3.57

The equations to be solved
$1.6771 = 4a + 6b$
$2.9601 = 6a + 14b$

$\log \bar{Y}_p = 0.2859 + 0.0889X$

about 23 percent

15

CYCLICAL VARIATION

Most businesses have periods of prosperity, recession, depression, and recovery. These movements are called *business cycles* if the duration of the cycle is more than a year. The annual data from frame #8 is used to illustrate how the cycle is isolated from the time series. The annual dollar volume of imports contains trend and cycle, designated by TC. If the original data are divided by trend (T), a cyclical relative (index) results. That is $[TC/T](100) = C$. Or, $[Y/\bar{Y}_p](100) = C$.

The straight-line equation from frame #8 is $\bar{Y}_p = 2.8 + 1.4X$ where imports are in billions and 1974 is the origin. Complete the table.

Year	*Imports* Y	$\bar{Y}_p$	$\frac{Y}{\bar{Y}_p}$	*Cyclical Index* C
1974	\$3	\$2.8	$\left[\left(\frac{3}{2.8}\right)\right]$	(100) = 107.1
1975	5	4.2	$\left[\left(\frac{5}{4.2}\right)\right]$	(100) = 119.0
1976	4	___	___	( ) = ___
1977	7	___	___	( ) = ___
1978	9	___	___	( ) = ___

The original data and the trend line are portrayed as follows.

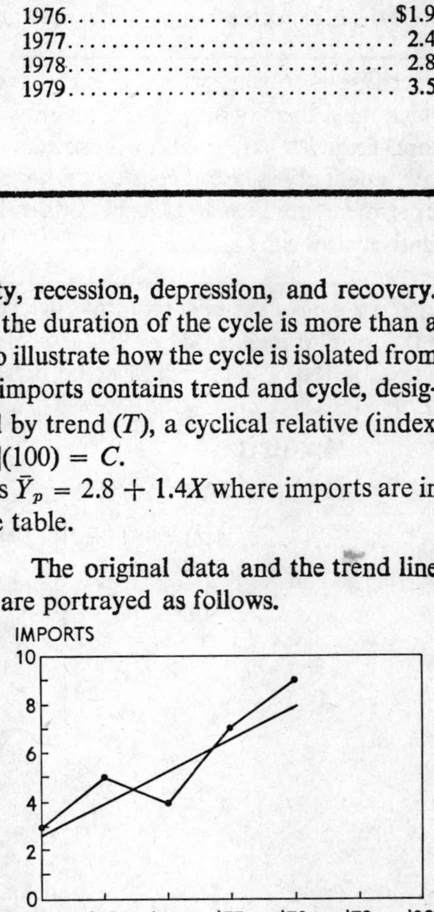

$\bar{Y}_p$	$Y_p/\bar{Y}_p$	C
\$5.6	(4/5.6) (100)	= 71.4
7.0	(7/7.0) (100)	= 100.0
8.4	(9/8.4) (100)	= 107.1

In 1976, imports were 28.6 percent below normal (i.e., 28.6 percent below the long-term trend). Imports were 7.1 percent above normal in 1978.

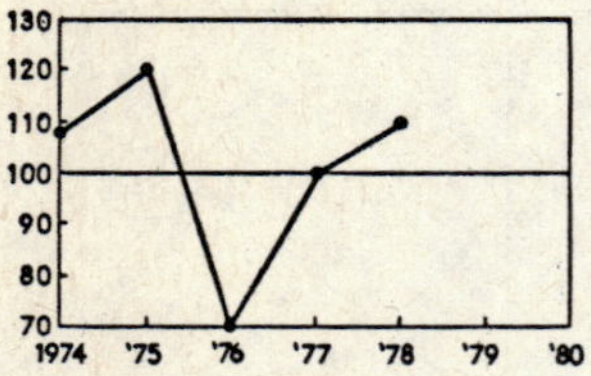

Plot the cyclical indexes.

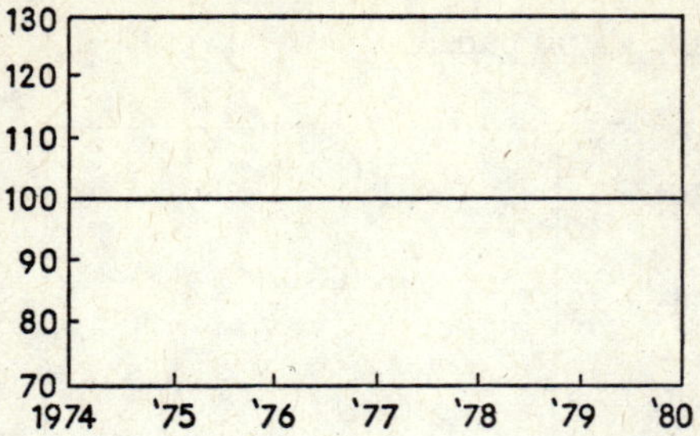

Imports were 7.1 percent above normal in 1974 and 19.0 percent above normal in 1975 (a period of relative prosperity). Interpret the 1976 and 1978 indexes.____

16

SEASONAL VARIATION

(in any order) trend, cycle, irregular

the first few months of the year, and during the summer

typical seasonal

Numerous methods have been developed to measure the typical seasonal fluctuation in a time series. The methods vary from a rather simple approach to sophisticated methods employing electronic computers. Four such methods are: (1) a method using averages, (2) a ratio-to-trend method, (3) a commonly used ratio-to-moving-average method, and (4) an exponential smoothing method.

The purpose of employing one of these methods is to isolate seasonal (S), i.e., exclude the other three components of a time series; namely, ________________, ________________, and ________________. The usual procedure is to start with a monthly series such as sales, production, or other data which may, or may not, have a repetitive seasonal pattern. The sales of a department store (Exhibit 1) are used for illustration. In order to determine whether the series does have a definable seasonal pattern, a *tier* chart may be drawn (Exhibit 2). Note that the department store usually has periods of high sales in the spring and at Christmas and relatively low sales ________________________ and ________________________. Using one of the methods mentioned (or others) a *typical seasonal* pattern is determined (Exhibit 3). These typical seasonals are in the form of indexes. The average of the 12 ____________ ____________ indexes is 100. The typical seasonal indexes have been plotted (Exhibit 4).

EXHIBIT 1

Sales ($000), 1973

Jan.	$401
Feb.	398
Mar.	403
Apr.	416
etc.	etc.

EXHIBIT 2

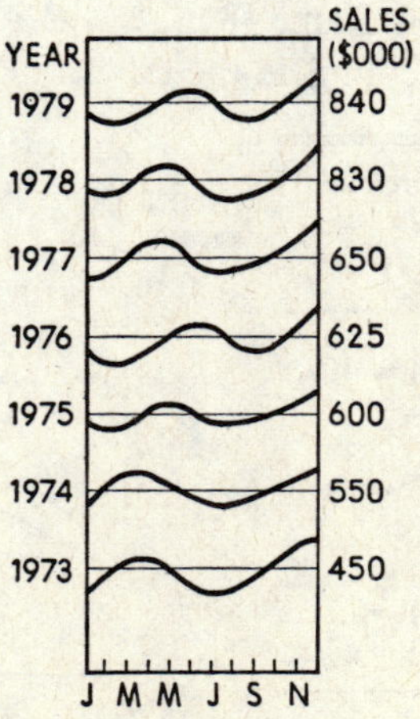

EXHIBIT 3

Typical Seasonal Indexes

Jan.	86.2
Feb.	81.3
Mar.	99.6
Apr.	101.3
May	98.7
June	97.1
July	99.8
Aug.	101.2
Sept.	103.6
Oct.	105.1
Nov.	110.9
Dec.	115.2

EXHIBIT 4

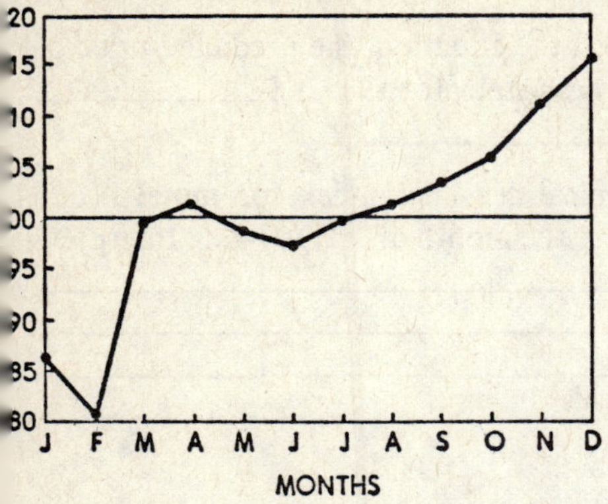

The typical seasonal index of 86.2 for January indicates that typically the sales of this department store are 13.8 percent below the average for the year. The typical seasonal index of 115.2 for December indicates that ______________________________.

Typical December sales are 15.2 percent above the average for the year

The typical seasonal pattern, which is a composite of past experience, can be used by the management of the department store to make comparisons with the typical seasonal pattern of all department stores. It can also be used s a bench mark against which current sales can be compared. For example, this year ıanagement tried several new sales innovations during the months of January and ebruary. The seasonal index for those two months dropped to 95.6 and 93.8 respecvely. Sales were still below the average for the year (100), but how did sales for those vo months this year compare with sales during a typical January and February? From Exhibit 3.) ______________________________.

The sales promotion was apparently a success. Sales for January and February of this year were above the typical sales for January and February determined from past experience.

Final Self-Review Examination

First, answer all of the questions. Then check your answers against those given at the end of this chapter. Scoring: 10 problems × 10 points each = 100 possible points.

17. The four components of a time series are ______________________________, ______________________________, ______________________________, and ______________________________.

18. Plot the following sales data and estimate the straight-line trend equation using the freehand method. The trend equation is: (*a*)______________________________

Year	*Sales ($000)*
1973	$ 2
1974	6
1975	4
1976	6
1977	10
1978	8

What is one weakness to the freehand approach? (*b*)______________________________

____

19. Now, using the semiaverage method, determine the linear-trend line for the sales data shown in frame #18. (Carry calculations to the nearest hundredth, such as 2.68.) The equation is ______________________________.

20. Referring again to the sales data (frame #18), determine the arithmetic straight-line trend equation using the least squares method. The equation is ______________________________.

21. Based on the straight-line trend equation (frame #20), the predicted sales for 1984 are $______________________________.

22. Based on the same equation (frame #20), the cyclical index for 1975 is (*a*)______________________________. Interpret (*b*)______________________________.

23. The per-share price of Amberbold Limited increased as shown.

Year	*Price*
1976	\$ 6.81
1977	8.74
1978	11.20
1979	14.50

A cursory examination of the data revealed that the price of Amberbold stock has been increasing at a somewhat constant rate (about 30 percent a year on the average). Thus, a semilogarithmic straight-line trend equation should be used. The equation is ____________.

24. Based on the semilog equation, the price of Amberbold stock increased ____________ percent on the average a year. (nearest percent)

25. Based on the equation, the predicted price of Amberbold stock for 1985 is \$____________.
____________.

26. The typical seasonal index for motel occupancy for the month of July is 140.6. Interpret.
____
____
____
____

Answers to Final Self-Review Examination

17. (In any order) trend, cycle, seasonal, irregular.
18. (*a*) $\bar{Y}_p = 3 + 1.4X$
    (*b*) Subjective judgment is involved drawing the freehand line.
19. $\bar{Y}_p = 2.67 + 1.33X$
20. $\bar{Y}_p = 2.85 + 1.26X$
21. \$16.71 (or \$16,710)
22. (*a*) 74.5, found by (4/5.37)(100)
    (*b*) Sales in 1975 were 25.5 percent below the trend line.
23. The two equations are
    I : $3.9852 = 4a + 6b$
    II: $6.5241 = 6a + 14b$
    $\log \bar{Y}_p = 0.83241 + 0.10926X$
24. Over 28 percent
25. \$65.40, found by $\log \bar{Y}_p = 0.83241 + 0.10926(9)$
26. Typically, motel occupancy in July is 40.6 percent above the average for the year.

Indexes

chapter

18

1

A typical television, radio, or newspaper release might be "Consumer prices rose again this month, according to the U.S. Department of Commerce. The Consumer Price Index was up one tenth to 196.8, meaning that prices this month were 96.8 percent above those in 1967." In addition to the well-known Consumer Price Index, there are hundreds of indexes published on a daily, weekly, monthly, quarterly, and annual basis by the federal government, universities, financial institutions, and others.

To illustrate the construction of an index, assume that the annual production of bituminous coal was 4 billion tons in 1974 and 5 billion tons in 1978. The index of production for 1978, based on 1974, was 125, computed by dividing 5 billion tons by 4 billion tons and then multiplying by 100; that is, $[5/4](100) = 125$.

If the price of Grade D plywood was $200 a thousand board feet in 1975 and $180 in 1979, the price index for plywood for 1979 based on 1975 (1975 = 100) is: _____. **90**

2

Note that:

1. **An index is actually a percent. The percent sign is seldom given, however.**
2. **Each index has a *base* period. The base period of the Consumer Price Index is 1967.**
3. The base number of practically all indexes equals 100. There is no specific reason, however, why 10, 1,000, or any other number cannot be used as a base.
4. Most indexes are carried either to the nearest tenth, such as the Consumer Price Index of 196.8 from frame #1, or to the nearest whole number, such as the bituminous coal index of 125.
5. If the base is 100, the percent change from the base period to the current month or year can be easily determined. For example, the Consumer Price Index of 196.8 indicates that prices increased _____._____ percent from the base period to the current month. The price index of 90.0 for plywood indicates that the price of plywood (increased/decreased) __________ by __________ percent from 1975 to 1979.

96.8

decreased
10

3

One might ask, Why are such indexes as the Consumer Price Index and indexes of industrial production, department store sales, and so on, compiled and published? Indexes facilitate a comparison and analysis of unlike series, such as production, employment, prices, and sales, by establishing a base period and converting subsequent numbers into percents (indexes). Converting data to indexes also makes it easier to compare the trend in a series composed of exceptionally large numbers. For example, if the total sales of a product were $295,932,456.94 in 1967, and increased to $296,-044,529.00 in 1978, the increase would appear significantly large. The 1978 sales expressed as an index based on 1967 sales, however, is 100.04. This indicates that sales increased only ______.

4/100 of 1 percent

Furthermore, an index is also a convenient way of expressing a change in the total of a heterogeneous group of items. The Index of Industrial Production, for example, includes many different items, such as steel production, television production, and automobile production, expressed in tons, barrels, yards, each, and many other different units.

Economists and others watch the Consumer Price Index and other index series for signs of excessive inflation, recession, and so forth. Some labor-management contracts have escalator clauses in them automatically providing a specified increase in wages should the Consumer Price Index rise a given number of points. Businessmen compare changes in their production or prices with other firms or the industry using indexes.

4

CONSTRUCTION OF INDEXES

Unweighted index numbers

Unweighted indexes are also called *simple* indexes, or *relatives*. The base for the following illustration was arbitrarily chosen as 1975. The index for 1978 is 150, found by $60/40 times 100. Complete the table.

Year	Bale Price of Jute	Index (1975 = 100)
1974	$36	______ = ______
1975	40	[$40/$40](100) = 100.0
1976	46	______ = ______
1977	53	______ = ______
1978	60	[$60/$40](100) = 150.0

[$36/$40](100) = 90.0

[$46/$40](100) = 115.0

[$53/$40](100) = 132.5

5

The relative (index) for 1978 of 150.0, using 1975 = 100, indicates that ______ ______. If the average of 1975 and 1976 were selected as the base (written 1975–76 = 100), the price relative (index) for 1978 would be ______.______.

the price of jute increased 50% from 1975 to 1978

139.5 found by [$60/$43] (100)

6

A slightly more complex problem would be to determine an index of food prices. Assume for this illustration that the typical family eats only three food items: bread, milk, and pomegranates. An unweighted index of food prices for 1979 in the following example would be computed by dividing the total of the prices for 1979 (p_n) by the 1967 (p_o) total. That is:

$$P = \frac{\Sigma p_n}{\Sigma p_o}(100) = \_\_\_\_(100) = \_\_\_\_.\_\_\_\_$$

$$P = \frac{164¢}{130¢}(100) = 126.2$$

Item	1967 Price p_o	1979 Price p_n
Bread (loaf)	30¢	28¢
Milk (quart)	40	36
Pomegranates (box)	60	100
Total	—	—

$\Sigma p_o = 130¢$ $\Sigma p_n = 164¢$

---

he method used in the preceding example is not appropriate. The unweighted price ıdex of 126.2 seems illogical because the two major food items (bread and milk) ecreased and only pomegranates, which are eaten infrequently, increased. It seems ɔgical, therefore, that the prices of bread and milk should be given more *weight* than ıe price of pomegranates.

Veighted indexes

The same data from frame #6 is used to illustrate the construction of a *weighted* rice index. The consumption of each food in the base period of 1967 is given in the cond column and is designated q_o. To determine the total amount spent for food in ıe base period, the quantity of each food item consumed is multiplied by the corre-ɔonding price. Find the total amount spent for food in the base period by completing ıe middle column.

In order to measure the effect of price, an assumption is made that the amount of ɔod consumed by a typical person did not change between the base period (1967) and 979. The 1974 prices (p_n) are multiplied by the corresponding quantities consumed in 967. Complete the right column in the following table designated as p_nq_o.

Item	1967 Price p_o	1967 Amount Consumed q_o	p_oq_o	1979 Price p_n	p_nq_o
Bread (loaf)	30¢	2,000	$600.00	28¢	$560.00
Milk (quart)	40	500	____	36	____
Pomegranates (box)	60	2	____	100	____
Total			$____		$____

$200.00	$180.00
1.20	2.00
$801.20	$742.00

---

etermine the weighted index of price for 1979, using 1967 as the base.

$$P = \frac{\Sigma p_nq_o}{\Sigma p_oq_o}(100) = \_\_\_\_\_\_(\_\_\_\_) = \_\_\_\_.\_\_\_\_$$

$$\frac{\$742.00}{\$801.20}(100) = 92.6$$

---

he unweighted price index of 126.2 computed in frame #6 indicated an increase of .2 percent in the price of food from 1967 to 1979. The price index found using the

The composite price of food declined 7.4 percent from 1967 to 1979.

The two major food items (bread and milk) declined in price, but only one minor item (pomegranates) increased in price. Thus, it is logical that the index is under 100.

weighted method (92.6) gives a more logical answer. Interpret the index of 92.

____

Why is weighted index of 92.6 a more logical answer? ______________________________

____

____

10

Using the weighted method to compute a price index, the quantity in the base perio is held constant. This method was developed by Etienne Laspeyres in the 1700's.

The Laspeyres method of weighting is also used to compute a quantity index. Th prices in the base year (1964) are held constant in the following illustration in order t determine the index of industrial production. Complete the table and find the weighte index of industrial production.

Item	*1964 Price* p_0	*1964 Quantity Produced* q_0	p_0q_0	*1978 Quantity Produced* q_n	p_0q_n
Automobile (each)	$2,000	10	$______	9	$______
Oil (barrel)	4	800	______	1,000	______
Transformers (each)	100	40	______	300	______
Color film (roll)	2	1,000	______	5,000	______
Total			$______		$______

p_0q_0	p_0q_n
$20,000	$18,000
3,200	4,000
4,000	30,000
2,000	10,000
$29,200	$62,000

$$\frac{\$62{,}000}{\$29{,}200}(100) = 212.3$$

$$Q = \frac{\Sigma p_0q_n}{\Sigma p_0q_0}(100) = \_\_\_\_\_\_\_\_\_\_ = \_\_\_\_\_\_\_\_\_\_$$

11

In addition to price indexes and quantity indexes, there are *value* indexes and *special purpose* indexes. As the name implies, a value index measures the change in the tota value of a group of products, commodities, and so on. A value index, such as the well known Index of Department Store Sales, needs both the base-year prices and bas quantities and the present-year prices and present-year quantities for its construction Complete the following table.

COMPUTATIONS FOR A VALUE INDEX

Item	*1970 Price* p_0	*1970 Quantity Sold* q_0	p_0q_0	*1979 Price* p_n	*1979 Quantity Sold* q_n	p_nq_n
TV sets (each)	$400	50	$______	$500	30	$______
Cologne (set)	5	300	______	4	200	______
Shoes (pair)	10	1,000	______	20	1,500	______
Girdles (each)	4	2,000	______	4	3,000	______
Total			$______			$______

p_0q_0	p_nq_n
$20,000	$15,000
1,500	800
10,000	30,000
8,000	12,000
$39,500	$57,800

The Index of Department Store Sales is found by dividing the total dollar volume of sales in 1979 by the total dollar volume of sales in the base period (1970). Design a formula, insert essential figures in the formula, and find the index.

$V =$ ______ $=$ ______ $=$ ______

$$V = \frac{\Sigma p_n q_n}{\Sigma p_o q_o}(100) = \frac{\$57{,}800}{\$39{,}500}(100) = 146.3$$

12

Special-purpose indexes are usually a combination of a number of price, quantity, and value indexes. The Forbes Index and the Business Week Index are two examples of ______-______ indexes. Various indicators and indexes selected by the statistician are arbitrarily weighted by him to find the composite weighted index. For example, note in the following table that in the judgment of the statistician, the Industrial Production Index should be weighted 50 percent. The Employment Index was arbitrarily weighted 30 percent and Money Turnover 20 percent. To determine the composite (weighted) index of business activity for 1977, the production index of 110.0 was weighted by 0.50, employment of 120.0 by 0.30, and money turnover by ______. The index of 109.0, computed by 55 + 36 + 18 for 1977, indicates that general business activity was up 9.0 percent over the 1974 level. Compute the index of business activity for 1978. ______.The index of business activity for 1978 indicates that______ ______ ______.

special purpose

0.20

103.0

general business activity increased three percent from 1974 to 1978.

Year	*Industrial Production Index*	*Employment Index*	*Money Turnover*
	Weight. . .0.50	*0.30*	*0.20*
1974	100.0	100.0	100.0
1977	110.0	120.0	90.0
1978	108.0	116.0	71.0

13

CRITERIA FOR THE CONSTRUCTION OF AN INDEX

One criterion for the selection of a base period for an economic and business index is that conditions be somewhat normal. Why wasn't 1933 given consideration as a base year? ______

It was a depression year

Changes in the basic consumption pattern dictate a revision of an index and a change in the base period from time to time. For example, outboard motors and phonograph records are now included in the CPI.

Another important consideration in the construction of an index is the selection of the items to be included and the weight allocated to each item. The Consumer Price Index includes about 400 consumer items, and the Wholesale Price Index about 2,000. In the Consumer Price Index, beer has a relative weight of 1.06 percent, indicating that ______ percent of a typical consumer's income is spent on beer.

1.06

14

SHIFTING THE BASE

If two or more series being compared are not on the same base, it is difficult to make any meaningful comparison between the series. Suppose that the increase in the prices received by farmers and the increase in all wholesale prices from 1972 to 1978 are to be compared. Note in the following table that the Index of Prices Received by Farmers is on a 1910–14 base but that the Wholesale Price Index is on a 1967 base. Complete the table by shifting both series to a 1972 base (1972 = 100).

Year	*Index of Prices Received by Farmers 1910–14 = 100*	*Index of Prices Received by Farmers 1972 = 100*	*Wholesale Price Index 1967 = 100*	*Wholesale Price Index 1972 = 100*
1972	320	$\frac{320}{320}(100) = 100$	119.1	100.0
1973	413	$\frac{413}{320}(100) = 129.1$	135.3	113.6
1978*	480	—( ) = —.–	220.0	—.–

Source: *Survey of Current Business,* November 1973, pp. S–7, S–8, and *Weekly Supplement,* March 31, 1978, p. 2.
* Estimated.

Farm Index $= \frac{480}{320}(100)$
$= 150.0$
W.P.I. = 184.7, found by
$\frac{220.0}{119.1}(100)$

15

Now that the two series are on a common base, make a comparison of the change in prices from 1972 to 1978. ______________________________
____
____

Wholesale prices increased at a more rapid rate (84.7%) than did farm prices (50.0%) between 1972 and 1978.

16

SPECIAL USES OF THE CONSUMER PRICE INDEX

Real income

The Consumer Price Index measures the change in prices of goods and services bought by city wage earners' and clerical workers' families from one time period (1967) to another time period. The CPI has a number of other applications. One use is to determine the "*real*" *income* of individuals. Two other popular terms are *deflated income* and *income expressed in constant dollars*.

To illustrate the concept of real income, assume that Mr. Typical Wage Earner had an income of \$6,000 in 1970 and that the base of the Consumer Price Index was shifted to 1970, i.e., 1970 = 100. His income this year is estimated to be \$12,000 and the CPI 200. It appears that since his income doubled, his standard of living is higher than in 1970. Note, however, that although his *money income* doubled from \$6,000 to \$12,000, the prices Mr. Typical Wage Earner pays for food, gasoline, clothing, and other items also doubled. Thus, his standard of living remained the ame from 1970 to the present time. So, his buying power (real income) is still $6,000. he computations for real income are as shown in the following table:

Year	Money Income	Consumer Price Index 1970 = 100	Real Income
70	$ 6,000	100	$\frac{\$6,000}{100}(100) = \$6,000$
esent year	$12,000	200	$\frac{\$12,000}{200}(100) = \$6,000$

he income of another wage earner increased from $14,000 in 1971 to $16,000 in 1978. ssume that the Consumer Price Index in 1971 was 140 (1967 = 100) and that the PI was 200 in 1978. The wage earner's real, or deflated, income in 1971 was ______ ad ______________ in 1978. Indicate what happened to his buying power eal income) from 1971 to 1978. Interpret. ______________________________ ______________________________. The ame concept is used to determine the real sales of a company.

$10,000 found by [$14,000/140](100)
$8,000 found by [$16,000/200](100)
His real income decreased $2,000, or 20 percent, from 1971 to 1978, indicating that he can buy less in 1978 than he did in 1971.

7

urchasing power of the dollar

The Consumer Price Index is also used to determine the *purchasing power of the ollar*. Again, assume that the CPI is 200 at the present time (1967 = 100). Thus, ices have doubled from the base period to the present. Another way of stating this to say that the purchasing power of the dollar has been cut in half. Thus, the purasing power of the dollar today, based on prices in the latter part of the 1960's, is aly $0.50 (computed by dividing $1 by 200 and multiplying the answer by 100).

Suppose that the Consumer Price Index was 125.0 in 1974 (1967 = 100). What as the purchasing power of the dollar in 1974 based on prices in the latter part of the 960's? ______________. What is the basic reason for the decline in e purchasing power of a dollar in the 7-year period? ______________________________

$0.80
Prices increased 25 percent during the period 1967 to 1974. Thus, a dollar in 1974 was worth only 80 cents compared with a dollar in the latter part of the 1960's.

inal Self-Review Examination

irst, answer all of the questions. Then check your aswers against those given at the end of this chapter. oring: 10 problems × 10 points each = 100 possie points.

3. Assume that the Index of Industrial Production was 139.2 for January 1978. (1967 = 100.) The base period is (*a*) ______________. The base number index is (*b*)______________. The index of 139.2 indicates that when all production was combined, it (increased/decreased) (*c*)______________ during a period of about (*d*)__________ years.

19. Give two reasons why index numbers are compiled and published.
(1)______________________________
____
(2)______________________________
____

20. Determine the unweighted price index, (simple index) (price relative) for 1979 based on 1977 (see the following table). (*a*)________

Year	Ton Price of Iron Ore
1977	$18
1978	22
1979	54

Interpret the index for 1979 (1977 = 100) (*b*)________________

If 1977–78 were used as the base period, the price relative for 1979 would be (*c*)________

Questions 21, 22, and 23 are based on the following table.

Item	1972 Price	1972 Amount Consumed	1978 Price	1978 Amount Consumed
Oil (barrel)	$ 4	100	5	200
Wool cloth (yard)	2	1,000	2	2,000
Steel (ton)	20	50	15	100

21. Using the Laspeyres method, the weighted index of price is ________.________ for 1978 (1972 = 100).

22. Using the Laspeyres method, the weighted index of quantity is ________.____ for 1978 (1972 = 100).

23. The index of value for 1978 based on 1972 is (*a*)________.________, indicating that the value of these items (increased/decreased) (*b*)________________ about (*c*)________.________ percent from 1972 to 1978.

24. A statistician wishes to design a special-purpose index to measure general business activity in the United States. The base period is to be 1969. In his judgment, the industrial production should be weighted 40, department store sales 30, employment 20, and money turnover (*a*)____________. Determine the special-purpose index of general business activity for 1979. (*b*)______.______

1969 = 100

Year	Index of Industrial Production	Index of Department Store Sales	Index of Employ-ment	Index c Money Turnove
1979	180	90	103	210

25. Indicate two criteria for the construction c an index.

____

26. The price changes in meats and vegetable from 1970 to 1978 are to be compared. However, the two price indexes are on differen bases, making a comparison difficult. Shif the bases and make a comparison of the tw price changes from 1970 to 1978.

Year	Index of the Price of Meats 1963 = 100	Index of the Price of Vegetables 1967 = 100
1970	150	120
1978	180	132

The Index of Meat Prices for 1978 (1970 = 100) is (*a*)________.________ and the Inde of Vegetable Prices for 1978 (1970 = 100) i (*b*)________.________. A comparison o them indicates that (*c*)________________

27. The Consumer Price Index and the money income of Mr. Smith for the years 1970, 1971 and 1978 follow.

Year	Consumer Price Index 1967 = 100	Mr. Smith's Income
1970	110	$ 8,600
1971	120	9,600
1978	144	14,400

Based on 1967, Mr. Smith's real income for 1978 was (*a*) \$_____________. His real income in 1971 was (*b*) \$__________. A comparison of the two real incomes indicates that (*c*)____

Based on the Consumer Price Index given, the purchasing power in 1978 was (*d*) \$__________.______ (1967 = 100). This indicates that if Mr. Absent-Minded misplaced \$1,000 in 1967, and found it in 1978, the \$1,000 could only purchase (*e*) \$______________ worth of goods.

nswers to Final Self-Review Examination

18. (*a*) 1967
 (*b*) 100
 (*c*) increased
 (*d*) 11

19. (In any order.) Indexes facilitate a comparison of unlike series such as production, employment, and sales. When the numbers being compared or analyzed are large (such as total department store sales), it is easier, and more meaningful, to compare percent changes.

20. (*a*) 300
 (*b*) Price of iron ore increased 200 percent from 1977 to 1979.
 (*c*) 270

21. [\$3,250/\$3,400](100) = 95.6

22. [\$6,800/\$3,400](100) = 200.0

23. (*a*) [\$6,500/\$3,400](100) = 191.2
 (*b*) increased
 (*c*) 91.2

24. (*a*) 10
 (*b*) 140.6

25. (In any order.) The base year, or years, should be somewhat normal. The base period should not be too far in the past, or too close to the present year. Consideration should be given to the items to be included in the index and the weight placed on each.

26. (*a*) 120
 (*b*) 110
 (*c*) Meat prices increased 20 percent from 1970 compared with a 10 percent increase in vegetable prices during the same period.

27. (*a*) \$10,000
 (*b*) \$8,000
 (*c*) Although his money income increased \$4,800 (\$14,400 – \$9,600), Mr. Smith's real income only increased \$2,000 (\$10,000 – \$8,000). This indicates, however, that his money increased at a more rapid rate than prices (as measured by the CPI) resulting in a gain in his standard of living.
 (*d*) \$.694
 (*e*) \$694

Glossary of Terms and Formulas

Arithmetic Mean ($\bar{X}$)

Ungrouped data: $\bar{X} = \frac{\Sigma X}{n}$

Grouped data: $\bar{X} = \frac{\Sigma fX}{n}$

The arithmetic average is the sum of all the observations divided by the total number of observations (Chapter 4).

Average Deviation (A.D. or M.D.)

Ungrouped data: A.D. $= \frac{\Sigma|X - \bar{X}|}{n}$

It is also called the *Mean Deviation.* The average deviation is the average of the absolute deviations from the mean, i.e., all deviations from the mean are considered positive (Chapter 5).

Bayes' Rule

$$P(B_i|A) = \frac{P(B_i) \cdot P(A|B_i)}{\sum_i P(B_i) \cdot P(A|B_i)}$$

It is a theorem (formula) for determining the posterior probability $P(B_i|A)$. This is accomplished by revising the prior probability B_i given that event A has occurred. There may be more than one prior probability. The large sigma indicates that all probabilities are to be summed given occurrence A (Chapter 12).

Chi-Square (χ^2)

$$\chi^2 = \sum \frac{(f_o - f_e)^2}{f_e}$$

One use of the statistic chi-square is testing the hypothesis that one set of observed frequencies is significantly different from an expected set of frequencies (Chapter 13).

Confidence Limits

For Variables: $\bar{X} \pm z(s_{\bar{x}})$
For Proportions: $p \pm z(s_p)$

Based on sample data, the confidence limits are two values between which the population mean (or proportion) will fall given a certain level of confidence—such as the 0.95 level (Chapter 9).

Correlation, Coefficient of (r or R)

$$r = \frac{n(\Sigma XY) - (\Sigma X)(\Sigma Y)}{\sqrt{[n(\Sigma X^2) - (\Sigma X)^2]\,[n(\Sigma Y^2) - (\Sigma Y)^2]}}$$

r is the simple coefficient of correlation. It measures the degree of relationship between a dependent variable Y and an independent variable X. In multiple correlation, R gives the degree of relationship between Y and $X_1, X_2 \ldots X_n$ (Chapters 15, 16).

Determination, Coefficient of (r^2 or R^2)

It is the coefficient of correlation squared. (See correlation coefficient for formula.) The coefficient of determination r in simple correlation analysis measures the percent of the variation in Y (the dependent variable) explained by X (the independent variable). In multiple correlation analysis, R^2 measures the percent variation in Y explained by the X's ($X_1, X_2 \ldots X_n$ (Chapter 15, 16).

Finite Multiplier

Computed by: $\sqrt{\frac{N - n}{N - 1}}$

The finite multiplier is also called the finite correction factor. It is applied to the standard error of the mean $s_{\bar{x}}$, or the standard error of the proportion s_p, in a sampling problem. It compensates for the size of the sample n relative to the size of the finite population N (Chapter 9).

Geometric Mean (G.M.)

G.M. $= \sqrt[n]{X_1 \cdot X_2 \cdot X_3 \ldots . X_n}$

It is defined as the nth root of the product of all of the observations in the series. It is usually computed using logarithms. A useful formula for finding e geometric mean increase in sales, production, c. from one period of time to another is:

$$G.M. = \sqrt[n-1]{\frac{\text{Value at end of period}}{\text{Value at beginning of period}}} - 1$$

hapter 4).

dex

As an example, a weighted price index can be und by:

$$P = \frac{\Sigma p_n q_o}{\Sigma p_o q_o}(100)$$

here are price, quality, value and special-purpose dexes. Expressed as a percent, an index can be ed to measure the percent change in one item, or composite of items, from one period of time esignated as the base) to another period of time hapter 18).

edian

$$\text{Median} = L + \frac{\frac{n}{2} - CF}{f}(i)$$

The observations are first arranged from low to gh or vice versa. The median is the point above nich and below which half of the observations lie hapter 4).

ode

$$\text{Mode} = L_1 + \frac{\Delta_1}{\Delta_1 + \Delta_2}(i)$$

It is defined as the value of the most frequently curring item (Chapter 4).

ondetermination, Coefficient of (k^2 or $1 - r^2$ or $- R^2$)

(See correlation coefficient for formula for r.) It the percent of the variation in the dependent vari- le Y not explained by the one independent variable in simple correlation analysis. In multiple correla- on analysis, $1 - R^2$ is a measure of the percent riation in Y not explained by the many inde- endent variables $X_1, X_2 \ldots X_n$ (Chapters 15, 16).

urchasing Power of the Dollar

Computed by: $\frac{\$1}{\text{CPI}}(100)$

It is the reciprocal of the Consumer Price Index and expresses the current value of a dollar in relation to the base period of the index. If the base of the index was 1967 and the purchasing power of the dollar for the current month was $0.85, it indicates that the 1967 dollar is now worth only 85 cents. (Chapter 18).

Quartile Deviation (Q.D.)

$$Q.D. = \frac{Q_3 - Q_1}{2}$$

It is also called the Semi-Interquartile Range. The quartile deviation is defined as half of the distance between the third and the first quartile (Chapter 5).

Range (R)

It is the distance between the highest and lowest value (Chapter 5).

Real Wages

Computed by: $\frac{\$\text{ Wages}}{\text{Consumer Price Index}}(100)$

Real wages, or real income, of an individual represents the dollar value of goods and services a wage earner can buy currently compared with the amount he could purchase in the base period of the index (Chapter 18).

Skewness, Coefficient of (Sk)

$$Sk = \frac{3(\bar{X} - \text{median})}{s}$$

Developed by Karl Pearson, the coefficient of skewness is a relative measure which reveals the degree and the direction (plus or minus) of the skewness of a frequency distribution. There are other similar measures (Chapter 5).

Standard Deviation (s or σ)

Ungrouped data: $s = \sqrt{\frac{\Sigma X^2}{n} - \bar{X}^2}$

Grouped data: $s = \sqrt{\frac{\Sigma f X^2}{n} - \bar{X}^2}$

The standard deviation is the square root of the sum of the squared deviations from the mean divided by the number of observations. It is the most commonly used measure to describe the dispersion in a normal distribution (Chapter 5).

Variance (s^2 or σ^2)

It is the standard deviation squared. See: Standard deviation for formula (Chapter 5).

Variation, Coefficient of (CV)

$$CV = \frac{s}{\bar{X}}(100)$$

It is a percent found by dividing the standard deviation of a distribution by its mean. It expresses the variation in relative terms, thus facilitating a comparison of the dispersion of two or more frequency distributions (Chapter 5).

z Value (z)

For two means:

$$z = \frac{\bar{X}_1 - \bar{X}_2}{\sqrt{\left(\frac{s_1}{\sqrt{n_1}}\right)^2 + \left(\frac{s_2}{\sqrt{n_2}}\right)^2}}$$

For two proportions:

$$z = \frac{p_1 - p_2}{\sqrt{\frac{\bar{P}(1 - \bar{P})}{n_1} + \frac{\bar{P}(1 - \bar{P})}{n_2}}}$$

One use of the z value is in testing a hypothesis involving the difference between two means or two proportions. A hypothesis is stated that two samples are from two identical populations or the same population. If the hypothesis is true, then the distribution of z values of many paired samples will approximate a normal distribution with a mean of zero (Chapter 10).

Appendix I. Logarithms

N	0	1	2	3	4	5	6	7	8	9
10	0000	0043	0086	0128	0170	0212	0253	0294	0334	0374
11	0414	0453	0492	0531	0569	0607	0645	0682	0719	0755
12	0792	0828	0864	0899	0934	0969	1004	1038	1072	1106
13	1139	1173	1206	1239	1271	1303	1335	1367	1399	1430
14	1461	1492	1523	1553	1584	1614	1644	1673	1703	1732
15	1761	1790	1818	1847	1875	1903	1931	1959	1987	2014
16	2041	2068	2095	2122	2148	2175	2201	2227	2253	2279
17	2304	2330	2355	2380	2405	2430	2455	2480	2504	2529
18	2553	2577	2601	2625	2648	2672	2695	2718	2742	2765
19	2788	2810	2833	2856	2878	2900	2923	2945	2967	2989
20	3010	3032	3054	3075	3096	3118	3139	3160	3181	3201
21	3222	3243	3263	3284	3304	3324	3345	3365	3385	3404
22	3424	3444	3464	3483	3502	3522	3541	3560	3579	3598
23	3617	3636	3655	3674	3692	3711	3729	3747	3766	3784
24	3802	3820	3838	3856	3874	3892	3909	3927	3945	3962
25	3979	3997	4014	4031	4048	4065	4082	4099	4116	4133
26	4150	4166	4183	4200	4216	4232	4249	4265	4281	4298
27	4314	4330	4346	4362	4378	4393	4409	4425	4440	4456
28	4472	4487	4502	4518	4533	4548	4564	4579	4594	4609
29	4624	4639	4654	4669	4683	4698	4713	4728	4742	4757
30	4771	4786	4800	4814	4829	4843	4857	4871	4886	4900
31	4914	4928	4942	4955	4969	4983	4997	5011	5024	5038
32	5051	5065	5079	5092	5105	5119	5132	5145	5159	5172
33	5185	5198	5211	5224	5237	5250	5263	5276	5289	5302
34	5315	5328	5340	5353	5366	5378	5391	5403	5416	5428
35	5441	5453	5465	5478	5490	5502	5514	5527	5539	5551
36	5563	5575	5587	5599	5611	5623	5635	5647	5658	5670
37	5682	5694	5705	5717	5729	5740	5752	5763	5775	5786
38	5798	5809	5821	5832	5843	5855	5866	5877	5888	5899
39	5911	5922	5933	5944	5955	5966	5977	5988	5999	6010
40	6021	6031	6042	6053	6064	6075	6085	6096	6107	6117
41	6128	6138	6149	6160	6170	6180	6191	6201	6212	6222
42	6232	6243	6253	6263	6274	6284	6294	6304	6314	6325
43	6336	6345	6355	6365	6375	6385	6395	6405	6415	6425
44	6435	6444	6454	6464	6474	6484	6493	6503	6513	6522
45	6532	6542	6551	6561	6571	6580	6590	6599	6609	6618
46	6628	6637	6646	6656	6665	6675	6684	6693	6702	6712
47	6721	6730	6739	6749	6758	6767	6776	6785	6794	6803
48	6812	6821	6830	6839	6848	6857	6866	6875	6884	6893
49	6902	6911	6920	6928	6937	6946	6955	6964	6972	6981
50	6990	6998	7007	7016	7024	7033	7042	7050	7059	7067
51	7076	7084	7093	7101	7110	7118	7126	7135	7143	7152
52	7160	7168	7177	7185	7193	7202	7210	7218	7226	7235
53	7243	7251	7259	7267	7275	7284	7292	7300	7308	7316
54	7324	7332	7340	7348	7356	7364	7372	7380	7388	7396
55	7404	7412	7419	7427	7435	7443	7451	7459	7466	7474
56	7482	7490	7497	7505	7513	7520	7528	7536	7543	7551
57	7559	7566	7574	7582	7589	7597	7604	7612	7619	7627
58	7634	7642	7649	7657	7664	7672	7679	7686	7694	7701
59	7709	7716	7723	7731	7738	7745	7752	7760	7767	7774
60	7782	7789	7796	7803	7810	7818	7825	7832	7839	7846
61	7853	7860	7868	7875	7882	7889	7896	7903	7910	7917
62	7924	7931	7938	7945	7952	7959	7966	7973	7980	7987
63	7993	8000	8007	8014	8021	8028	8035	8041	8048	8055
64	8062	8069	8075	8082	8089	8096	8102	8109	8116	8122
65	8129	8136	8142	8149	8156	8162	8169	8176	8182	8189
66	8195	8202	8209	8215	8222	8228	8235	8241	8248	8254
67	8261	8267	8274	8280	8287	8293	8299	8306	8312	8319
68	8325	8331	8338	8344	8351	8357	8363	8370	8376	8382
69	8388	8395	8401	8407	8414	8420	8426	8432	8439	8445
70	8451	8457	8463	8470	8476	8482	8488	8494	8500	8506
71	8513	8519	8525	8531	8537	8543	8549	8555	8561	8567
72	8573	8579	8585	8591	8597	8603	8609	8615	8621	8627
73	8633	8639	8645	8651	8657	8663	8669	8675	8681	8686
74	8692	8698	8704	8710	8716	8722	8727	8733	8739	8745
75	8751	8756	8762	8768	8774	8779	8785	8791	8797	8802
76	8808	8814	8820	8825	8831	8837	8842	8848	8854	8859
77	8865	8871	8876	8882	8887	8893	8899	8904	8910	8915
78	8921	8927	8932	8938	8943	8949	8954	8960	8965	8971
79	8976	8982	8987	8993	8998	9004	9009	9015	9020	9025
80	9031	9036	9042	9047	9053	9058	9063	9069	9074	9079
81	9085	9090	9096	9101	9106	9112	9117	9122	9128	9133
82	9138	9143	9149	9154	9159	9165	9170	9175	9180	9186
83	9191	9196	9201	9206	9212	9217	9222	9227	9232	9238
84	9243	9248	9253	9258	9263	9269	9274	9279	9284	9289
85	9294	9299	9304	9309	9315	9320	9325	9330	9335	9340
86	9345	9350	9355	9360	9365	9370	9375	9380	9385	9390
87	9395	9400	9405	9410	9415	9420	9425	9430	9435	9440
88	9445	9450	9455	9460	9465	9469	9474	9479	9484	9489
89	9494	9499	9504	9509	9513	9518	9523	9528	9533	9538
90	9542	9547	9552	9557	9562	9566	9571	9576	9581	9586
91	9590	9595	9600	9605	9609	9614	9619	9624	9628	9633
92	9638	9643	9647	9652	9657	9661	9666	9671	9675	9680
93	9685	9689	9694	9699	9703	9708	9713	9717	9722	9727
94	9731	9736	9741	9745	9750	9754	9759	9763	9768	9773
95	9777	9782	9786	9791	9795	9800	9805	9809	9814	9818
96	9823	9827	9832	9836	9841	9845	9850	9854	9859	9863
97	9868	9872	9877	9881	9886	9890	9894	9899	9903	9908
98	9912	9917	9921	9926	9930	9934	9939	9943	9948	9952
99	9956	9961	9965	9969	9974	9978	9983	9987	9991	9996

Appendix II. Factors for Control Charts

Number of Items in Sample,	Chart for Averages	Chart for Ranges		
	Factors for Control Limits	Factors for Central Line	Factors for Control Limits	
n	A_2	d_2	D_3	D_4
2	1.880	1.128	0	3.267
3	1.023	1.693	0	2.575
4	.729	2.059	0	2.282
5	.577	2.326	0	2.115
6	.483	2.534	0	2.004
7	.419	2.704	.076	1.924
8	.373	2.847	.136	1.864
9	.337	2.970	.184	1.816
10	.308	3.078	.223	1.777
11	.285	3.173	.256	1.744
12	.266	3.258	.284	1.716
13	.249	3.336	.308	1.692
14	.235	3.407	.329	1.671
15	.223	3.472	.348	1.652

Source: Adapted from American Society for Testing and Materials, *Manual on Quality Control of Materials*, 1951, Table B2, p. 115. For a more detailed table and explanation, see Acheson J. Duncan, *Quality Control and Industrial Statistics* (3rd ed.; Homewood, Ill.: Richard D. Irwin, Inc., 1965) Table M, p. 927.

n	√n	√10n	n	√n	√10n	n	√n	√10n
1.00	1.00000	3.16228	1.50	1.22474	3.87298	2.00	1.41421	4.47214
1.01	1.00499	3.17805	1.51	1.22882	3.88587	2.01	1.41774	4.48330
1.02	1.00995	3.19374	1.52	1.23288	3.89872	2.02	1.42127	4.49444
1.03	1.01489	3.20936	1.53	1.23693	3.91152	2.03	1.42478	4.50555
1.04	1.01980	3.22490	1.54	1.24097	3.92428	2.04	1.42829	4.51664
1.05	1.02470	3.24037	1.55	1.24499	3.93700	2.05	1.43178	4.52769
1.06	1.02956	3.25576	1.56	1.24900	3.94968	2.06	1.43527	4.53872
1.07	1.03441	3.27109	1.57	1.25300	3.96232	2.07	1.43875	4.54973
1.08	1.03923	3.28634	1.58	1.25698	3.97492	2.08	1.44222	4.56070
1.09	1.04403	3.30151	1.59	1.26095	3.98748	2.09	1.44568	4.57165
1.10	1.04881	3.31662	1.60	1.26491	4.00000	2.10	1.44914	4.58258
1.11	1.05357	3.33167	1.61	1.26886	4.01248	2.11	1.45258	4.59347
1.12	1.05830	3.34664	1.62	1.27279	4.02492	2.12	1.45602	4.60435
1.13	1.06301	3.36155	1.63	1.27671	4.03733	2.13	1.45945	4.61519
1.14	1.06771	3.37639	1.64	1.28062	4.04969	2.14	1.46287	4.62601
1.15	1.07238	3.39116	1.65	1.28452	4.06202	2.15	1.46629	4.63681
1.16	1.07703	3.40588	1.66	1.28841	4.07431	2.16	1.46969	4.64758
1.17	1.08167	3.42053	1.67	1.29228	4.08656	2.17	1.47309	4.65833
1.18	1.08628	3.43511	1.68	1.29615	4.09878	2.18	1.47648	4.66905
1.19	1.09087	3.44964	1.69	1.30000	4.11096	2.19	1.47986	4.67974
1.20	1.09545	3.46410	1.70	1.30384	4.12311	2.20	1.48324	4.69042
1.21	1.10000	3.47851	1.71	1.30767	4.13521	2.21	1.48661	4.70106
1.22	1.10454	3.49285	1.72	1.31149	4.14729	2.22	1.48997	4.71169
1.23	1.10905	3.50714	1.73	1.31529	4.15933	2.23	1.49332	4.72229
1.24	1.11355	3.52136	1.74	1.31909	4.17133	2.24	1.49666	4.73286
1.25	1.11803	3.53553	1.75	1.32288	4.18330	2.25	1.50000	4.74342
1.26	1.12250	3.54965	1.76	1.32665	4.19524	2.26	1.50333	4.75395
1.27	1.12694	3.56371	1.77	1.33041	4.20714	2.27	1.50665	4.76445
1.28	1.13137	3.57771	1.78	1.33417	4.21900	2.28	1.50997	4.77493
1.29	1.13578	3.59166	1.79	1.33791	4.23084	2.29	1.51327	4.78539
1.30	1.14018	3.60555	1.80	1.34164	4.24264	2.30	1.51658	4.79583
1.31	1.14455	3.61939	1.81	1.34536	4.25441	2.31	1.51987	4.80625
1.32	1.14891	3.63318	1.82	1.34907	4.26615	2.32	1.52315	4.81664
1.33	1.15326	3.64692	1.83	1.35277	4.27785	2.33	1.52643	4.82701
1.34	1.15758	3.66060	1.84	1.35647	4.28952	2.34	1.52971	4.83735
1.35	1.16190	3.67423	1.85	1.36015	4.30116	2.35	1.53297	4.84768
1.36	1.16619	3.68782	1.86	1.36382	4.31277	2.36	1.53623	4.85798
1.37	1.17047	3.70135	1.87	1.36748	4.32435	2.37	1.53948	4.86826
1.38	1.17473	3.71484	1.88	1.37113	4.33590	2.38	1.54272	4.87852
1.39	1.17898	3.72827	1.89	1.37477	4.34741	2.39	1.54596	4.88876
1.40	1.18322	3.74166	1.90	1.37840	4.35890	2.40	1.54919	4.89898
1.41	1.18743	3.75500	1.91	1.38203	4.37035	2.41	1.55242	4.90918
1.42	1.19164	3.76829	1.92	1.38564	4.38178	2.42	1.55563	4.91935
1.43	1.19583	3.78153	1.93	1.38924	4.39318	2.43	1.55885	4.92950
1.44	1.20000	3.79473	1.94	1.39284	4.40454	2.44	1.56205	4.93964
1.45	1.20416	3.80789	1.95	1.39642	4.41588	2.45	1.56525	4.94975
1.46	1.20830	3.82099	1.96	1.40000	4.42719	2.46	1.56844	4.95984
1.47	1.21244	3.83406	1.97	1.40357	4.43847	2.47	1.57162	4.96991
1.48	1.21655	3.84708	1.98	1.40712	4.44972	2.48	1.57480	4.97996
1.49	1.22066	3.86005	1.99	1.41067	4.46094	2.49	1.57797	4.98999

n	√n	√10n	n	√n	√10n	n	√n	√10n
2.50	1.58114	5.00000	3.00	1.73205	5.47723	3.50	1.87083	5.91608
2.51	1.58430	5.00999	3.01	1.73494	5.48635	3.51	1.87350	5.92453
2.52	1.58745	5.01996	3.02	1.73781	5.49545	3.52	1.87617	5.93296
2.53	1.59060	5.02991	3.03	1.74069	5.50454	3.53	1.87883	5.94138
2.54	1.59374	5.03984	3.04	1.74356	5.51362	3.54	1.88149	5.94979
2.55	1.59687	5.04975	3.05	1.74642	5.52268	3.55	1.88414	5.95819
2.56	1.60000	5.05964	3.06	1.74929	5.53173	3.56	1.88680	5.96657
2.57	1.60312	5.06952	3.07	1.75214	5.54076	3.57	1.88944	5.97495
2.58	1.60624	5.07937	3.08	1.75499	5.54977	3.58	1.89209	5.98331
2.59	1.60935	5.08920	3.09	1.75784	5.55878	3.59	1.89473	5.99166
2.60	1.61245	5.09902	3.10	1.76068	5.56776	3.60	1.89737	6.00000
2.61	1.61555	5.10882	3.11	1.76352	5.57674	3.61	1.90000	6.00833
2.62	1.61864	5.11859	3.12	1.76635	5.58570	3.62	1.90263	6.01664
2.63	1.62173	5.12835	3.13	1.76918	5.59464	3.63	1.90526	6.02495
2.64	1.62481	5.13809	3.14	1.77200	5.60357	3.64	1.90788	6.03324
2.65	1.62788	5.14782	3.15	1.77482	5.61249	3.65	1.91050	6.04152
2.66	1.63095	5.15752	3.16	1.77764	5.62139	3.66	1.91311	6.04979
2.67	1.63401	5.16720	3.17	1.78045	5.63028	3.67	1.91572	6.05805
2.68	1.63707	5.17687	3.18	1.78326	5.63915	3.68	1.91833	6.06630
2.69	1.64012	5.18652	3.19	1.78606	5.64801	3.69	1.92094	6.07454
2.70	1.64317	5.19615	3.20	1.78885	5.65685	3.70	1.92354	6.08276
2.71	1.64621	5.20577	3.21	1.79165	5.66569	3.71	1.92614	6.09098
2.72	1.64924	5.21536	3.22	1.79444	5.67450	3.72	1.92873	6.09918
2.73	1.65227	5.22494	3.23	1.79722	5.68331	3.73	1.93132	6.10737
2.74	1.65529	5.23450	3.24	1.80000	5.69210	3.74	1.93391	6.11555
2.75	1.65831	5.24404	3.25	1.80278	5.70088	3.75	1.93649	6.12372
2.76	1.66132	5.25357	3.26	1.80555	5.70964	3.76	1.93907	6.13188
2.77	1.66433	5.26308	3.27	1.80831	5.71839	3.77	1.94165	6.14003
2.78	1.66733	5.27257	3.28	1.81108	5.72713	3.78	1.94422	6.14817
2.79	1.67033	5.28205	3.29	1.81384	5.73585	3.79	1.94679	6.15630
2.80	1.67332	5.29150	3.30	1.81659	5.74456	3.80	1.94936	6.16441
2.81	1.67631	5.30094	3.31	1.81934	5.75326	3.81	1.95192	6.17252
2.82	1.67929	5.31037	3.32	1.82209	5.76194	3.82	1.95448	6.18061
2.83	1.68226	5.31977	3.33	1.82483	5.77062	3.83	1.95704	6.18870
2.84	1.68523	5.32917	3.34	1.82757	5.77927	3.84	1.95959	6.19677
2.85	1.68819	5.33854	3.35	1.83030	5.78792	3.85	1.96214	6.20484
2.86	1.69115	5.34790	3.36	1.83303	5.79655	3.86	1.96469	6.21289
2.87	1.69411	5.35724	3.37	1.83576	5.80517	3.87	1.96723	6.22093
2.88	1.69706	5.36656	3.38	1.83848	5.81378	3.88	1.96977	6.22896
2.89	1.70000	5.37587	3.39	1.84120	5.82237	3.89	1.97231	6.23699
2.90	1.70294	5.38516	3.40	1.84391	5.83095	3.90	1.97484	6.24500
2.91	1.70587	5.39444	3.41	1.84662	5.83952	3.91	1.97737	6.25300
2.92	1.70880	5.40370	3.42	1.84932	5.84808	3.92	1.97990	6.26099
2.93	1.71172	5.41295	3.43	1.85203	5.85662	3.93	1.98242	6.26897
2.94	1.71464	5.42218	3.44	1.85472	5.86515	3.94	1.98494	6.27694
2.95	1.71756	5.43139	3.45	1.85742	5.87367	3.95	1.98746	6.28490
2.96	1.72047	5.44059	3.46	1.86011	5.88218	3.96	1.98997	6.29285
2.97	1.72337	5.44977	3.47	1.86279	5.89067	3.97	1.99249	6.30079
2.98	1.72627	5.45894	3.48	1.86548	5.89915	3.98	1.99499	6.30872
2.99	1.72916	5.46809	3.49	1.86815	5.90762	3.99	1.99750	6.31664

* Adapted with permission of the publisher from *Macmillan Selected Mathematical Tables* by Earle R. Hedrick. Copyright 1936 by The Macmillan Company.

Appendix III (*Continued*)

n	$\sqrt{n}$	$\sqrt{10n}$	n	$\sqrt{n}$	$\sqrt{10n}$	n	$\sqrt{n}$	$\sqrt{10n}$	n	$\sqrt{n}$	$\sqrt{10n}$	n	$\sqrt{n}$	$\sqrt{10n}$	n	$\sqrt{n}$	$\sqrt{10n}$
4.00	2.00000	6.32456	**4.50**	2.12132	6.70820	**5.00**	2.23607	7.07107	**5.50**	2.34521	7.41620	**6.00**	2.44949	7.74597	**6.50**	2.54951	8.06226
4.01	2.00250	6.33246	4.51	2.12368	6.71565	5.01	2.23830	7.07814	5.51	2.34734	7.42294	6.01	2.45153	7.75242	6.51	2.55147	8.06846
4.02	2.00499	6.34035	4.52	2.12603	6.72309	5.02	2.24054	7.08520	5.52	2.34947	7.42967	6.02	2.45357	7.75887	6.52	2.55343	8.07465
4.03	2.00749	6.34823	4.53	2.12838	6.73053	5.03	2.24277	7.09225	5.53	2.35160	7.43640	6.03	2.45561	7.76531	6.53	2.55539	8.08084
4.04	2.00998	6.35610	4.54	2.13073	6.73795	5.04	2.24499	7.09930	5.54	2.35372	7.44312	6.04	2.45764	7.77174	6.54	2.55734	8.08703
4.05	2.01246	6.36396	4.55	2.13307	6.74537	5.05	2.24722	7.10634	5.55	2.35584	7.44983	6.05	2.45967	7.77817	6.55	2.55930	8.09321
4.06	2.01494	6.37181	4.56	2.13542	6.75278	5.06	2.24944	7.11337	5.56	2.35797	7.45654	6.06	2.46171	7.78460	6.56	2.56125	8.09938
4.07	2.01742	6.37966	4.57	2.13776	6.76018	5.07	2.25167	7.12039	5.57	2.36008	7.46324	6.07	2.46374	7.79102	6.57	2.56320	8.10555
4.08	2.01990	6.38749	4.58	2.14009	6.76757	5.08	2.25389	7.12741	5.58	2.36220	7.46994	6.08	2.46577	7.79744	6.58	2.56515	8.11172
4.09	2.02237	6.39531	4.59	2.14243	6.77495	5.09	2.25610	7.13442	5.59	2.36432	7.47663	6.09	2.46779	7.80385	6.59	2.56710	8.11788
4.10	2.02485	6.40312	**4.60**	2.14476	6.78233	**5.10**	2.25832	7.14143	**5.60**	2.36643	7.48331	**6.10**	2.46982	7.81025	**6.60**	2.56905	8.12404
4.11	2.02731	6.41093	4.61	2.14709	6.78970	5.11	2.26053	7.14843	5.61	2.36854	7.48999	6.11	2.47184	7.81665	6.61	2.57099	8.13019
4.12	2.02978	6.41872	4.62	2.14942	6.79706	5.12	2.26274	7.15542	5.62	2.37065	7.49667	6.12	2.47386	7.82304	6.62	2.57294	8.13634
4.13	2.03224	6.42651	4.63	2.15174	6.80441	5.13	2.26495	7.16240	5.63	2.37276	7.50333	6.13	2.47588	7.82943	6.63	2.57488	8.14248
4.14	2.03470	6.43428	4.64	2.15407	6.81175	5.14	2.26716	7.16938	5.64	2.37487	7.50999	6.14	2.47790	7.83582	6.64	2.57682	8.14862
4.15	2.03715	6.44205	4.65	2.15639	6.81909	5.15	2.26936	7.17635	5.65	2.37697	7.51665	6.15	2.47992	7.84219	6.65	2.57876	8.15475
4.16	2.03961	6.44981	4.66	2.15870	6.82642	5.16	2.27156	7.18331	5.66	2.37908	7.52330	6.16	2.48193	7.84857	6.66	2.58070	8.16088
4.17	2.04206	6.45755	4.67	2.16102	6.83374	5.17	2.27376	7.19027	5.67	2.38118	7.52994	6.17	2.48395	7.85493	6.67	2.58263	8.16701
4.18	2.04450	6.46529	4.68	2.16333	6.84105	5.18	2.27596	7.19722	5.68	2.38238	7.53658	6.18	2.48596	7.86130	6.68	2.58457	8.17313
4.19	2.04695	6.47302	4.69	2.16564	6.84836	5.19	2.27816	7.20417	5.69	2.38537	7.54321	6.19	2.48797	7.86766	6.69	2.58650	8.17924
4.20	2.04939	6.48074	**4.70**	2.16795	6.85565	**5.20**	2.28035	7.21110	**5.70**	2.38747	7.54983	**6.20**	2.48998	7.87401	**6.70**	2.58844	8.18535
4.21	2.05183	6.48845	4.71	2.17025	6.86294	5.21	2.28254	7.21803	5.71	2.38956	7.55645	6.21	2.49199	7.88036	6.71	2.59037	8.19146
4.22	2.05426	6.49615	4.72	2.17256	6.87023	5.22	2.28473	7.22496	5.72	2.39165	7.56307	6.22	2.49399	7.88670	6.72	2.59230	8.19756
4.23	2.05670	6.50384	4.73	2.17486	6.87750	5.23	2.28692	7.23187	5.73	2.39374	7.56968	6.23	2.49600	7.89303	6.73	2.59422	8.20366
4.24	2.05913	6.51153	4.74	2.17715	6.88477	5.24	2.28910	7.23878	5.74	2.39583	7.57628	6.24	2.49800	7.89937	6.74	2.59615	8.20975
4.25	2.06155	6.51920	4.75	2.17945	6.89202	5.25	2.29129	7.24569	5.75	2.39792	7.58288	6.25	2.50000	7.90569	6.75	2.59808	8.21584
4.26	2.06398	6.52687	4.76	2.18174	6.89928	5.26	2.29347	7.25259	5.76	2.40000	7.58947	6.26	2.50200	7.91202	6.76	2.60000	8.22192
4.27	2.06640	6.53452	4.77	2.18403	6.90652	5.27	2.29565	7.25948	5.77	2.40208	7.59605	6.27	2.50400	7.91833	6.77	2.60192	8.22800
4.28	2.06882	6.54217	4.78	2.18632	6.91375	5.28	2.29783	7.26636	5.78	2.40416	7.60263	6.28	2.50599	7.92465	6.78	2.60384	8.23408
4.29	2.07123	6.54981	4.79	2.18861	6.92098	5.29	2.30000	7.27324	5.79	2.40624	7.60920	6.29	2.50799	7.93095	6.79	2.60576	8.24015
4.30	2.07364	6.55744	**4.80**	2.19089	6.92820	**5.30**	2.30217	7.28011	**5.80**	2.40832	7.61577	**6.30**	2.50998	7.93725	**6.80**	2.60768	8.24621
4.31	2.07605	6.56506	4.81	2.19317	6.93542	5.31	2.30434	7.28697	5.81	2.41039	7.62234	6.31	2.51197	7.94355	6.81	2.60960	8.25227
4.32	2.07846	6.57267	4.82	2.19545	6.94262	5.32	2.30651	7.29383	5.82	2.41247	7.62889	6.32	2.51396	7.94984	6.82	2.61151	8.25833
4.33	2.08087	6.58027	4.83	2.19773	6.94982	5.33	2.30868	7.30068	5.83	2.41454	7.63544	6.33	2.51595	7.95613	6.83	2.61343	8.26438
4.34	2.08327	6.58787	4.84	2.20000	6.95701	5.34	2.31084	7.30753	5.84	2.41661	7.64199	6.34	2.51794	7.96241	6.84	2.61534	8.27043
4.35	2.08567	6.59545	4.85	2.20227	6.96419	5.35	2.31301	7.31437	5.85	2.41868	7.64853	6.35	2.51992	7.96869	6.85	2.61725	8.27647
4.36	2.08806	6.60303	4.86	2.20454	6.97137	5.36	2.31517	7.32120	5.86	2.42074	7.65506	6.36	2.52190	7.97496	6.86	2.61916	8.28251
4.37	2.09045	6.61060	4.87	2.20681	6.97854	5.37	2.31733	7.32803	5.87	2.42281	7.66159	6.37	2.52389	7.98123	6.87	2.62107	8.28855
4.38	2.09284	6.61816	4.88	2.20907	6.98570	5.38	2.31948	7.33485	5.88	2.42487	7.66812	6.38	2.52587	7.98749	6.88	2.62298	8.29458
4.39	2.09523	6.62571	4.89	2.21133	6.99285	5.39	2.32164	7.34166	5.89	2.42693	7.67463	6.39	2.52784	7.99375	6.89	2.62488	8.30060
4.40	2.09762	6.63325	**4.90**	2.21359	7.00000	**5.40**	2.32379	7.34847	**5.90**	2.42899	7.68115	**6.40**	2.52982	8.00000	**6.90**	2.62679	8.30662
4.41	2.10000	6.64078	4.91	2.21585	7.00714	5.41	2.32594	7.35527	5.91	2.43105	7.68765	6.41	2.53180	8.00625	6.91	2.62869	8.31264
4.42	2.10238	6.64831	4.92	2.21811	7.01427	5.42	2.32809	7.36206	5.92	2.43311	7.69415	6.42	2.53377	8.01249	6.92	2.63059	8.31865
4.43	2.10476	6.65582	4.93	2.22036	7.02140	5.43	2.33024	7.36885	5.93	2.43516	7.70065	6.43	2.53574	8.01873	6.93	2.63249	8.32466
4.44	2.10713	6.66333	4.94	2.22261	7.02851	5.44	2.33238	7.37564	5.94	2.43721	7.70714	6.44	2.53772	8.02496	6.94	2.63439	8.33067
4.45	2.10950	6.67083	4.95	2.22486	7.03562	5.45	2.33452	7.38241	5.95	2.43926	7.71362	6.45	2.53969	8.03119	6.95	2.63629	8.33667
4.46	2.11187	6.67832	4.96	2.22711	7.04273	5.46	2.33666	7.38918	5.96	2.44131	7.72010	6.46	2.54165	8.03741	6.96	2.63818	8.34266
4.47	2.11424	6.68581	4.97	2.22935	7.04982	5.47	2.33880	7.39594	5.97	2.44336	7.72658	6.47	2.54362	8.04363	6.97	2.64008	8.34865

n	$\sqrt{n}$	$\sqrt{10n}$	n	$\sqrt{n}$	$\sqrt{10n}$	n	$\sqrt{n}$	$\sqrt{10n}$	n	$\sqrt{n}$	$\sqrt{10n}$	n	$\sqrt{n}$	$\sqrt{10n}$	n	$\sqrt{n}$	$\sqrt{10n}$
7.00	2.64575	8.36660	7.50	2.73861	8.66025	8.00	2.82843	8.94427	8.50	2.91548	9.21954	9.00	3.00000	9.48683	9.50	3.08221	9.74679
7.01	2.64764	8.37257	7.51	2.74044	8.66603	8.01	2.83019	8.94986	8.51	2.91719	9.22497	9.01	3.00167	9.49210	9.51	3.08383	9.75192
7.02	2.64953	8.37854	7.52	2.74226	8.67179	8.02	2.83196	8.95545	8.52	2.91890	9.23038	9.02	3.00333	9.49737	9.52	3.08545	9.75705
7.03	2.65141	8.38451	7.53	2.74408	8.67756	8.03	2.83373	8.96103	8.53	2.92062	9.23580	9.03	3.00500	9.50263	9.53	3.08707	9.76217
7.04	2.65330	8.39047	7.54	2.74591	8.68332	8.04	2.83549	8.96660	8.54	2.92233	9.24121	9.04	3.00666	9.50789	9.54	3.08869	9.76729
7.05	2.65518	8.39643	7.55	2.74773	8.68907	8.05	2.83725	8.97218	8.55	2.92404	9.24662	9.05	3.00832	9.51315	9.55	3.09031	9.77241
7.06	2.65707	8.40238	7.56	2.74955	8.69483	8.06	2.83901	8.97775	8.56	2.92575	9.25203	9.06	3.00998	9.51840	9.56	3.09192	9.77753
7.07	2.65895	8.40833	7.57	2.75136	8.70057	8.07	2.84077	8.98332	8.57	2.92746	9.25743	9.07	3.01164	9.52365	9.57	3.09354	9.78264
7.08	2.66083	8.41427	7.58	2.75318	8.70632	8.08	2.84253	8.98888	8.58	2.92916	9.26283	9.08	3.01330	9.52890	9.58	3.09516	9.78775
7.09	2.66271	8.42021	7.59	2.75500	8.71206	8.09	2.84429	8.99444	8.59	2.93087	9.26823	9.09	3.01496	9.53415	9.59	3.09677	9.79285
7.10	2.66458	8.42615	7.60	2.75681	8.71780	8.10	2.84605	9.00000	8.60	2.93258	9.27362	9.10	3.01662	9.53939	9.60	3.09839	9.79796
7.11	2.66646	8.43208	7.61	2.75862	8.72353	8.11	2.84781	9.00555	8.61	2.93428	9.27901	9.11	3.01828	9.54463	9.61	3.10000	9.80306
7.12	2.66833	8.43801	7.62	2.76043	8.72926	8.12	2.84956	9.01110	8.62	2.93598	9.28440	9.12	3.01993	9.54987	9.62	3.10161	9.80816
7.13	2.67021	8.44393	7.63	2.76225	8.73499	8.13	2.85132	9.01665	8.63	2.93769	9.28978	9.13	3.02159	9.55510	9.63	3.10322	9.81326
7.14	2.67208	8.44985	7.64	2.76405	8.74071	8.14	2.85307	9.02219	8.64	2.93939	9.29516	9.14	3.02324	9.56033	9.64	3.10483	9.81835
7.15	2.67395	8.45577	7.65	2.76586	8.74643	8.15	2.85482	9.02774	8.65	2.94109	9.30054	9.15	3.02490	9.56556	9.65	3.10644	9.82344
7.16	2.67582	8.46168	7.66	2.76767	8.75214	8.16	2.85657	9.03327	8.66	2.94279	9.30591	9.16	3.02655	9.57079	9.66	3.10805	9.82853
7.17	2.67769	8.46759	7.67	2.76948	8,75785	8.17	2.85832	9.03881	8.67	2.94449	9.31128	9.17	3.02820	9.57601	9.67	3.10966	9.83362
7.18	2.67955	8.47349	7.68	2.77128	8.76356	8.18	2.86007	9.04434	8.68	2.94618	9.31665	9.18	3.02985	9.58123	9.68	3.11127	9.83870
7.19	2.68142	8.47939	7.69	2.77308	8.76926	8.19	2.86182	9.04986	8.69	2.94788	9.32202	9.19	3.03150	9.58645	9.69	3.11288	9.84378
7.20	2.68328	8.48528	7.70	2.77489	8.77496	8.20	2.86356	9.05539	8.70	2.94958	9.32738	9.20	3.03315	9.59166	9.70	3.11448	9.84886
7.21	2.68514	8.49117	7.71	2.77669	8.78066	8.21	2.86531	9.06091	8.71	2.95127	9.33274	9.21	3.03480	9.59687	9.71	3.11609	9.85393
7.22	2.68701	8.49706	7.72	2.77849	8.78635	8.22	2.86705	9.06642	8.72	2.95296	9.33809	9.22	3.03645	9.60208	9.72	3.11769	9.85901
7.23	2.68887	8.50294	7.73	2.78029	8.79204	8.23	2.86880	9.07193	8.73	2.95466	9.34345	9.23	3.03809	9.60729	9.73	3.11929	9.86408
7.24	2.69072	8.50882	7.74	2.78209	8.79773	8.24	2.87054	9.07744	8.74	2.95635	9.34880	9.24	3.03974	9.61249	9.74	3.12090	9.86914
7.25	2.69258	8.51469	7.75	2.78388	8.80341	8.25	2.87228	9.08295	8.75	2.95804	9.35414	9.25	3.04138	9.61769	9.75	3.12250	9.87421
7.26	2.69444	8.52056	7.76	2.78568	8.80909	8.26	2.87402	9.08845	8.76	2.95973	9.35949	9.26	3.04302	9.62289	9.76	3.12410	9.87927
7.27	2.69629	8.52643	7.77	2.78747	8.81476	8.27	2.87576	9.09395	8.77	2.96142	9.36483	9.27	3.04467	9.62808	9.77	3.12570	9.88433
7.28	2.69815	8.53229	7.78	2.78927	8.82043	8.28	2.87750	9.09945	8.78	2.96311	9.37017	9.28	3.04631	9.63328	9.78	3.12730	9.88939
7.29	2.70000	8.53815	7.79	2.79106	8.82610	8.29	2.87924	9.10494	8.79	2.96479	9.37550	9.29	3.04795	9.63846	9.79	3.12890	9.89444
7.30	2.70185	8.54400	7.80	2.79285	8.83176	8.30	2.88097	9.11043	8.80	2.96648	9.38083	9.30	3.04959	9.64365	9.80	3.13050	9.89949
7.31	2.70370	8.54985	7.81	2.79464	8.83742	8.31	2.88271	9.11592	8.81	2.96816	9.38616	9.31	3.05123	9.64883	9.81	3.13209	9.90454
7.32	2.70555	8.55570	7.82	2.79643	8.84308	8.32	2.88444	9.12140	8.82	2.96985	9.39149	9.32	3.05287	9.65401	9.82	3.13369	9.90959
7.33	2.70740	8.56154	7.83	2.79821	8.84873	8.33	2.88617	9.12688	8.83	2.97153	9.39681	9.33	3.05450	9.65919	9.83	3.13528	9.91464
7.34	2.70924	8.56738	7.84	2.80000	8.85438	8.34	2.88791	9.13236	8.84	2.97321	9.40213	9.34	3.05614	9.66437	9.84	3.13688	9.91968
7.35	2.71109	8.57321	7.85	2.80179	8.86002	8.35	2.88964	9.13783	8.85	2.97489	9.40744	9.35	3.05778	9.66954	9.85	3.13847	9.92472
7.36	2.71293	8.57904	7.86	2.80357	8.86566	8.36	2.89137	9.14330	8.86	2.97658	9.41276	9.36	3.05941	9.67471	9.86	3.14006	9.92975
7.37	2.71477	8.58487	7.87	2.80535	8.87130	8.37	2.89310	9.14877	8.87	2.97825	9.41807	9.37	3.06105	9.67988	9.87	3.14166	9.93479
7.38	2.71662	8.59069	7.88	2.80713	8.87694	8.38	2.89482	9.15423	8.88	2.97993	9.42338	9.38	3.06268	9.68504	9.88	3.14325	9.93982
7.39	2.71846	8.59651	7.89	2.80891	8.88257	8.39	2.89655	9.15969	8.89	2.98161	9.42868	9.39	3.06431	9.69020	9.89	3.14484	9.94485
7.40	2.72029	8.60233	7.90	2.81069	8.88819	8.40	2.89828	9.16515	8.90	2.98329	9.43398	9.40	3.06594	9.69536	9.90	3.14643	9.94987
7.41	2.72213	8.60814	7.91	2.81247	8.89382	8.41	2.90000	9.17061	8.91	2.98496	9.43928	9.41	3.06757	9.70052	9.91	3.14802	9.95490
7.42	2.72397	8.61394	7.92	2.81425	8.89944	8.42	2.90172	9.17606	8.92	2.98664	9.44458	9.42	3.06920	9.70567	9.92	3.14960	9.95992
7.43	2.72580	8.61974	7.93	2.81603	8.90505	8.43	2.90345	9.18150	8.93	2.98831	9.44987	9.43	3.07083	9.71082	9.93	3.15119	9.96494
7.44	2.72764	8.62554	7.94	2.81780	8.91067	8.44	2.90517	9.18695	8.94	2.98998	9.45516	9.44	3.07246	9.71597	9.94	3.15278	9.96995
7.45	2.72947	8.63134	7.95	2.81957	8.91628	8.45	2.90689	9.19239	8.95	2.99166	9.46044	9.45	3.07409	9.72111	9.95	3.15436	9.97497
7.46	2.73130	8.63713	7.96	2.82135	8.92188	8.46	2.90861	9.19783	8.96	2.99333	9.46573	9.46	3.07571	9.72625	9.96	3.15595	9.97998
7.47	2.73313	8.64292	7.97	2.82312	8.92749	8.47	2.91033	9.20326	8.97	2.99500	9.47101	9.47	3.07734	9.73139	9.97	3.15753	9.98499
7.48	2.73496	8.64870	7.98	2.82489	8.93308	8.48	2.91204	9.20869	8.98	2.99666	9.47629	9.48	3.07896	9.73653	9.98	3.15911	9.98999
7.49	2.73679	8.65448	7.99	2.82666	8.93868	8.49	2.91376	9.21412	8.99	2.99833	9.48156	9.49	3.08058	9.74166	9.99	3.16070	9.99500

Appendix IV. The Area under the Normal Curve

This table shows the area under the normal curve between the mean and a selected *z* value.

Example:

The area under the normal curve between the mean and a *z* of 1.00 is 0.3413 of the total (34.13 percent of the total). The total area is 1.0.

z/σ	.00	.01	.02	.03	.04	.05	.06	.07	.08	.09
0.0	.0000	.0040	.0080	.0120	.0160	.0199	.0239	.0279	.0319	.0359
0.1	.0398	.0438	.0478	.0517	.0557	.0596	.0636	.0675	.0714	.0753
0.2	.0793	.0832	.0871	.0910	.0948	.0987	.1026	.1064	.1103	.1141
0.3	.1179	.1217	.1255	.1293	.1331	.1368	.1406	.1443	.1480	.1517
0.4	.1554	.1591	.1628	.1664	.1700	.1736	.1772	.1808	.1844	.1879
0.5	.1915	.1950	.1985	.2019	.2054	.2088	.2123	.2157	.2190	.2224
0.6	.2257	.2291	.2324	.2357	.2389	.2422	.2454	.2486	.2518	.2549
0.7	.2580	.2612	.2642	.2673	.2704	.2734	.2764	.2794	.2823	.2852
0.8	.2881	.2910	.2939	.2967	.2995	.3023	.3051	.3078	.3106	.3133
0.9	.3159	.3186	.3212	.3238	.3264	.3289	.3315	.3340	.3365	.3389
1.0	.3413	.3438	.3461	.3485	.3508	.3531	.3554	.3577	.3599	.3621
1.1	.3643	.3665	.3686	.3708	.3729	.3749	.3770	.3790	.3810	.3830
1.2	.3849	.3869	.3888	.3907	.3925	.3944	.3962	.3980	.3997	.4015
1.3	.4032	.4049	.4066	.4082	.4099	.4115	.4131	.4147	.4162	.4177
1.4	.4192	.4207	.4222	.4236	.4251	.4265	.4279	.4292	.4306	.4319
1.5	.4332	.4345	.4357	.4370	.4382	.4394	.4406	.4418	.4429	.4441
1.6	.4452	.4463	.4474	.4484	.4495	.4505	.4515	.4525	.4535	.4545
1.7	.4554	.4564	.4573	.4582	.4591	.4599	.4608	.4616	.4625	.4633
1.8	.4641	.4649	.4656	.4664	.4671	.4678	.4686	.4693	.4699	.4706
1.9	.4713	.4719	.4726	.4732	.4738	.4744	.4750	.4756	.4761	.4767
2.0	.4772	.4778	.4783	.4788	.4793	.4798	.4803	.4808	.4812	.4817
2.1	.4821	.4826	.4830	.4834	.4838	.4842	.4846	.4850	.4854	.4857
2.2	.4861	.4864	.4868	.4871	.4875	.4878	.4881	.4884	.4887	.4890
2.3	.4893	.4896	.4898	.4901	.4904	.4906	.4909	.4911	.4913	.4916
2.4	.4918	.4920	.4922	.4925	.4927	.4929	.4931	.4932	.4934	.4936
2.5	.4938	.4940	.4941	.4943	.4945	.4946	.4948	.4949	.4951	.4952
2.6	.4953	.4955	.4956	.4957	.4959	.4960	.4961	.4962	.4963	.4964
2.7	.4965	.4966	.4967	.4968	.4969	.4970	.4971	.4972	.4973	.4974
2.8	.4974	.4975	.4976	.4977	.4977	.4978	.4979	.4979	.4980	.4981
2.9	.4981	.4982	.4982	.4983	.4984	.4984	.4985	.4985	.4986	.4986
3.0	.49865	.4987	.4987	.4988	.4988	.4989	.4989	.4989	.4990	.4990
3.1	.49903	.4991	.4991	.4991	.4992	.4992	.4992	.4992	.4993	.4993
3.2	.4993129	.4993	.4994	.4994	.4994	.4994	.4994	.4995	.4995	.4995
3.3	.4995166	.4995	.4995	.4996	.4996	.4996	.4996	.4996	.4996	.4997
3.4	.4996631	.4997	.4997	.4997	.4997	.4997	.4997	.4997	.4998	.4998
3.5	.4997674	.4998	.4998	.4998	.4998	.4998	.4998	.4998	.4998	.4998
3.6	.4998409	.4998	.4999	.4999	.4999	.4999	.4999	.4999	.4999	.4999
3.7	.4998922	.4999	.4999	.4999	.4999	.4999	.4999	.4999	.4999	.4999
3.8	.4999277	.4999	.4999	.4999	.4999	.4999	.4999	.5000	.5000	.5000
3.9	.4999519	.5000	.5000	.5000	.5000	.5000	.5000	.5000	.5000	.5000
4.0	.4999683									
4.5	.4999966									
5.0	.4999997133									

Example: The number on the χ^2 scale for 10 d.f. corresponding to the area of 0.05 in the one tail is 18.3.

d/f	0.30	0.20	0.10	0.05	0.025	0.010	0.005	0.001
1	1.07	1.64	2.71	3.84	5.02	6.63	7.88	10.8
2	2.41	3.22	4.61	5.99	7.38	9.21	10.6	13.8
3	3.67	4.64	6.25	7.82	9.35	11.3	12.8	16.3
4	4.88	5.99	7.78	9.49	11.1	13.3	14.9	18.5
5	6.06	7.29	9.24	11.1	12.8	15.1	16.7	20.5
6	7.23	8.56	10.6	12.6	14.4	16.8	18.5	22.5
7	8.38	9.80	12.0	14.1	16.0	18.5	20.3	24.3
8	9.52	11.0	13.4	15.5	17.5	20.1	22.0	26.1
9	10.7	12.2	14.7	16.9	19.0	21.7	23.6	27.9
10	11.8	13.4	16.0	18.3	20.5	23.2	25.2	29.6
11	12.9	14.6	17.3	19.7	21.9	24.7	26.8	31.3
12	14.0	15.8	18.5	21.0	23.3	26.2	28.3	32.9
13	15.1	17.0	19.8	22.4	24.7	27.7	29.8	34.5
14	16.2	18.2	21.1	23.7	26.1	29.1	31.3	36.1
15	17.3	19.3	22.3	25.0	27.5	30.6	32.8	37.7
16	18.4	20.5	23.5	26.3	28.8	32.0	34.3	39.3
17	19.5	21.6	24.8	27.6	30.2	33.4	35.7	40.8
18	20.6	22.8	26.0	28.9	31.5	34.8	37.2	42.3
19	21.7	23.9	27.2	30.1	32.9	36.2	38.6	43.8
20	22.8	25.0	28.4	31.4	34.2	37.6	40.0	45.3
21	23.9	26.2	29.6	32.7	35.5	38.9	41.4	46.8
22	24.9	27.3	30.8	33.9	36.8	40.3	42.8	48.3
23	26.0	28.4	32.0	35.2	38.1	41.6	44.2	49.7
24	27.1	29.6	33.2	36.4	39.4	43.0	45.6	51.2
25	28.2	30.7	34.4	37.7	40.6	44.3	46.9	52.6
26	29.2	31.8	35.6	38.9	41.9	45.6	48.3	54.1
27	30.3	32.9	36.7	40.1	43.2	47.0	49.6	55.5
28	31.4	34.0	37.9	41.3	44.5	48.3	51.0	56.9
29	32.5	35.1	39.1	42.6	45.7	49.6	52.3	58.3
30	33.5	36.3	40.3	43.8	47.0	50.9	53.7	59.7

Source: Catherine M. Thompson, "Tables of the Percentage Points of the χ^2-Distribution," *Biometrika,* Vol. XXXII (1941), pp. 188–89. The remainder of the table is abridged with permission from Table IV of R. A. Fisher and F. Yates, *Statistical Tables for Biological, Agricultural and Medical Research* (Edinburgh: Oliver & Boyd, Ltd.).

Values in the table are for the function:

$$P(x) = \frac{\mu^{x}e^{-\mu}}{x(x-1)(x-2)\text{—}1}$$

x	$P(x)$ for specified values of μ									
	$\mu = 0.1$	$\mu = 0.2$	$\mu = 0.3$	$\mu = 0.4$	$\mu = 0.5$	$\mu = 0.6$	$\mu = 0.7$	$\mu = 0.8$	$\mu = 0.9$	$\mu = 1.0$
0	.9048374	.8187308	.7408182	.6703200	.606531	.548812	.496585	.449329	.406570	.367879
1	.0904837	.1637462	.2222455	.2681280	.303265	.329287	.347610	.359463	.365913	.367879
2	.0045242	.0163746	.0333368	.0536256	.075816	.098786	.121663	.143785	.164661	.183940
3	.0001508	.0010916	.0033337	.0071501	.012636	.019757	.028388	.038343	.049398	.061313
4	.0000038	.0000546	.0002500	.0007150	.001580	.002964	.004968	.007669	.011115	.015328
5	.0000001	.0000022	.0000150	.0000572	.000158	.000356	.000696	.001227	.002001	.003066
6		.0000001	.0000008	.0000038	.000013	.000036	.000081	.000164	.000300	.000511
7				.0000002	.000001	.000003	.000008	.000019	.000039	.000073
8							.000001	.000002	.000004	.000009
9										.000001

x	$\mu = 2.0$	$\mu = 3.0$	$\mu = 4.0$	$\mu = 5.0$	$\mu = 6.0$	$\mu = 7.0$	$\mu = 8.0$	$\mu = 9.0$	$\mu = 10.0$
0	.135335	.049787	.018316	.006738	.002479	.000912	.000335	.000123	.000045
1	.270671	.149361	.073263	.033690	.014873	.006383	.002684	.001111	.000454
2	.270671	.224042	.146525	.084224	.044618	.022341	.010735	.004998	.002270
3	.180447	.224042	.195367	.140374	.089235	.052129	.028626	.014994	.007567
4	.090224	.168031	.195367	.175467	.133853	.091226	.057252	.033737	.018917
5	.036089	.100819	.156293	.175467	.160623	.127717	.091604	.060727	.037833
6	.012030	.050409	.104196	.146223	.160623	.149003	.122138	.091090	.063055
7	.003437	.021604	.059540	.104445	.137677	.149003	.139587	.117116	.090079
8	.000859	.008102	.029770	.065278	.103258	.130377	.139587	.131756	.112599
9	.000191	.002701	.013231	.036266	.068838	.101405	.124077	.131756	.125110
10	.000038	.000810	.005292	.018133	.041303	.070983	.099262	.118580	.125110
11	.000007	.000221	.001925	.008242	.022529	.045171	.072190	.097020	.113736
12	.000001	.000055	.000642	.003434	.011264	.026350	.048127	.072765	.094780
13		.000013	.000197	.001321	.005199	.014188	.029616	.050376	.072908
14		.000003	.000056	.000472	.002228	.007094	.016924	.032384	.052077
15		.000001	.000015	.000157	.000891	.003311	.009026	.019431	.034718
16			.000004	.000049	.000334	.001448	.004513	.010930	.021699
17			.000001	.000014	.000118	.000596	.002124	.005786	.012764
18				.000004	.000039	.000232	.000944	.002893	.007091
19				.000001	.000012	.000085	.000397	.001370	.003732
20					.000004	.000030	.000159	.000617	.001866
21					.000001	.000010	.000061	.000264	.000889
22						.000003	.000022	.000108	.000404
23						.000001	.000008	.000042	.000176
24							.000003	.000016	.000073
25							.000001	.000006	.000029
26								.000002	.000011
27								.000001	.000004
28									.000001
29									.000001

Source: E. C. Molina, *Poisson's Exponential Binomial Limit* (Princeton, N.J.: D. Van Nostrand Co., Inc., 1942). Reprinted by permission.

Appendix VII. Binomial Distribution

$$P\{r\} = \frac{n!}{r!(n-r)!} p^r q^{n-r}$$

n	r	.05	.10	.15	.20	.25	p .30	.35	.40	.45	.50
1	0	.9500	.9000	.8500	.8000	.7500	.7000	.6500	.6000	.5500	.5000
	1	.0500	.1000	.1500	.2000	.2500	.3000	.3500	.4000	.4500	.5000
2	0	.9025	.8100	.7225	.6400	.5625	.4900	.4225	.3600	.3025	.2500
	1	.0950	.1800	.2550	.3200	.3750	.4200	.4550	.4800	.4950	.5000
	2	.0025	.0100	.0225	.0400	.0625	.0900	.1225	.1600	.2025	.2500
3	0	.8574	.7290	.6141	.5120	.4219	.3430	.2746	.2160	.1664	.1250
	1	.1354	.2430	.3251	.3840	.4219	.4410	.4436	.4320	.4084	.3750
	2	.0071	.0270	.0574	.0960	.1406	.1890	.2389	.2880	.3341	.3750
	3	.0001	.0010	.0034	.0080	.0156	.0270	.0429	.0640	.0911	.1250
4	0	.8145	.6561	.5220	.4096	.3164	.2401	.1785	.1296	.0915	.0625
	1	.1715	.2916	.3685	.4096	.4219	.4116	.3845	.3456	.2995	.2500
	2	.0135	.0486	.0975	.1536	.2109	.2646	.3105	.3456	.3675	.3750
	3	.0005	.0036	.0115	.0256	.0469	.0756	.1115	.1536	.2005	.2500
	4	.0000	.0001	.0005	.0016	.0039	.0081	.0150	.0256	.0410	.0625
5	0	.7738	.5905	.4437	.3277	.2373	.1681	.1160	.0778	.0503	.0312
	1	.2036	.3280	.3915	.4096	.3955	.3602	.3124	.2592	.2059	.1562
	2	.0214	.0729	.1382	.2048	.2637	.3087	.3364	.3456	.3369	.3125
	3	.0011	.0081	.0244	.0512	.0879	.1323	.1811	.2304	.2757	.3125
	4	.0000	.0004	.0022	.0064	.0146	.0284	.0488	.0768	.1128	.1562
	5	.0000	.0000	.0001	.0003	.0010	.0024	.0053	.0102	.0185	.0312
6	0	.7351	.5314	.3771	.2621	.1780	.1176	.0754	.0467	.0277	.0156
	1	.2321	.3543	.3993	.3932	.3560	.3025	.2437	.1866	.1359	.0938
	2	.0305	.0984	.1762	.2458	.2966	.3241	.3280	.3110	.2780	.2344
	3	.0021	.0146	.0415	.0819	.1318	.1852	.2355	.2765	.3032	.3125
	4	.0001	.0012	.0055	.0154	.0330	.0595	.0951	.1382	.1861	.2344
	5	.0000	.0001	.0004	.0015	.0044	.0102	.0205	.0369	.0609	.0938
	6	.0000	.0000	.0000	.0001	.0002	.0007	.0018	.0041	.0083	.0156
7	0	.6983	.4783	.3206	.2097	.1335	.0824	.0490	.0280	.0152	.0078
	1	.2573	.3720	.3960	.3670	.3115	.2471	.1848	.1306	.0872	.0547
	2	.0406	.1240	.2097	.2753	.3115	.3177	.2985	.2613	.2140	.1641
	3	.0036	.0230	.0617	.1147	.1730	.2269	.2679	.2903	.2918	.2734
	4	.0002	.0026	.0109	.0287	.0577	.0972	.1442	.1935	.2388	.2734
	5	.0000	.0002	.0012	.0043	.0115	.0250	.0466	.0774	.1172	.1641
	6	.0000	.0000	.0001	.0004	.0013	.0036	.0084	.0172	.0320	.0547
	7	.0000	.0000	.0000	.0000	.0001	.0002	.0006	.0016	.0037	.0078
8	0	.6634	.4305	.2725	.1678	.1002	.0576	.0319	.0168	.0084	.0039
	1	.2793	.3826	.3847	.3355	.2670	.1977	.1373	.0896	.0548	.0312
	2	.0515	.1488	.2376	.2936	.3115	.2065	.2587	.2090	.1569	.1094

n	r	.05	.10	.15	.20	.25	p .30	.35	.40	.45	.50
8	3	.0054	.0331	.0839	.1468	.2076	.2541	.2786	.2787	.2568	.2188
	4	.0004	.0046	.0185	.0459	.0865	.1361	.1875	.2322	.2627	.2734
	5	.0000	.0004	.0026	.0092	.0231	.0467	.0808	.1239	.1719	.2188
	6	.0000	.0000	.0002	.0011	.0038	.0100	.0217	.0413	.0403	.1094
	7	.0000	.0000	.0000	.0001	.0004	.0012	.0033	.0079	.0164	.0312
	8	.0000	.0000	.0000	.0000	.0000	.0001	.0002	.0007	.0017	.0039
9	0	.6302	.3874	.2316	.1342	.0751	.0404	.0207	.0101	.0046	.0020
	1	.2985	.3874	.3679	.3020	.2253	.1556	.1004	.0605	.0339	.0176
	2	.0629	.1722	.2597	.3020	.3003	.2668	.2162	.1612	.1110	.0703
	3	.0077	.0446	.1069	.1762	.2336	.2668	.2716	.2508	.2119	.1641
	4	.0006	.0074	.0283	.0661	.1168	.1715	.2194	.2508	.2600	.2461
	5	.0000	.0008	.0050	.0165	.0389	.0735	.1181	.1672	.2128	.2461
	6	.0000	.0001	.0006	.0028	.0087	.0210	.0424	.0743	.1160	.1641
	7	.0000	.0000	.0000	.0003	.0012	.0039	.0098	.0212	.0407	.0703
	8	.0000	.0000	.0000	.0000	.0001	.0004	.0013	.0035	.0083	.0176
	9	.0000	0000	0000	0000	0000	0000	0001	.0003	.0008	.0020
10	0	.5987	.3487	.1969	.1074	.0563	.0282	.0135	.0060	.0025	.0010
	1	.3151	.3874	.3474	.2684	.1877	.1211	.0725	.0403	.0207	.0098
	2	.0746	.1937	.2759	.3020	.2816	.2335	.1757	.1209	.0763	.0439
	3	.0105	.0574	.1298	.2013	.2503	.2668	.2522	.2150	.1665	.1172
	4	.0010	.0112	.0401	.0881	.1460	.2001	.2377	.2508	.2384	.2051
	5	.0001	.0015	.0085	.0264	.0584	.1029	.1536	.2007	.2340	.2461
	6	.0000	.0001	.0012	.0055	.0162	.0368	.0689	.1115	.1596	.2051
	7	.0000	.0000	.0001	.0008	.0031	.0090	.0212	.0425	.0746	.1172
	8	.0000	.0000	.0000	.0001	.0004	.0014	.0043	.0106	.0229	.0439
	9	.0000	.0000	.0000	.0000	.0000	.0001	.0005	.0016	.0042	.0098
	10	.0000	.0000	.0000	.0000	.0000	.0000	.0000	.0001	.0003	.0010
11	0	.5688	.3138	.1673	.0859	.0422	.0198	.0088	.0036	.0014	.0005
	1	.3293	.3835	.3248	.2362	.1549	.0932	.0518	.0266	.0125	.0054
	2	.0867	.2131	.2866	.2953	.2581	.1998	.1395	.0887	.0513	.0269
	3	.0137	.0710	.1517	.2215	.2581	.2568	.2254	.1774	.1259	.0806
	4	.0014	.0158	.0536	.1107	.1721	.2201	.2428	.2365	.2060	.1611
	5	.0001	.0025	.0132	.0388	.0803	.1321	.1830	.2207	.2360	.2256
	6	.0000	.0003	.0023	.0097	.0268	.0566	.0985	.1471	.1931	.2256
	7	.0000	.0000	.0003	.0017	.0064	.0173	.0379	.0701	.1128	.1611
	8	.0000	.0000	.0000	.0002	.0011	.0037	.0102	.0234	.0462	.0806
	9	.0000	.0000	.0000	.0000	.0001	.0005	.0018	.0052	.0126	.0269
	10	.0000	.0000	.0000	.0000	.0000	.0000	.0002	.0007	.0021	.0054
	11	.0000	.0000	.0000	.0000	.0000	.0000	.0000	.0000	.0002	.0005

Index

This book has been set in 10 and 9 point Times Roman, leaded 2 points. Chapter numbers are in 16 and 30 point Helvetica and chapter titles are in 18 point Helvetica Medium. The size of the type page is 42 x 52½ picas.